The History of Motor Sport

This book explores, analyses, and explains the significance of motor sport in a number of selected countries throughout the world, to provide a focus on its numerous disciplines and outline how each of these varies in popularity from country to country. In so doing, this volume arrives at a more informed understanding of the role of motor sport in ideological and sporting terms and thereby contributes to the increasing momentum of academic research in this field. When examining sport, its meanings, and significance in society, the accent is often on individuals and teams that represent a nation or a particular ideological standpoint. Rarely does attention turn to other sporting forms and yet it is here that a remarkable story is revealed.

This collection represents the first occasion ever when the full extent of the impact of motor sport on certain countries is thoughtfully considered. It tracks its evolution out from its conception in central Europe, into the southern part of the continent and onwards throughout the Americas.

This book was published as a special issue of the *International Journal of the History of Sport*.

David Hassan is a Senior Lecturer in Sport Studies at the University of Ulster. He is Academic Editor of *Sport in Society* (Taylor & Francis Ltd.) and has guest edited a number of leading journals in the field. He is Series Editor (with Dr. Allan Edwards) of *Foundations of Sport Management* (a new Routledge series) and has published extensively in the social, political and historical significance of sport.

The History of Motor Sport
A Case Study Analysis

Edited by
David Hassan

LONDON AND NEW YORK

First published 2012
by Routledge
2 Park Square, Milton Park, Abingdon, Oxon, OX14 4RN

Simultaneously published in the USA and Canada
by Routledge
711 Third Avenue, New York, NY 10017

Routledge is an imprint of the Taylor & Francis Group, an informa business

British Library Cataloguing in Publication Data
A catalogue record for this book is available from the British Library

ISBN13: 978-0-415-67788-2

Typeset in Times New Roman
by Taylor & Francis Books

Disclaimer
The publisher would like to make readers aware that the chapters in this book are referred to as articles as they had been in the special issue. The publisher accepts responsibility for any inconsistencies that may have arisen in the course of preparing this volume for print.

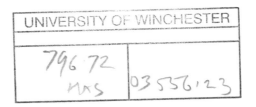

MIX
Paper from
responsible sources
FSC® C004839

Printed and bound in Great Britain by the MPG Books Group

Contents

SERIES EDITORS' FOREWORD

On January 1, 2010 *Sport in the Global Society*, created by Professor J.A. Mangan in 1997, was divided into two parts: *Historical Perspectives* and *Contemporary Perspectives*. These new categories involve predominant rather than exclusive emphases. The past is part of the present and the present is part of the past. The Editors of *Historical Perspectives* are Mark Dyreson and Thierry Terret.

The reasons for the division are straightforward. SGS has expanded rapidly since its creation with over one hundred publications in some twelve years. Its editorial teams will now benefit from sectional specialist interests and expertise. *Historical Perspectives* draws on IJHS monograph reviews, themed collections and conference/workshop collections. It is, of course, international in content.

Historical Perspectives continues the tradition established by the original incarnation of *Sport in the Global Society* by promoting the academic study of one of the most significant and dynamic forces in shaping the historical landscapes of human cultures. Sport spans the contemporary globe. It captivates vast audiences. It defines, alters, and reinforces identities for individuals, communities, nations, empires, and the world. Sport organizes memories and perceptions, arouses passions and tensions, and reveals harmonies and cleavages. It builds and blurs social boundaries, animating discourses about class, gender, race, and ethnicity. Sport opens new vistas on the history of human cultures, intersecting with politics and economics, ideologies and theologies. It reveals aesthetic tastes and energizes consumer markets.

By the end of the twentieth century a critical mass of scholars recognized the importance of sport in their analyses of human experiences and *Sport in the Global Society* emerged to provide an international outlet for the world's leading investigators of the subject. As Professor Mangan contended in the original series foreword: "The story of modern sport is the story of the modern world—in microcosm; a modern global tapestry permanently being woven. Furthermore, nationalist and imperialist, philosopher and politician, radical and conservative have all sought in sport a manifestation of national identity, status and superiority. Finally for countless millions sport is the personal pursuit of ambition, assertion, well-being and enjoyment."

Sport in the Global Society: Historical Perspectives continues the project, building on previous work in the serious and excavating new terrain. It remains a consistent and coherent response to the attention the academic community demands for the serious study of sport.

Mark Dyreson
Thierry Terret

SPORT IN THE GLOBAL SOCIETY

Series Editors: Mark Dyreson and Thierry Terret

THE HISTORY OF MOTOR SPORT

A Case Study Analysis

Sport in the Global Society: Historical Perspectives
Series Editors: Mark Dyreson and Thierry Terret

Titles in the Series

Sport in the Global Society
Past SGS publications prior to 2010

Africa, Football and FIFA
Politics, Colonialism and Resistance
Paul Darby

Amateurism in British Sport
'It Matters Not Who Won or Lost'
*Edited by Dilwyn Porter and Stephen
Wagg*

Amateurism in Sport
An Analysis and Defence
Lincoln Allison

America's Game(s)
A Critical Anthropology of Sport
*Edited by Benjamin Eastman, Sean
Brown and Michael Ralph*

American Sports
An Evolutionary Approach
Edited by Alan Klein

A Social History of Indian Football
Striving to Score
*Kausik Bandyopadhya and Boria
Majumdar*

A Social History of Swimming in England, 1800–1918
Splashing in the Serpentine
Christopher Love

A Sport-Loving Society
Victorian and Edwardian Middle-Class
England at Play
Edited by J.A. Mangan

Athleticism in the Victorian and Edwardian Public School
The Emergence and Consolidation of an
Educational Ideology, New Edition
J.A. Mangan

Australian Beach Cultures
The History of Sun, Sand and Surf
Douglas Booth

Barbarians, Gentlemen and Players
A Sociological Study of the Development of Rugby Football, Second Edition
Eric Dunning and Kenneth Sheard

Beijing 2008: Preparing for Glory
Chinese Challenge in the 'Chinese Century'
Edited by J.A. Mangan and Dong Jinxia

Body and Mind
Sport in Europe from the Roman Empire
to the Renaissance
John McClelland

British Football and Social Exclusion
Edited by Stephen Wagg

Capoeira
The History of an Afro-Brazilian Martial Art
Matthias Röhrig Assunção

Crafting Patriotism for Global Dominance
America at the Olympics
Mark Dyreson

Fringe Nations in Soccer
Making it Happen
Edited by Kausik Bandyopadhyay and
Sabyasachi Malick

From Fair Sex to Feminism
Sport and the Socialization of Women in
the Industrial and Post-Industrial Eras
Edited by J.A. Mangan and Roberta J.
Park

Gender, Sport, Science
Selected Writings of Roberta J. Park
Edited by J.A. Mangan and Patricia
Vertinsky

Globalised Football
Nations and Migration, the City and the
Dream
Edited by Nina Clara Tiesler and João
Nuno Coelho

Italian Fascism and the Female Body
Sport, Submissive Women and Strong
Mothers
Gigliola Gori

Japan, Sport and Society
Tradition and Change in a Globalizing
World
Edited by Joseph Maguire and
Masayoshi Nakayama

Law and Sport in Contemporary Society
Edited by Steven Greenfield and Guy
Osborn

Leisure and Recreation in a Victorian
Mining Community
The Social Economy of Leisure in
North-East England, 1820–1914
Alan Metcalfe

Lost Histories of Indian Cricket
Battles off the Pitch
Boria Majumdar

Making European Masculinities
Sport, Europe, Gender
Edited by J.A. Mangan

Making Men
Rugby and Masculine Identity
Edited by John Nauright and Timothy J.
L. Chandler

Making the Rugby World
Race, Gender, Commerce
Edited by Timothy J.L. Chandler and
John Nauright

Militarism, Hunting, Imperialism
'Blooding' The Martial Male
J.A. Mangan and Callum McKenzie

Militarism, Sport, Europe
War Without Weapons
Edited by J.A. Mangan

Modern Sport: The Global Obsession
Essays in Honour of J.A.Mangan
Edited by Boria Majumdar and Fan
Hong

Muscular Christianity and the Colonial
and Post-Colonial World
Edited by John J. MacAloon

Native Americans and Sport in North
America
Other Peoples' Games
Edited by C. Richard King

Olympic Legacies – Intended and Unin-
tended
Political, Cultural, Economic and Educational
Edited by J.A. Mangan and Mark Dyr-
eson

Playing on the Periphery
Sport, Identity and Memory
Tara Brabazon

Pleasure, Profit, Proselytism
British Culture and Sport at Home and
  Abroad 1700–1914
Edited by J.A. Mangan

Rain Stops Play
Cricketing Climates
Andrew Hignell

Reformers, Sport, Modernizers
Middle-Class Revolutionaries
Edited by J.A. Mangan

Rugby's Great Split
Class, Culture and the Origins of Rugby
  League Football
Tony Collins

Running Cultures
Racing in Time and Space
John Bale

Scoring for Britain
International Football and International
  Politics, 1900–1939
Peter J. Beck

Serious Sport
J.A. Mangan's Contribution to the His-
  tory of Sport
Edited by Scott Crawford

Shaping the Superman
Fascist Body as Political Icon – Aryan
  Fascism
Edited by J.A. Mangan

Sites of Sport
Space, Place and Experience
*Edited by John Bale and Patricia Ver-
  tinksy*

Soccer and Disaster
International Perspectives
*Edited by Paul Darby, Martin Jones and
  Gavin Mellor*

Soccer in South Asia
Empire, Nation, Diaspora
Edited by Paul Dimeo and James Mills

Soccer's Missing Men
Schoolteachers and the Spread of Asso-
  ciation Football
J.A. Mangan and Colm Hickey

Soccer, Women, Sexual Liberation
Kicking off a New Era
Edited by Fan Hong and J.A. Mangan

Sport: Race, Ethnicity and Indigenity
Building Global Understanding
Edited by Daryl Adair

Sport and American Society
Exceptionalism, Insularity, 'Imperialism'
*Edited by Mark Dyreson and J.A.
  Mangan*

**Sport and Foreign Policy in a Globalizing
  World**
*Edited by Steven J. Jackson and Stephen
  Haigh*

Sport and International Relations
An Emerging Relationship
*Edited by Roger Levermore and Adrian
  Budd*

Sport and Memory in North America
Edited by Steven Wieting

Sport, Civil Liberties and Human Rights
*Edited by Richard Giulianotti and David
  McArdle*

Sport, Culture and History
Region, Nation and Globe
Brian Stoddart

Sport in Asian Society
Past and Present
Edited by Fan Hong and J.A. Mangan

Sport in Australasian Society
Past and Present
Edited by J.A. Mangan and John Nauright

Sport in Europe
Politics, Class, Gender
Edited by J.A. Mangan

Sport in Films
Edited by Emma Poulton and Martin Roderick

Sport in Latin American Society
Past and Present
Edited by Lamartine DaCosta and J.A. Mangan

Sport in South Asian Society
Past and Present
Edited by Boria Majumdar and J.A. Mangan
Sport in the Cultures of the Ancient World
New Perspectives
Edited by Zinon Papakonstantinou

Sport, Media, Culture
Global and Local Dimensions
Edited by Alina Bernstein and Neil Blain

Sport, Nationalism and Orientalism
The Asian Games
Edited by Fan Hong

Sport Tourism
Edited by Heather J. Gibson

Sporting Cultures
Hispanic Perspectives on Sport, Text and the Body
Edited by David Wood and P. Louise Johnson

Sporting Nationalisms
Identity, Ethnicity, Immigration and Assimilation
Edited by Mike Cronin and David Mayall

Superman Supreme
Fascist Body as Political Icon – Global Fascism
Edited by J.A. Mangan

Terrace Heroes
The Life and Times of the 1930s Professional Footballer
Graham Kelly

The Balkan Games and Balkan Politics in the Interwar Years 1929-1939
Politicians in Pursuit of Peace
Penelope Kissoudi

The Changing Face of the Football Business
Supporters Direct
Edited by Sean Hamil, Jonathan Michie, Christine Oughton and Steven Warby

The Commercialisation of Sport
Edited by Trevor Slack

The Cultural Bond
Sport, Empire, Society
Edited by J.A. Mangan

The First Black Footballer
Arthur Wharton 1865–1930: An Absence of Memory
Phil Vasili

The Football Manager
A History
Neil Carter

The Future of Football
Challenges for the Twenty-First Century
Edited by Jon Garland, Dominic Malcolm and Mike Rowe

xiii

Notes on Contributors

Thomas Ameye is preparing a doctoral dissertation at the Research Centre for the History of Sport and Kinesiology at K.U. Leuven. His dissertation intends an in-depth analysis of the rise, evolution, institutionalisation and legitimisation of Olympism in Belgium, and its international impact. In 2006, Thomas Ameye was laureate of the Postgraduate Research Grant Programme of the IOC's Olympic Studies Centre, and, in 2010, was awarded the Ian Buchanan Memorial Scholarship of the International Society of Olympic Historians. Since August 2010, he holds a post in the National Cycling Museum, Roeselare, Belgium.

Pascal Delheye studied physical education, sport management and history at the universities of Leuven and Lyon. His doctoral research, for which he won the Young Investigators Award of the European College of Sport Science in 2003, focused on the history of physical education and its origin as an academic discipline. After post-doctoral research at the universities of Leuven and Berkeley, he became head of the Research Centre for the History of Sport and Kinesiology at K.U. Leuven in 2008.

Victor Andrade de Melo is Professor of the Post-Graduation Program of Comparative History/Federal, University of Rio de Janeiro and Coordinator of 'Sport': Laboratory of History of Sport and Leisure (www.sport.ufrj.ifcs.br).

Bieke Gils completed her undergraduate degree in 2006 at K.U. Leuven, and received her human kinetics master's degree in 2009 from the University of Windsor, Ontario, Canada. Bieke Gils is currently a PhD student in the School of Human Kinetics at the University of British Columbia, Vancouver, Canada. She was recently awarded the Fred Hume Graduate Scholarship in Sport History (2009–2010). She is still affiliated to the Research Centre for the History of Sport and Kinesiology of K.U. Leuven. Bieke's research interests are sport and gender history. Her current research interests include female aerialists (aviators, trapeze artists and ski-jumpers) in the 1920s and 1930s.

Teresa González Aja is Professor of History and Politics of Sport at the Polytechnic University of Madrid; Head of the department of Social Sciences of Sport; President, College of Fellows of CESH (European Commitee for Sport History); ISHPES Council Member; and author of different publications on Francoism and the image of sport in the arts.

David Hassan is a Senior Lecturer in the School of Sports Studies at the University of Ulster Jordanstown. He is Academic Editor of *Sport in Society* and Series Editor of

Foundations of Sport Management (Routledge). He has published extensively in the social, historical and political significance of sport for the past decade.

Éamon Ó. Cofaigh teaches French and Irish in the National University of Ireland, Galway and is nearing completion of a PhD on Sport and Leisure in Twentieth Century France.

Philip O'Kane is a member of the Faculty of Arts at the University of Ulster, Magee. Philip holds a BA (Hons) degree in History from Queens University Belfast, a MA in Modern History from the University of Ulster and an LLB, also from the University of Ulster. His research interests centre around culture and identity, with a particular emphasis on sport.

Ben Shackleford currently works as a senior researcher for the US Internal Revenue Service. Before joining the Federal Government as social scientist, Ben earned a doctorate in the History and Sociology of Science and Technology at the Georgia Institute of Technology. While at Georgia Tech, Ben was a Raymond Riddle Fellow at the Center for Industry in the Modern South, a Senior Research Fellow at the Smithsonian Institution Lemelson Center for the Study of Innovation, published several scholarly articles on the history of motorsport, and edited the memoirs of famed auto racing mechanic, inventor, and alternate energy guru Henry 'Smokey' Yunick. His own experience as a mechanic and crew chief in the American Le Mans Series, International Motor Sports Association, Sports Car Club of America and, Historic Sportscar Racing series' help Ben provide unique perspective in his doctoral dissertation which covered the social history of Stock Car Racing in America.

Prologue: The Cultural Significance and Global Importance of Motor Sport

David Hassan

University of Ulster at Jordanstown, UK

This special issue intends to explore, analyse and explain the significance of motor sport in a number of selected countries throughout the world, to provide a focus on its numerous disciplines and outline how each of these varies in popularity from country to country. In so doing it is hoped to arrive at a more informed understanding of the role of motor sport in ideological and sporting terms and thereby begin to address the almost complete absence of academic research in this field to date. When examining sport, its meanings and significance in society, the accent is often on individuals and teams that represent a nation or a particular ideological standpoint. Rarely does attention turn to other sporting forms and yet it is here that a remarkable story is revealed.

At the same time that various sports were organising in codified forms and governing bodies were establishing themselves globally, the motor car was emerging as a source of fascination right across the world. The concept of racing these motor vehicles, and later other forms of motorised transport, emerged on mainland Europe but quickly spread throughout North America into South America and elsewhere. Indeed it's apparent that what we were witnessing was an early but extremely popular form of sporting globalisation. It is remarkable therefore that in the expansive body of literature examining sport and globalisation that there is almost no mention of motor sport. Not only is motor sport universally popular – the World Rally Championship alone commanded a global television audience of 800 million in 2007 – but the discipline is organised on a transnational basis and is closely tied to the automobile industry, one of the world's foremost manufacturing sectors. The motor sport industry is worth an estimated £50 billion per annum and considerably more when one considers the platform for additional sales that its leading events present for automobile manufacturers, especially in developing markets. Yet all the while almost nothing has existed within academic scholarship concerning the emergence, evolution and cultural significance of motor sport, its marquee events or even analysis of how the development of motor sport has exercised an influence upon other industrial sectors, such as aviation. An attempt to address these omissions constituted the primary motivation for this collection, which brings together the scholarship of a range of academics, many of whom were writing about sport for the first time, to commence a process of systematic research into the emergence of motorised vehicles as a popular form of sporting pastime and competition.

Content

What becomes apparent within this collection is the cultural centrality of motor sport within many developed nation states and this is especially the case within Europe. Éamon Ó Cofaigh's opening contribution draws attention to the role of France, the established birthplace of motor sport, in the late nineteenth century during a period when the automobile itself was struggling for widespread acceptance. Motor vehicles were generally received with a combination of awe and intrigue but for some sections of European society their emergence gave rise to a considerable degree of resistance. Indeed it was the French aristocracy that pioneered these new inventions and subsequently began a programme of advocacy among the population at large. The article relays the initial emergence of city-to-city races, which were to become extremely popular across a number of European nation-states and elsewhere, before motor racing began to establish dedicated spaces in which men and their machines could compete. Ó Cofaigh also turns the spotlight on Gordon Bennett, widely accepted as being in the vanguard of the development of international motor sport, and tracks his personal contribution to this field. Finally the latter part of this article highlights the cultural significance of the Le Mans 24-hour race, which is not only a significant event in its own right but constitutes one third of the elusive 'Triple Crown' of motor racing, which is the subject of O'Kane's contribution to this collection, one that will be previewed later in this prologue.

However it is apparent that the emergence of motor sport in the late nineteenth century and early twentieth century had its genesis in northern central Europe, and this is a theme further developed in the outstanding contribution of Thomas Ameye, Bieke Gils and Pascal Delheye. They track the importance of motor sport in Belgium from the belle époque, when the nation was at the forefront of development across a range of cultural fields. More tellingly Ameye et al. detail the seamless shift from the bicycle to the automobile and in turn to the airplane during a time span either side of the dawn of the twentieth century, and which lasted little over a decade. Interestingly, although these developments may indicate that, in Belgium at least, the process of evolution was reserved for the bourgeoisie, in fact this work demonstrates that the working classes could achieve a degree of upward mobility too by engaging in such practices. The theme running though this article, however, is one of national pride in the very important role played by Belgians in the development of both the early automobile and, in turn, its impact upon other industries, including the aviation sector.

The significant contribution of motor sport to the wider political realm is at the core of an article by Teresa González Aja, which tracks the evolution of the Spanish nation from dictatorship, principally in the guise of General Franco, to democracy, during which the personal triumphs of the motorcyclist Angel Nieto provide a convenient prism through which to view this movement. Aja details how motorcycling, in this case, was a minority sport in Spain during its early years, but very quickly the regime realised that it represented a convenient method of advancing propaganda and began to channel funds towards it. The article also examines the iconography of the sporting hero and how his/her achievements can be partially appropriated by the nation state to advance a range of positive agendas.

Ultimately the success of motorcyclists such as Angel Nieto convinced Spain's ruling authorities of the value of investing in new circuits and the benefit of relaxing its attitude towards the foreign importation of goods, including motorcycles, into Spain. In a setting in which the game of association football appears to cast a long shadow over other sporting forms, Aja's contribution reminds the student of Spanish, and indeed European, sport about the existence of other avenues for investigation when examining the impact of political ideologies upon sport.

Thereafter the collection metaphorically moves from two wheels to four in the form of Victor Andrade de Melo's detailed and thoughtful analysis of motor racing in Brazil. Here de Melo briefly examines the remarkable, some would argue exceptional, achievements of Brazilian drivers within Formula One racing; but the main focus of the work is on the early automobile races that took place in the country, dating back to the opening decade of the twentieth century. It is from this period that the basis for Brazil's subsequent dominance of motor sport and its close association with F1 can be traced. Here de Melo, almost regretfully, poses the question as to why Brazil, which for much of its history has remained an economically underdeveloped nation, continues to produce exceptional racing car drivers. In so doing he brings into sharp focus the ever-present debate surrounding the perceived extravagance of motor sport and perhaps more significantly the opportunity costs involved in staging major sports events of this kind.

It is a debate implicit throughout the work of Hassan and O'Kane who examine the history and impact of the iconic Paris to Dakar Rally, including the emergence of corporate social responsibility within the wider field of motor sport. The Paris to Dakar Rally is among the world's most iconic events; one built less upon speed and more upon endurance as well as driver ingenuity. Yet the race has been the source of considerable controversy in recent years because of its negative impact upon the host environment and its people, and because of threats against competitors from a number of unspecified terrorist groupings. The latter has resulted in the race being staged in South America for the last two years with no impending prospect of it returning to its spiritual home, at least in the short term. Prior to this the race was already considered noteworthy because of the number of deaths and injuries arising from it, including among the indigenous people of the Saharan region, not to mention the considerable impact it had caused to the delicate desert ecosystem. It is timely therefore that this article examines the 'dark side' of motor racing and challenges the reader to consider the full extent of motor racing's impact in the modern world.

Thereafter the remarkable detail contained within O'Kane's single-authored piece on the 'Triple Crown' of motor racing reminds the reader of the iconic status of the Indianapolis 500, the Le Mans 24-hour race and the Monaco Grand Prix, which individually and collectively command unparalleled levels of respect among motor sport aficionados. It also serves to highlight the importance of America as a site for motor sport and in so doing fulfils the collection's key aim of providing a selective appreciation of motor sport across Europe, Africa and both North and South America.

However the chequered flag is not finally waved until Ben Shackleford offers a valuable overview of the inception and evolution of NASCAR racing in the USA. The latter is particularly popular in the Southern states (as opposed to the omnipotence of Indycar racing in the north of the country) and Shackleford does a remarkable job in interpreting this cultural distinction as part of a detailed investigation into a field that has rarely, if ever, received adequate levels of scholarly attention. Indeed Shackleford's work is indicative of the collection as a whole in that it uncovers new and invigorating areas of research and yet at the same time merely offers an initial grounding in this field and instead points the way for others to follow.

Motor Sport in France: Testing-ground for the World

Éamon Ó. Cofaigh

Department of French, National University of Ireland, Galway, Ireland

The birth of the automobile in the late nineteenth century was greeted with a mixture of awe, scepticism and sometimes even disdain from sections of the European public. In this article, the steps taken in France to pioneer and promote this new invention are examined. Unreliable and noisy, the early automobile owes a debt of gratitude to the French aristocracy who organised and codified motor racing in an effort to test these new inventions while at the same time introduce them to a wider public. City-to-city races demonstrated the potential of the automobile before the initiative of Gordon Bennett proved to be the catalyst for the birth of international motor sport as we recognise it today. Finally this article looks at the special connection between Le Mans and the automobile. Le Mans has, through its 24-hour race, maintained a strong link with the development of everyday automobile tourism and offers the enthusiast an alternative to the machines that reach incredible speeds on modern-day closed circuits. This article examines how French roads were veritable testing grounds for the earliest cars and how the public roads of Le Mans maintain the tradition to this day.

France played a major role in the early development of the motor car. French craftsmen looked to the automobile as a vehicle capable of transforming the fortunes of smaller enterprises willing to take a gamble on the new invention. Central to this process was motor sport, which came into being in France in the 1890s, based on the model of the bicycle races that had successfully provided a bridge between the nation's major towns. Turn-of-the-century city-to-city races provided stern tests for these early vehicles while simultaneously providing an advertising platform upon which manufacturers could display their models, albeit to an initially reluctant public. Pioneering manufacturers such as Renault and Peugeot quickly realised that it was necessary to participate in these events to ensure the commercial viability of their vehicles.

Motor sport in its infancy was an important testing ground for these newly invented motorised vehicles as early races gave manufacturers the opportunity to test the reliability of their cars over long distances on public roads. The new sport was inevitably extremely expensive and it was thus France's upper classes who were the first to test and promote the automobile. As motor sport gradually began to democratise the car, Gordon Bennett served as an important catalyst in the growth of the sport when he inaugurated the first international races, precursors to the first international Grand Prix. Le Mans, just 200km to the west of Paris, also played an active role in the early development of motoring. In this article, the genesis of motor racing in France will be discussed, demonstrating how sport helped the automobile to establish a foothold in society. The impact of an American, Gordon Bennett, in placing the sport on the international stage will also be examined. More specifically, a case study of Le Mans will show how this city, birthplace of the Grand Prix, has become synonymous with French motor sport, having hosted its iconic 24-hour race for over 80 years.

Pre-1900

Although the internal combustion engine was invented by Gottlieb Daimler in Germany in the 1880s, the automobile developed more quickly in France for a number of reasons. Firstly, the more developed road network in France allowed the transition from horse-drawn vehicles to the automobile to be made without too much difficulty. Napoleon Bonaparte's creation at the turn of the nineteenth century of a star-shaped road network with Paris as the hub allowed easy access to and from the capital. Paris was, itself, capable of accommodating the motor car, having been rebuilt in the mid-nineteenth century by Baron Haussman under the orders of Napoleon III. Fashionable houses were built on elegant boulevards with open intersections which had been designed to deter the building of barricades by rebels, but which now allowed for the coexistence of horseless and horse-drawn carriages.

A second major factor was the foresight of French entrepreneurs, anxious to make up ground lost as a result of France's belated and partial industrial revolution. The traditional *famille artisanale* only began to industrialise in the latter half of the nineteenth century. These small businesses typically engaged in trades such as metal- and woodworking and thus had both the necessary flexibility and the existing infrastructure to turn their workshops into automobile manufacturing plants. These family-run workshops rapidly established themselves as the core of what came to be known as the Second Industrial Revolution in France. Thus, by the turn of the century, France had over 600 car manufacturers compared with fewer than 100 in the rest of Western Europe and the United States put together.[1]

The French aristocracy was mainly responsible for the first attempts to codify the sport. The bourgeois actively supported and participated in sports and indeed, the *Jockey-club de Paris*, a gathering of the elite of nineteenth-century French society, was an example of this close link. It was two members of this exclusive club who formed two-thirds of the founding members of the *Automobile Club de France* (ACF) in 1895. The Count de Dion, Baron de Zuylen and Paul Meyan, a journalist with *Le Figaro* and editor of the newsletter *La France Automobile*, met in September 1895 to create the world's first automobile club. De Dion was nominated club president, a post he immediately ceded to de Zuylen as he saw his position as a major manufacturer of the time as a conflict of interest in the promotion of the car. Although the creation of the *Association Internationale des Automobile Clubs Reconnus* (AIACR) in 1904 may be seen as the logical development of a governing body for automobile clubs, this predecessor to the FIA (*Fédération Internationale de l'Automobile*), which came into being in 1947, was essentially the body with which the ACF organised its international races. Its headquarters is located next door to that of the ACF at 8 Place de la Concorde and had, until 1963, the same presidents as that of the ACF. Indeed, the link between motor sport and aristocracy endured through much of the twentieth century; to this day, only three out of the ten presidents of what is now known as the FIA have not had noble titles.

The growth in automobile racing was also to have its effects on the highly politicised arena of journalism. The Comte Albert de Dion and Pierre Giffard found themselves on opposite sides of one of the largest political scandals in French history: the Dreyfus Affair. Giffard founded *Le Vélo* in 1892 and pursued an active role in promoting both the bicycle and automobile; as a result, his paper was widely used for the advertising of these vehicles. One such manufacturer was the Comte de Dion, a vocal anti-Dreyfusard. De Dion became involved in a highly publicised spat with the French president Émile Loubet at the Auteuil races and for which he was jailed for 15 days. Having been heavily criticised by Giffard in the newspaper he sponsored extensively, de Dion removed his advertising from *Le Vélo* and set about creating a new newspaper. He and a number of other industrialists, including Michelin created *L'Auto-Vélo* in 1900 with Henri Desgranges as editor-in-chief. It became *L'Auto* in January 1903 when Giffard successfully sued the paper for infringement on his own paper's name. Hence it was *L'Auto* in 1903 that was responsible for the creation and organisation of the *Tour de France*.

The popular press at the time was also experiencing substantial development with growing levels of literacy in society as each newspaper was striving to come up with ideas to increase its readership. A strong link developed between journalism and the expansion of sport. As sport was of growing interest, it was seen by journalists as a means of acquiring and then maintaining a high readership. The coverage of a sporting event that lasted over a number of days or even weeks was used as a tool to promote the purchase of newspapers on a regular basis. Pierre Giffard, editor-in-chief of *Le Petit Journal*, the largest-selling newspaper of the 1890s, organised in 1891 a bicycle race from Bordeaux to Paris; this was followed in the same year by Paris-Brest-Paris. These bicycle races allowed Giffard to create a daily column relating to the race build-up and the preparations involved in it, encouraging readers to buy their paper each day, for the duration of the race period, in order to learn about the progress each competitor was making on a daily basis.[2] This paper-selling technique was the reason for the creation by *L'Auto* of the *Tour de France*. It was only a matter of time before this practice was adapted and used as a model to promote a motoring event.

The first attempts to test the efficiency of automobiles in public were organised as early as 1887 when the French newspaper *Le Vélocipède illustré* announced the holding of a 'reliability' trial. The event involved a short run from Paris to Versailles. Only one competitor showed up, however, and the event had to be abandoned. The following year the same trial was organised and this time two automobiles were present; the trial was carried out and completed but little importance has been given to it since the two cars involved were both from the same manufacturer, the Comte de Dion. An automobile was allowed take part in the Paris-Brest-Paris bicycle race of 1891. This race also saw the first instance of pneumatic tyres used in a race. The Frères Michelin convinced the renowned cyclist Charles Terront to use their invention on his entry. While having to stop to repair numerous punctures, the pneumatics' ability to cope with the rough terrain helped Terront to a famous victory. The race winner actually finished the course some 17 minutes before the car did, which is perhaps indicative of why the first race was not to take place for another number of years.

Pierre Giffard, having sponsored the Paris-Brest-Paris bike race, decided to apply his model to a motoring trial. Having seen the automobile at first hand in 1891, Giffard organised and publicised a trial for *voitures sans chevaux* (horseless carriages) to be held on the public roads between Paris and Rouen in 1894. It was not a race but a reliability trial intended to assess the potential of the motor car. Unlike previous attempts, this event mustered a large level of interest, not least due to its constant front-page promotion by Giffard in *Le Petit Journal*. It gradually began to catch the attention of the public and what has been qualified as a 'significant' crowd turned out in Porte-Maillot for the departure on 11 June 1894.[3] Of the 102 entrants, 21 actually appeared on the start line and 17 made it to the finish. As reliability and practicality were the order of the day, the automobile that finished first was not necessarily awarded first prize. The Comte de Dion, on a steam engine of his own invention, crossed the line first; his vehicle, as it required a stoker, was deemed to be impractical and first prize was jointly awarded to the second and third-placed marques, both of which were petrol-powered. De Dion covered the distance of 127km in a time of six hours and 48 minutes, giving him an average speed of just over 18 km/h – but it must be taken into account that all competitors stopped for lunch during the event.

Giffard was immediately approached to organise an automobile race in 1895 but declined as he was unwilling to run an event on open roads with vehicles capable of reaching what was perceived at the time to be dangerously high speeds. De Dion and Baron de Zuylen duly organised the Paris-Bordeaux-Paris race. The choice of route may have been modelled on the first city-to-city bicycle race, which was successfully run from Bordeaux to Paris in 1891. This route was also chosen in order to show those still sceptical about the automobile that it could not only cover a large distance with a minimum of mechanical issues but also, by linking two of France's largest cities, demonstrate the utilitarian role of the car. De Dion, in the rules, shows that he is aware of what is at stake:

> It is important to remind competitors that the rules which they must follow have been devised in their own interest as well as endeavouring to demonstrate the progress made in automobile construction which was the principal reason behind the committee's decision to organise this race. Consequently, the committee asks that competitors never lose sight of the fact that this 1,200 kilometre test, in which they are taking part, could be decisive from the point of view of daily usage, today and in the future, of automotive transport.[4]

While car trials were a thing of the past, with people wanting to know which car was the fastest, practicality remained a primordial concern, as although Emile Levassor on a Panhard finished the race first, in a time of 48 hours and 48 minutes (24.5 km/h), he wasn't awarded first prize due to the fact that his automobile only had two seats and was thus not considered viable. However his achievement is remembered by a statue situated at the start/finish line in Porte-Maillot, Paris. Commissioned by the ACF in 1898, a year after Levassor's death, the monument was originally to be sculpted by Jules Dalou, but upon his death in 1902, one of his students, Camille Lefèvre, completed the Greco-Roman-style triumphal arch in 1907. The arch, which depicts Levassor in his car being watched by onlookers, is situated in the Place Porte-Maillot and recently celebrated its hundredth birthday.

The newborn ACF decided to hold city-to-city races on an annual basis. Race organisers chose routes that always incorporated Paris as starting point but which gradually moved further away in their destination. Paris-Bordeaux-Paris covered a total distance of almost 1200km; the following year the race distance was extended to more than 1700 km for the Paris-Marseille-Paris race. The year 1898 may have seen a shorter race but with a much more significant destination as the race was from Paris to Amsterdam; actual political borders were crossed as the automobile was proving capable of linking countries. Races linking Paris with Berlin, Vienna and Madrid followed; these were interspersed with some national competitions including the holding of the *Tour de France automobile* in 1899, organised by Paul Meyan and *Le Matin*, a full four years before the cycling version.

The largest sporting event to take place in 1903 was not, as most would assume, the inaugural *Tour de France* bicycle race but the Paris-Madrid road race organised by the ACF, which left from Versailles on 24 May 1903 in front of a reputed 200,000 spectators.[5] A further two million people lined the roads from Paris to Bordeaux and, according to newspaper reports the entire 200,000 population of Bordeaux came out to see the arrival at the end of the first major stage of this race. A spate of fatal accidents, however, brought about the cancellation of the Bordeaux-Madrid stage of the race. Among the victims was Marcel Renault, brother of Louis, co-founder of the company that still dominates today. As the automobile was becoming more famous it was also beginning to find detractors in journalistic and literary fields; among others, Léon Bloy stated in *Le Journal* of 26 May 1903 that 'all ambitious automobilists *are premeditated killers'*.[6] 'Motor racing had taken a firm hold of the imagination of the French public, however, and the promotional potential of up to three million people attending a single race could not be ignored. The ill-fated Paris-Madrid race signalled the banning of city-to-city races in France as it was deemed impossible to adequately marshal motor races on open roads. An early form of circuit racing came into being as a result of which roads were closed to public use to form a circuit; this became the compromise required for the authorities to allow racing to continue.

While these races were important for the establishment of reliability, many manufacturers were not convinced about the feasibility of the internal combustion engine and the late 1890s saw the beginning of a struggle for power between three types of vehicle: internal combustion, steam and electric. Each vehicle had its own qualities and weaknesses. Electric cars were quiet and reliable, but their batteries never lasted more than 40 or 50 kilometres and, given the fact that they were difficult to recharge outside urban environs, were essentially seen as city cars. Steam-powered automobiles worked along the same lines as locomotive engines albeit in a much smaller form: these cars required a *chauffeur* (literally *heater*) to feed the engine with fuel in order to provide the steam to propel the car. Steam cars, therefore, required two people to run and were quite large and cumbersome. They were also slow to start as 20 minutes were generally needed for an automobile to build up a head of steam. Internal combustion engines were noisy, smelly and largely unreliable; however, they could cover large distances and for those who converted from steam, their *chauffeur* now drove the car.

La France Automobile, which was essentially the journalistic organ of the ACF, in an attempt to find an answer to this debate, initiated a series of short speed tests in the late 1890s A straight stretch of road the Parc Agricole d'Achères near Paris was the venue chosen for these sprints and in 1898 Gaston de Chasseloup-Laubat set the world's first land speed record when he achieved 63km/h driving a Jeantaud, an electric vehicle. In 1899, Camille Jenatzy, nicknamed 'The Red Devil', broke the 100km/h barrier for the first time, driving another electric car which he aptly named *La Jamais Contente* ('never satisfied'). This high point also proved to be the beginning of the electric car's downfall as it was becoming more and more apparent that there was no scope for improvement in the power or longevity of electric batteries. Steam, and more particularly internal combustion, remained a more viable option. Léon Serpollet procured the bragging rights for steam when he broke the land speed record in April 1902 driving his *Oeuf de Pâques* ('Easter Egg') along the Promenade des Anglais in Nice, to record a speed of 120km/h. Within a matter of months prominent American William K Vanderbilt II drove a French Mors at 122km/h to become the first internal-combustion-powered automobile to hold the land speed record. This signalled the beginning of the end for steam power as petrol, in winning both reliability and speed trials, was proving its ability to answer the needs of all drivers. Across the Atlantic, the success of the Stanley Steamer and the Doble steam car meant that steam power retained a commercial market in the United States until the late 1920s; however, the advent of electric ignition for internal combustion, which greatly simplified starting a car, along with greater affordability, allowed Henry Ford and his Model T take control of the automotive market in the States.[7]

Gordon Bennett: Modern Motor Sport Arrives

Wealthy American journalist Gordon James Bennett played a significant role in the promotion of international motor racing. He sponsored the world's first international race, inviting competitors from different countries to compete for the Gordon Bennett trophy. Gordon James Bennett (1841–1918) was born in the Alpes Maritimes, France. He was the son of an Irish-American mother and a Scottish-American father who owned the famous *New York Herald*, the leading American newspaper of the day. When he took over the reins from his father in 1866, he was 25 and keen to spread the family firm abroad. Gordon Bennett had a natural sense of the newsworthy and publicised his *Herald* with a series of publicity stunts, such as Arctic and African expedition sponsorships, predecessors to the Citroën 'raids' of the 1920s and 1930s as they used exploration to promote sales. Bennett was also an avid sailor having won the first transatlantic yacht race in 1866. As a sports fan and seeing sports promotion as a means of improving newspaper readership, much like Giffard, he inaugurated competitions in yachting, football and boxing.

Bennett moved to Paris in 1877 where he established the *Paris Herald*; he was, therefore, in France at the birth of the motor car and was ideally placed to observe its progress. Consequently, in announcing the inauguration of his *Coupe Internationale*, his aim was to expand motor sport into an international phenomenon. The first international races followed a set of rules devised by Bennett but enforced by the ACF. Each annual race was open to a maximum of three entries per nation and they were to be held in the country of the winner of the previous year's race. The cars of each nation were to be painted a national colour irrespective of their manufacturer. French cars were painted blue, American cars red, Belgians yellow, Italians black and Germans white. As there was no British entry in the inaugural race and since the three traditional colours from the British flag were taken by other countries, the Napier driven by Selwyn Edge in 1901, and which won in 1902, was green – and this is reputedly the source of British Racing Green.

While initially quite farcical affairs, with only France filling its quota of three cars, it was not until the French were defeated that manufacturers and the public opened their eyes to the worth of the competition. In its third year, a British car, a Napier, won the Paris-Vienna race, albeit in rather fortunate circumstances as the three leading cars, all of which were French, each broke down in quick succession. This victory, however, brought to an end a perception of French invincibility felt not only by the French themselves but also by other nations. A dramatic rise in the number of entries in the French qualifying competition for the following year is indicative of the importance attached to this result in France. Equally, 1903 saw the largest number of entries in the race, twice the number of the previous year, and full quotas of competitors for the first time from Germany, Britain and the USA.

As the 1902 race had been won by a British driver, it was now Britain's responsibility to host the race and this proved problematic. Britain had always been hostile towards the automobile and the 'Red Flag Law' set a speed limit of 12 miles per hour on all British roads and stipulated that all motor cars be preceded by a man on foot waving a red flag. Although this law had been repealed by 1903, speed limits were still maintained so it was decided that the race be hosted in Ireland where a relaxation of speed laws was permitted on rural roads but not in towns. The racing track consisted of two circuits forming a figure '8' centred on the town of Athy, Co. Kildare. On seven points where the track passed through towns, there were non-racing zones where the cars followed a bicycle through the town. This was the first example of an international motor race taking place outside France; it was also the first time motor sport was attracting global attention. Camille Jenatzy, driving a Mercedes, won the race, taking the Gordon Bennett Trophy to Germany along with the privilege of hosting the following race.

The final two Gordon Bennett races in 1904 and 1905 took place in a highly charged political atmosphere. The Franco-Prussian war of 1870 was still part of mentalities and this was no more evident than in Alsace, which had been ceded by France to what was to become Germany in the aftermath of their high-profile military defeat. Léon Théry's 1904 victory on German soil and subsequent triumphant return to France through Alsace where he and his supporters were ordered to hide their Tricolours demonstrated the potential of the motor car to become a symbol of national pride.[8] The ostentatious welcoming of Théry by the president of France on the Champs-Elysées further augmented the political impact of the event.[9] These races took place on a backdrop of a series of events that would ultimately bring about the First World War. Germany's policy of *Weldpolitik* and the subsequent signing of the *Entente Cordiale* in 1904 between the United Kingdom and France heightened national tension and the automobile, symbol of progress, of modernity and of technicity became a powerful player in this cold war. The final Gordon Bennett race took place in France and was the centre of media attention across the globe. Léon Théry's triumph for a second year in a row was front page news simultaneously in France, Britain and the USA among other countries; in doing so it relegated the Russo-Japanese War to page 2.[10]

The Gordon Bennett Cup (1900–5) internationalised motor sport at a time when it seemed that France would continue to monopolise the sport for years to come. Bennett harnessed the French method of organising racing, even going so far as to use the ACF to organise his races. He based his initial race in France but, by stipulating that the winner must host the following year's event, he opened the door for other nations, in time, to establish themselves in motor racing; this also provided a focal point to develop this growth. Bennett's cup acted as a catalyst for motor sport development as it evolved into a phenomenon visible on the world stage. These races, however, left France increasingly frustrated. While other nations often struggled to assemble a team, France held annual qualifiers to choose its representatives. Thus, with only three French cars out of 29 qualifying for the 1904 race, manufacturers such as Clément-Bayard, Darracq, De Dietrich, Gobron-Brillié, Hotchkiss, Panhard, Serpollet and Turcat-Méry found themselves absent from the international sporting spotlight. When the Gordon Bennett Cup was born in 1899, the motor industry was still struggling to make its products viable, but by 1905, the USA had overtaken France as the world's largest automobile producer.[11] Turn-of-the-century motor racing was a reliability exercise more so than a sporting event; however, the success of the Gordon Bennett Cup meant that the sport was becoming, to an even greater extent, an arena in which constructors marketed their products. Responding to the French inability to cater for all its manufacturers, the ACF decided to boycott the 1906 Gordon Bennett competition. It inaugurated a race in which all car producers could have a chance to compete without limiting entries. Bennett, in turn, withdrew sponsorship from his motor race and created the *Coupe Aéronautique Gordon Bennett* in 1906 for balloons, an event which exists to this day. He followed this, in 1909, by sponsoring in Rheims 'The Gordon Bennett', an airplane race which continued until the First World War. It is particularly apt that the street named in Bennett's honour in Paris is located beside the Stade Roland Garros – Garros was a renowned First World War pilot and the first person to fly across the Mediterranean.

Le Mans: Continuities and Changes

For the second part of this article, one area in France and its role in the growth of motor racing will be discussed. When the name Le Mans is mentioned, it is the 24-hour car race that springs to mind for the majority of people. While it is true the Le Mans *24 Heures* is universally recognised, the role of this town in the evolution of motor sport goes back much further than the 1923 start date of the first 24-hour race. As host of the world's first Grand Prix in 1906, Le Mans holds a singular place in motor sporting history but the automobile tracks stretch back even further in the history of the town and is an area which can justifiably claim to be the hub of motor sport in France.

The department of La Sarthe was home of the *famille Bollée*. Originally bell makers, this *famille artisanale* took up car construction when steam locomotion was being developed. Amédée Bollée invented *l'obéissante*,[12] a 12-seat estate that was advertised as the 'first road locomotive' in 1873. This vehicle made national news in 1875 when Bollée drove it the 200km that separate Le Mans and Paris. In 1878 *la Mancelle*, meaning a female native of Le Mans,[13] became the first automotive vehicle to be presented at the *Exposition Universelle de Paris*. Such was the lack of familiarity with this new mode of transport that, being steam powered, it was classified in this *Exposition* in the railroad section. Their *Nouvelle* took part in, as previously mentioned, the first ever automobile race, the 1895 Paris-Bordeaux-Paris. Many different vehicles built by the Bollée family won various small races over this period, including Paris-Dieppe (1897) and Paris-Trouville (1898), and in 1898 Léon

Bollée took part in the highly publicised world land speed record attempts averaging 60km/h. The Bollée family was a prime example of the success that could be had with the automobile. Its success inspired an ethic of innovation in the region of La Sarthe, an ethic that infused the ambition of an entire community to mobilise in order to attract what was to become the largest race of the time to their département.[14]

In late 1905 the ACF announced that a new *Grand Prix*[15] would be held the following year, allowing three entries from each automobile manufacturer. The newspaper *L'Auto* announced 'the Race for the Circuit' on 1 December 1905. Among the 17 proposals was one from Georges Durand on behalf of the *Circuit du Mans*, received on 15 December, just 14 days after the original advertisement. Durand had, before the end of 1905, acquired the financial backing of the *Conseil Général* of the Sarthe and had convinced the board members of the ACF to visit the proposed circuit, a triangular formation joining the towns of Le Mans, St Calais and La Ferté Bernard. After examining the proposal and visiting the proposed circuit between 14 and 16 January the ACF declared on 17 January 1906 that La Sarthe would host the inaugural *Grand Prix de l'ACF* in 1906. The *Automobile Club de la Sarthe* was created on 24 January 1906 and immediately made the Baron de Zuylen (the then president of the ACF) and Amédée Bollée honorary presidents. Durand was elected general secretary, having turned down the opportunity to become president. An energetic fund-raising campaign ensued, the circuit was duly prepared and on 26–7 June, the race took place on the 103.16km circuit which every car had to complete six times on each of the two days. Twenty-three French cars took part in this race, which despite a significant attendance constituted a loss for the ACS, with most of the spectators deciding to watch the race from areas where it was free to do so rather than paying entry into the main stand. This setback notwithstanding, the entire weekend was deemed a success by the ACF and Le Mans went down in history for having hosted the first Grand Prix.

In an effort to promote the Grand Prix series, the ACF moved the 1907 and 1908 editions of the race to other circuits and Le Mans found itself in need of a way of remaining at the cutting edge of innovation. The next big step in technology was also embraced with the creation of the *Aéro-Club du Mans* in 1908. Ballooning was becoming more and more popular and, in August 1908, Léon Bollée, son of Amédée, took the next logical step in aviation promotion by welcoming Wilbur Wright to Le Mans; where the main straight of the Le Mans Grand Prix circuit, *La Ligne Droite des Hunaudières* (the 'Mulsanne Straight' in English), was used for a series of flight exhibitions over a number of days. Wright left after a week of stunning the large numbers of spectators, among whom was Louis Bleriot, who became the first man to fly across the English Channel.

A period of lack of interest in motor sport in France followed, the country having lost the national Grand Prix events two years in a row to German competition. Thus French manufacturers took the radical decision to pull out of competitive international motor racing. Consequently the ACF decided to discontinue the Grand Prix after just three years of its taking place. This first depression in French motor racing would appear to be linked to disenchantment among French manufacturers, with the realisation that what they had seen as perhaps a God-given right to finish ahead of all competition was no longer the case. Rather than lose to what they saw as inferior competition, French manufacturers decided to withdraw from competition altogether. Smaller national races were still popular and Le Mans continued to host events through this period of transition. As general secretary of the

Automobile Club de la Sarthe (ACS), Durand decided, in 1911, to host the first *Grand Prix de France* in Le Mans on a circuit of just over 54km. This new Grand Prix, which was seen as a distinct entity from the *Grand Prix de l'ACF*, turned out to be such a success that the following year the *Grand Prix de l'ACF* was revived and run in Amiens while the *Grand Prix de France* remained in Le Mans. That two Grand Prix were held in France within one calendar year was indicative of the swing in popularity once again in favour of motor racing.

Georges Durand and the Circuit du Mans had one more role to play before the birth of its most famous offspring: the *24 heures du Mans*. Durand took the decision to attempt to bring French motor racing out of the doldrums for a second time, by launching the *Coupe des Voiturettes* in 1920. This was the first motor race to take place in the wake of the Great War. While the whole of France was still reeling from the effects of this conflict, Durand saw an opportunity for the ACS to once again come to the fore in the world of motor racing. This initiative provided the impetus for the hosting of the first post-war *Grand Prix de l'ACF*, run in Le Mans the following year.

Le Mans is arguably best known for its 24-hour race, the launching of which came, as has been seen, on the back of more than 20 years of groundwork and was to become the world's most famous annual race. The *24 Heures du Mans* was the brainchild of Georges Durand who, upon becoming worried about the enduring relevance of motor sport in its current form, held a meeting during the *Salon de l'Automobile* of 1922 with Charles Faroux of the newspapers *L'Auto* and *La Vie Automobile* and with Émile Coquille of Rudge-Whitworth, well-known wheel makers. It was decided that motor racing needed to be simplified and made more accessible. It was by now apparent that cars were reasonably reliable and could reach high speeds. The problem was that race cars were moving further and further away from the actual vehicles on the roads at the time and the technical advances were no longer of direct benefit to the everyday driver. Coquille was of the belief that car lights and starters were particularly behind the times and that, in the interests of building a safer car, a high-profile night race was needed. Durand suggested instead a 24-hour race as this would not only put the lights to the test but it would also test man and machine to the limit. It was agreed that the race of 'tourism cars' would take place during the second half of the month of June, when days are at their longest, and that the race was to run from four o'clock in the afternoon until the same time the following day.

The 'Le Mans start' was the initiative introduced to test the cars' starters: this involved the drivers lining up on one side of the road and, once the French flag was dropped at four o'clock sharp French time, they would run across the road, jump into their vehicle, start it up and drive off. The advent of racing harnesses did nothing to stop this practice and it took the actions of a racing driver to show the lunacy of competing at getting into racing harnesses. In 1969, instead of running across to his car, Jacky Ickx, the eventual winner, made the point of walking slowly across the track and belting up carefully before driving off. The following year would see the race start with the drivers already strapped into their cars. The Le Mans start did, however, ensure that Durand and Coquille accomplished the two goals they had set for themselves: testing the starters and lights of the cars.

The *Le Mans 24 heures* has continued to be used as a testing ground for new technologies and, in fact, aerodynamics improved immensely over the early years due to the long straights on the circuit. Disc brakes were first used at Le Mans in 1953.

Alternative fuel sources have also been tested there, from ethanol, used on a class-winning Porsche in 1980, to a diesel powered Audi that won three successive races from 2006 to 2008. Audi managed to achieve from diesel a similar speed to that obtained normally from a petrol car. This, allied with the fuel economy of diesel, meant that the Audi pitted fewer times than other cars, giving it the necessary margin to win. Peugeot has since followed Audi's lead and launched its 2007 challenger: a diesel powered car piloted by, among others, Jacques Villeneuve.

Le Mans is also the site of the single most devastating accident in motor sport, an accident that had severe repercussions not only in France but throughout the world. This is an accident also described vividly in the contribution of Philip O'Kane to this collection. In 1955, just seven hours into the race; French driver Pierre Levegh, driving a Mercedes, was forced to swerve wildly by another car, lost control of his own car and flew into a packed stand. He died instantly along with 82 spectators. The decision to continue the race was taken in order to allow emergency services access to the circuit, as stopping the race would have flooded the roads with over 200,000 people. Later in the race, Mercedes withdrew its two other participating cars and retired entirely from competitive racing until 1987. When the curtain drew on this event, it saw the cancellation of a number of races throughout the world, including the Grand Prix de France for that year. It also brought about a complete ban on circuit racing in Switzerland, a ban that exists to this day.

The *Le Mans 24 heures* has a mythical quality about it. It is difficult to define why it has acceded to this status but its significant history certainly contributes to this. The year 2007 saw over 250,000 spectators attend the race, the largest crowd ever seen there. This enduring and growing popularity also has much to do with the fact that it is one of the only races left in the world that actually uses public roads as part of the circuit. Much like the *Tour de France*, the *24 Heures* evokes strong feelings in spectators as it strives to maintain a relevance to the everyday person. The use of public roads for both events is extremely significant in this light. In the *Tour de France*, locals from each town appear to cheer on competitors from the area taking part on their roads in this prestigious event and, equally, there is a sense of pride evident in seeing the biggest names in the world taking part alongside French cars on an everyday road in France. In Le Mans, the Bugatti Circuit (named in honour of Ettore Bugatti, a famous French car manufacturer of Italian extraction) joins up with public roads, for one weekend of the year, to form the 13km track which is covered on average 250 times over the 24 hours of the race. The fascination of seeing these spectacular cars race on public roads, which have been closed to traffic just for this special weekend in June, is immense. It is the ultimate homage to the history and tradition of motor sport in La Sarthe that the main thoroughfare that joins it with Paris and which connects Paris to the west of the country is closed for this spectacle.

The notoriety of the Le Mans race is an international phenomenon. In 1955, the same year as the Le Mans accident, Nescafé launched in the English-speaking world a new coffee called 'Blend 37', the name of which is explained on the label. Apparently, Didier Cambreson drove his car, number 37, for the entire 1937 race after his partner failed to show up. He managed to complete this feat by drinking Blend 37 and he eventually finished the race in a very creditable 37th position. The fact that the story is untrue is unimportant; it is the epic nature of the supposed feat that impresses. One driver completing the entire 24-hour race without a break, except to drink this coffee, is the stuff of mythical legend. The typically French-sounding driver managing against all the odds to complete the most demanding race of them all fits perfectly with the lore associated with Le Mans. What is revealing is that this epic mystification of Le Mans is not a specifically French characteristic but it is a trend that has been exported successfully throughout the motoring world. This form of advertising Blend 37 was obviously effective as Nescafé went on to sponsor many racing cars with this particular brand.

When Le Mans is mentioned, it is these images that are evoked: the Le Mans start, the tradition of one of the oldest races in the world, the ritual closing of the *route nationale* to conjoin the race circuit with the Bugatti track. All of the above contribute to make the *Le Mans 24 heures* the legendary race it remains today. The Le Mans ethic of endurance is also reflected in the longevity of the race; it is a very proud statistic that only once in 80 years, other than during the Second World War, did the race not take place. It even took place during the social unrest of 1968, although it was pushed to September of that year until events had calmed down to a certain extent. The department of La Sarthe, of which Le Mans is the capital, has over the years made a concerted effort to promote sport in the area. The historical presence of the race has been used as a springboard to launch professional clubs in other sports and Le Mans is now the home to premier-division professional football and basketball teams. Le Mans Sarthe Basket won the national league in 2006 and Le Mans UC72 was promoted to the French first division for the first time ever in 2004 while its stadium, The *Stade Léon Bollée*, is to be replaced by a new complex in 2010, which will be the first commercially named stadium in France. Current French Prime Minister François Fillon, during his mandate as president of the Sarthe General Council, centralised funding for all sporting activity in the department and ensured adequate cooperation between these three larger sports in order to run them in harmony with each other. Le Mans has actively striven to make the most of the sporting atmosphere that exists in the region and has used its history in motor sport to create a certain aura which is seen to be distinct from that of the globalising image linked to Formula One. In 2007, the idea of the *Grand Prix de France* returning to Le Mans was mooted by the FIA; however, the possibility was rejected by the *Automobile Club de l'Ouest*, its president Jean-Claude Plassart stating in *L'Équipe* of 16 May 2008 that 'We have built our reputation on endurance and it is imperative that we do not blur this image'.

When international motor racing has become irrelevant to many; when, to many, Grand Prix Formula One is nothing more than rich kids driving around in aerodynamic cocoons that bear no more than a passing resemblance to road cars; when World Championship Rallying is being hit by withdrawals from its most prominent constructors, Le Mans' enduring popularity remains absolute. From its beginning, as a cradle for motor sport, through the early days of Grand Prix racing right up to its current position, at the forefront of motor racing in France, Le Mans continues to gather bigger viewing and attendance figures, year in year out, while all forms of motor sport are coming under increasing pressure to merely survive. Its rich legacy is one of perseverance, innovation and sheer hard work, much like the 24-hour race for which it is famous.

Conclusion

The role of France as testing ground for motor racing has existed from the very beginning of the sport. The first races ever run took place with Paris as its focal point and the first attempts at its codification were a result of France's desire to accept and promote this new technological innovation. The early growth stemmed the initiative taken by French *familles artisanales* to adapt their work and build what, hopefully, would be the future of horseless transport. This desire was then adopted by the French bourgeoisie who embraced the idea of organising and taking part in races in order to build the reliability and reputation of the self-propelled vehicles. Gordon Bennett modified the French turn-of-the-century races and successfully internationalised them through the use of French facilities to lay the groundwork until other countries were capable of taking up the baton. Le Mans assumed the reins in the further advancement of the product; its name will forever be associated with the hosting of the first international Grand Prix, but it is for its endurance race that this city is truly famous. The Le Mans 24-hour race was initially established to test motoring products that were superfluous in larger races. Le Mans has successfully maintained this link with everyday automobile tourism and, as such, has established a much more enduring relationship with supporters. The *Le Mans 24 heures* is, in many ways, a reflection of the ground-breaking turn-of-the-century races, just as these races were established to improve the automobile on its steep learning curve; the Le Mans ethic to test cars to their limit gives the event relevance far beyond seeing who finishes first.

Notes

1. Laux, *In First Gear*, 40.
2. Cf. Dauncey, 'Entre presse et spectacle sportif', 35–7.
3. Varey, *1000 Historic Automobile Sites*, 332.
4. Paris-Bordeaux race rules
5. Dauncey and Hare, *The Tour de France, 1903–2003*, 60.
6. Quoted in Laux, *In First Gear*, 40.
7. The advent of the assembly line, Fordism and Taylorism helped Ford produce cheaper cars which sold much larger numbers than the workshop-built models in France.
8. Besqueut, *La Coupe Gordon Bennet 1905*, 7.
9. Breyer, *La belle époque à 30 à l'heure*, 71.
10. Besqueut, *La Coupe Gordon Bennet 1905*, 5.
11. Laux, *In First Gear*, 210.
12. Female form of the adjective 'obedient'.
13. The gendered names given to these vehicles are indicative of the patriarchal society in which they existed.
14. Cf. Plessix, 'Au Berceau des Sports Mecaniques', 207–9.
15. The term 'Grand Prix' was a borrowing from horse racing, which inaugurated a 'Grand Prix de Dieppe' in 1870; however, the origins of the term may actually stem from the world of art, where a 'Grand Prix de Rome' was made available from as early as 1803. This term was also applied to races previously hosted by the ACF. The Paris-Bordeaux-Paris race was thus retrospectively named *Le premier Grand Prix de l'ACF*.

References

Besqueut, P. *La coupe Gordon Bennet 1905*. Clermont-Ferrand: la Montagne, 1985.
Breyer, V. *La belle époque à 30 à l'heure*. Paris: France-Empire, 1984.
Dauncey, H. 'Entre presse et spectacle sportif, l'itinéraire pionnier de Pierre Giffard (1853–1922)'. *Le Temps des Médias* 2, no. 8 (2007): 35–46.
Dauncey, H., and G. Hare. *The Tour de France 1903–2003: A Century of Sporting Structures, Meanings and Values*. London and Portland, OR: Frank Cass, 2003.
Laux, J.M. *In First Gear: The French Automobile Industry to 1914*. Montreal: McGill-Queen's University Press, 1976.
Plessix, R. 'Au Berceau des Sports Mecaniques: Le Mans', in *Jeux et Sports dans l'histoire*. ed. Comite des Travaux Historiques et Scientifiques. Paris: CTHS, 1992, 205–28.
Varey, M. *1000 Historic Automobile Sites*. Oakland, CA: Elderberry Press, 2003.

Daredevils and Early Birds: Belgian Pioneers in Automobile Racing and Aerial Sports During the Belle Époque

Thomas Ameye, Bieke Gils[1] and Pascal Delheye

Research Centre for the History of Sport and Kinesiology, Katholieke Universiteit Leuven, Tervuursevest 101, B-3001, Heverlee, Belgium

During the belle époque, Belgium was a trend-setting nation in many domains, including motorised sports. Belgian automobile racers and pilots shattered world records and became international stars. Striking was the shift in sports. Indeed, around 1896, sporting members of the leisure class stepped from the bicycle into the automobile and, around 1908, from the automobile into the airplane. Although these motorised sports were extremely expensive, this article shows that sportsmen and sportswomen from the working class could achieve upward social mobility through their performances. The achievements of these motorised pioneers had a major impact and wide-ranging significance. They laid the foundations for the expansion of the automobile industry and the emergence of civilian and military aviation.

Introduction

The pioneering role of Belgians in motorised sports has received little attention in the international literature. Even most Belgians do not know that the first motorised vehicle was already invented in the seventeenth century by the West Flemish Jesuit Ferdinand Verbiest,[2] that the internal combustion petrol engine was designed by their countryman Jean-Joseph Etienne Lenoir around 1860, that Pierre de Crawhez introduced racing on a closed circuit, that Camille Jenatzy was the first racer in the world to surpass 100km/h (see Figure 1) and that Hélène Dutrieu was the first woman to undertake a long-distance flight. Neither has the transition from cycling to automobile racing and from automobile racing to aviation been mapped in detail.[3] This is the intention of the present article. The shifting sport careers of Pierre de Caters, Hélène Dutrieu and Jan Olieslagers are used as examples of this evolution. The biographical information presented in this paper rests heavily on secondary literature. The biographies of de Caters, Dutrieu and Olieslagers are thus not necessarily 'renewing' and by no means complete. They are, on the other hand, instrumental to the interpretation presented in the last section of this article. Within the scope of this article, it is not possible to detail the adventurous careers of other Belgian pioneers such as Jozef Christiaens, Arthur Duray, Jules Tyck, Charles Van

Figure 1. Camille Jenatzy, a Belgian automobile racer, was the first in the world to surpass the 100 km/h barrier. This took place in 1899 in Archères (France) in his electrically driven car 'La Jamais Contente'. Interestingly, a comic movie entitled *La Toujours Contente* is scheduled to be shown in Belgian theatres by the end of 2011. Urbanus, the most successful Belgian comedian ever, will play the character of Armand Piston, a big admirer of Jenatzy who wants to build his own car.

den Born, John Verrept, Fernand Verschaeve *et al.* However, to gain a better understanding of the shift in sports we draw considerable attention to Belgium's broader socio-cultural context.

The very first official automobile race (Paris-Bordeaux-Paris) took place in France in 1895.[4] Among the automobiles – powered by petroleum, steam, or electricity – that drew up at the start line was a Belgian car, a Vincke-Delmer.[5] Nicolaas Vincke was the first Belgian automobile manufacturer to market automobiles and to participate in competitive racing.[6] The first automobile race in Belgium was organised in 1896 in Spa by the newly founded Automobile Club de Belgique.[7] Shortly after the Belgian Chevalier René de Knyff had won the prestigious Paris-Bordeaux race on 11 May 1898,[8] the first 'city-to-city' race on Belgian soil was held in June 1898 between Spa and Brussels. Forty participants appeared at the starting line, and the race was won by the Belgian Baron Pierre de Crawhez in his Panhard of French manufacture. The successes of René de Knyff and Pierre de Crawhez can be considered as the prelude to a glorious period for motorised sports in Belgium.[9]

The automobile and later the airplane were outstanding examples of the triumph of technology during the so-called belle époque.[10] The belle époque (1890–1914) was characterised by a flourishing bourgeois culture and an optimistic belief in progress, symbolised most prominently by the Eiffel Tower in Paris. The activities of engineers dominated this era and the wonders of science and technology grew exponentially (electricity, the telephone, radiotelegraphy etc.). Inventions were presented at 'astonishing' world's fairs. Culturally, not only was the rise of photography and cinematography striking, but also the emergence of new forms of art and architecture, such as art nouveau.[11] Belgian nationals played a very prominent role in this innovative era. While architects such as Victor Horta and Henry van de Velde gained international recognition, entrepreneurs like Edouard Empain and Ernest Solvay established international imperia. Around 1900, Belgium stood at the top of its economic power and cultural influence. With less than six million inhabitants it was – after Great Britain – the second industrial authority in the world thanks to its open, export-oriented and expansive market.[12] The 'greatness' of the country was exposed at world's fairs in Antwerp (1885, 1894), Brussels (1888, 1897, 1910), Liège (1905) and Ghent (1913).[13]

This period of prosperity and luxury for the 'leisure class' was – not surprisingly – very important for the institutionalisation of modern sports (football, cycling, tennis, yachting, motorised sports etc.). Young male members of the upper classes established and/or frequented English-style sports clubs.[14] These clubs not only denied democratic access due to requirements of leisure time and the money needed to buy sports equipment, but sometimes the statutes of the sports clubs – as in the case of the Racing Club de France – explicitly forbade membership to 'mechanics, labourers and artisans'.[15] The distinction between amateur sport (sports as an athlete's avocation) and professional sport (sports as an athlete's vocation) was a central issue in the sports milieu.[16] Baron Pierre de Coubertin, founder of the modern Olympic Games, even focussed on the problems regarding amateurism to arouse interest for his 'Olympic movement' during the congress he organised in Paris in June 1894. At this congress it was decided to establish an International Olympic Committee (IOC) and to re-establish the Olympic Games – with the first modern games to be held in Athens in 1896, which were exclusively accessible for amateurs.[17]

Belgians, too, played a leading role in the field of sport – in 1881 the Antwerp *Turner* Nicolaas Jan Cupérus was the founding president of the Fédération Européenne de Gymnastique, the first international sport federation – and in the discussions on amateurism. At the congress of the International Cyclists Association, organised in Antwerp in August 1894 and chaired by Raoul Claes, president of the Ligue Vélocipédique Belge, the classification of amateurs versus professionals in cycling was first internationally standardised.[18] It was Raoul Claes, too, who was contacted by Pierre de Coubertin to suggest a Belgian member for the IOC.[19] After conferences in Paris (1894) and in Le Havre (1897), a third Olympic congress was organised in 1905 in Brussels, and one year later the Belgian Olympic Committee was established on the occasion of the Intercalated Games in Athens in 1906.[20] Remarkable in this context is that the promoters of sport commenced to link the importance of physical activity to Belgium's expansion policy. They justified physical education and sport by citing its alleged positive impact on physical, moral and social development in support of world expansion. In all this England, industrial superpower and cradle of modern sport, served as the model.[21]

The differences between amateur and professional sport, as touched upon above, indicate that the period of the belle époque was ambivalent. It is an illusion to think that the elevated prosperity and (the belief in) unlimited expansion generated wealth and opportunities for everyone. Gita Deneckere has shown that the 'grandeur' of the belle époque has to be put in perspective.[22] Not only was the majority of the population unable to escape the hard reality of an impoverished existence, the triumphalistic achievements were only possible on the backs of the working class in Belgium and the slaves in the Congo. For instance, the colossal architectural and urban projects of King Leopold II of Belgium were made possible by the human exploitation in his colony.[23] As it will be demonstrated further in this article, the lucrative rubber industry contributed to the expansion of the Belgian automobile sector, with King Leopold II as catalyst.

Moreover, the bourgeois belief in progress was ambiguous and accompanied by thoughts of downfall and 'degeneration'. Jo Tollebeek has argued that degeneration thinking was the reverse side of the faith in progress:

> It was precisely the optimistic faith in the continual progress that led to the fear that this process would be interrupted, that the constant efforts to arrive at a better world would take their toll and decline would set it. And more, that the better world itself involved dangers for further growth and would ultimately undermine itself.[24]

Along with the emergence of new social movements – e.g. workmen, women, Flemish nationalists – fear of modernisation and massification grew among the members of the bourgeoisie and the aristocracy. This fear triggered defence mechanisms.[25] Hence, amateurism became a defence mechanism against the professional sport of the '*classes dangereuses*'.[26] Nevertheless, as this article is intended to illustrate, it was possible for members of the working class and for women to achieve upward social mobility via their sports performances.

Pierre de Caters (1875–1944)

Baron Pierre de Caters was born on 25 December 1875 in Berchem near Antwerp. He attended Greek-Latin secondary school and entered the Royal Military Academy in 1896. A year later, however, he broke off his military training and commenced engineering studies at the Montefiore Institute in Liège. He practised football, tennis, fencing and boxing, but his preference was for bicycle racing.[27] In 1898, thanks to his financial means – he inherited the complete fortune of his aunt (see Figure 2) – de Caters was able to acquire his first automobile; a 4 h.p. Mors from Paris. According to Michel Mandl and Guido Wuyts, he was persuaded into car racing by the successful Belgian racer Camille Jenatzy, whom he had met in the cycling milieu.[28]

Figure 2.   Baron Pierre de Caters in his Mercedes at the starting line of the Gordon Bennett race in 1904 in the German Taunus Mountains. His wealthy aunt, Mathilde de Caters, had named him as her sole heir in her will, which enabled him to profile himself in expensive motorised sports. Nevertheless, according to his grandson Guy de Caters, the extravagance of his projects caused him to reach the limit of his resources. © Frans Mielants.

On 16 December 1898, Pierre de Caters was one of the 26 founding members of the elite Automobile Club Anversois (of which he would become president in 1902).[29] His hunger for more cars was insatiable and he bought a De Dion, a 24 h.p. Mors and a 60 h.p. Mors from Paris, a Daimler from Stuttgart, a Vincke from Mechelen (Belgium), and a Snoeck Bolide from Ensival-lez-Verviers (Belgium).[30] In this Snoeck Bolide, he took part on 24 June 1900 in the *Course de Côte de Spa-Malchamps* (Belgium), which was won by Camille Jenatzy.[31] In order to be better able to work on his cars, de Caters set up a large garage in the carriage house of Catershof, the family estate in 's-Gravenwezel near Antwerp. In cooperation with Jenatzy, he placed an order of 60,000 francs[32] for the construction of a Voiture Mixte Jenatzy at the Fabrique Nationale d'Armes in Herstal (Belgium). The results with this car, which de Caters and Jenatzy had designed themselves with both an electric and a petroleum engine, fell short and were disappointing.[33] De Caters was more successful in a Mors. He came in first during the *Meeting d'Anvers* on 1 May 1901 and, with Jenatzy as his mechanic, he won, on 3 September 1901, the first *Semaine Automobile d'Ostende*, as well as the first 'flying kilometre' race organised by the Automobile Club Anversois.[34] Also in 1902 he raised the world speed record to 120km/h during the Paris-Vienna race.[35]

In 1903, Pierre de Caters participated for the first time in the legendary Gordon Bennett Cup race, which was organised, starting in 1900, by the publisher of the *New York Herald* 'to promote the [automobile] industry by affording an opportunity for competition between the manufacturers of different countries'. With Jenatzy and the American Foxhall Parker Keene, de Caters was, as captain, part of the German Mercedes team. At the start of the last round, de Caters was still in fourth place, but he had to quit the race only some ten kilometres from the finish when the rear axle of his Mercedes gave out.[36] Eventually, the victory went to his teammate and fellow countryman, Camille Jenatzy. The latter's victory was the first great international success for Mercedes, and the constructor thus awarded Jenatzy a prize of $25,000 and gave him a racing car that was worth $17,000. From his tyre manufacturer, Jenatzy received an extra $8,000. With the first place for Jenatzy and the second place for René de Knyff,[37] who drove a Panhard for France, this edition of the Gordon Bennett had a Belgian colour, which was also noted by *The New York Times*:

> A curious fact in connection with the race is that a majority of the racers are of English and American birth, and that while the German team won the trophy with the French team second, there was not a single German in the race, and but one Frenchman. Jenatzy, the winner, is a Belgian by birth, and so are Baron de Caters of the German team and Chevalier de Knyff of the French team, while Farman of the French team is English born and Keene of the German team is an American, making a total of four Americans, four Englishmen, three Belgians and one Frenchman in the race. Thus Belgium, though not entered or officially represented in the race, supplied a full team of three men who won both first and second places. As far as the nationality of the drivers counts, the result was a Belgian triumph.[38]

Besides car racing, Pierre de Caters was involved in several related activities. In 1905, he issued a challenge that would annually reward the manufacturers of the car with the engine that was the easiest to repair and thus be the most practical. The accompanying cup, a work of art valued at 5,000 francs, would be the property of the winner for one year.[39] Pierre de Caters also displayed his passion for cycle racing by offering a first prize – an automobile with a value between 8,000 and 10,000 francs – to the organising committee of the cycling race for amateurs from Paris to

Brussels in 1906.[40] De Caters also took part in motorboat races. He set world records in April 1906 for the one kilometre, ten kilometres, and 50 kilometres in Monaco, and in August he won the *Semaine Autonautique d'Ostende*.[41]

Furthermore, in the summer of 1906, Pierre de Caters, became involved in the establishment of a new Belgian-Italian automobile brand: Hermes Italiana SA (HISA). The headquarters of HISA were located both in Naples (Italy) and in Liège (Belgium) and from 1907 on in Bressoux, a suburb of Liège, where a factory was built. In 1907 de Caters took part in the *Coupe de la Commission Sportive de l'Automobile Club de France* in a HISA but he could not complete the course. Moreover, as not enough cars could be sold, the company had to close down on 2 August 1909.[42] At that time de Caters had already left automobile racing for aerial sport.[43]

Pierre de Caters was the first Belgian to make the transfer from automobile sport to aviation sport. In the beginning of September 1908, de Caters visited the training grounds of Issy-les-Moulineaux near Paris. He was impressed by several French flying pioneers and decided to buy the world's first triplane, designed by Ambroise Goupy and built by Voisin. The airplane was disassembled, crated and sent to Catershof where it was re-assembled.[44] On the family estate, a field of 1,800 by 1,500 metres was cleared of pine trees and a hangar was built for the airplane. The airplane itself was given a 50 h.p. Belgian Vivinus engine. It was tested for the first time on 17 October 1908. Finally, on 25 October 1908, de Caters succeeded in making a flight of 800 metres, albeit at an altitude of about 1.5 metres, and thereby crowned himself as the first Belgian aviator.[45] Apparently, he was dissatisfied with the results, for he ordered a biplane from Voisin. Voisin himself came with a crew to expedite the assembly of the biplane. In the meantime, the Aéro-Club de Belgique offered a prize for the first Belgian who could complete a flight of 1,000 metres. However, de Caters's first attempt on 20 December 1908 failed. Pierre de Caters's first airplane, the Goupy-Voisin triplane, was exhibited at the *Salon de l'Automobile et du Cycle* in Brussels in January 1909, where it was the central attraction.[46]

At the beginning of 1909, Pierre de Caters also started the construction of an airfield with hangars and access roads in Sint-Job-in-'t-Goor near Antwerp. While waiting for its completion, he practised on the military base in Mourmelon-le-Grand (France). There he also bought his third Voisin. In 1909, he already had participated in flight meetings in Monaco, Douai, Frankfurt and Berlin. During the international *Luftschiffart Ausstellung* in Frankfurt, with a flight of 35 minutes and 8 seconds, he broke the world time-flying record of the French aviator Louis Blériot. This way he earned a considerable amount of prize money, some 40,000 marks.[47]

The first flight in Belgium, by Farman on 27 May 1908 during the Ghent aviation week, quickly spawned successors: in 1909 aviation meetings were organised in Stockel, Tournai, Spa and Antwerp.[48] The *Semaine d'Aviation d'Anvers* (Antwerp) took place from 23 October to 2 November 1909 and was the first meeting where aviators from Belgium came into action. It was organised by the newly founded Aéro-Club d'Anvers, of which de Caters was vice president, and the Automobile-Club Anversois.[49] Pierre de Caters participated with three French biplanes of the Voisin type. He and his fellow aviator from Antwerp, Jan Olieslagers, who flew a French monoplane of the Blériot type, managed, in spite of the bad weather, to amaze the crowds. The *Semaine d'Aviation d'Anvers* catalysed Belgian aviation and set Belgian aviators out to explore the international airspace further. Thus, for example, de Caters was the first pilot to fly in Poland, Turkey and Egypt. On 24

October 1909, after his return to Belgium, he was the first Belgian to fly the distance of one kilometre and so collected the prize of the Aéro-Club de Belgique. On 3 December 1909, the Aéro-Club de Belgique issued him the first Belgian flying licence.[50]

On 17 February 1910, the French company Aviator opened a branch in Belgium of which Pierre de Caters's cousin, Max de Caters, became chairman. While the workshops of the constructor were originally set up in Zeebrugge (on the Belgian coast), they were quickly moved to Pierre's private airfield in Sint-Job-in-'t-Goor. Pierre provided publicity for his cousin's company by, for example, flying with an Aviator at the *Meeting d'Aviation* in Stockel (Brussels) in 1910.[51] Moreover, de Caters tried to convince the army to buy his airplanes. After all, an agreement for the training of pilots and/or the sale of Aviator airplanes could bring in a lot of money. However, his military endeavours were not fruitful and in November 1910 de Caters left with Jules Tyck, a young Antwerp aviator, for a lucrative demonstration tour in India. The Antwerp businessman René Bauwens acted as their manager. Initially de Caters and Tyck each received 25,000 francs from Bauwens. Until he was compensated for his initial expenditures of 50,000 francs, Bauwens received 60% of the entrance fees (as opposed to 20% for each de Caters and Tyck).[52] During their tour, de Caters was awarded the French *Croix de Chevalier de la Légion d'Honneur* and, three years later, in February 1914, the Belgian award of *Officier de l'Ordre de Léopold*.[53]

On 1 August 1914, on the eve of the First World War, Pierre de Caters volunteered for service in the army and became reserve lieutenant. A year later, at the age of 40, he was assigned the leadership of the military École d'Aviation d'Étampes, near Paris, which the French government had placed at the disposal of the Belgian Army. Pierre de Caters performed his function as commandant until he was sent on an aviation mission to Washington and New York in the summer of 1916.[54] According to the *New York Times*, de Caters 'after arranging for the purchase of a quantity of supplies' left for Bordeaux on 28 October 1916 aboard the French liner Rochambeau.[55] Whether or not he returned to the École d'Aviation d'Étampes is unknown. In any case, his military file, kept in the Archives of the Royal Museum of the Armed Forces and of Military History in Brussels, indicates that, from 15 July 1917 on, he was granted leave without pay from the Minister of War, Charles de Broqueville, and his successor Armand De Ceuninck. This allowed him to establish in Paris, together with engineer Mathieu van Roggen, a *Société Anonyme des Combustibles Économiques* for the production of turf briquettes to replace coal.[56] After the war, he probably continued his industrial activities. What is certain is that he gave up his activities in aviation entirely. Pierre de Caters died on 25 March 1944 in Paris, where he had settled after the First World War.[57]

Hélène Dutrieu (1877–1961)

Hélène Dutrieu was born in Tournai on 10 July 1877, the daughter of Florent Dutrieu, an artillery officer, and Clothilde van Thieghem. The family ran into financial problems, so the 14-year-old Hélène had to leave school and go out to work. Through her older brother, Eugène Dutrieu, who was already known in France with his bicycle circus Excelsior-Dutrieu, Hélène dedicated herself to bicycle racing.[58] In 1895 she participated for the first time in a bicycle race for women, which was organised in the velodrome in Tournai. She soon excelled in this sport, and, in 1895 and 1897, captured the hour record (distance covered in one hour on a bicycle).

In 1897, she won a prestigious speed race in Ostend, and, in 1898, she won the Grand Prix d'Europe, as well as a 12-day race in London. Because of her striking athletic achievements, King Leopold II awarded her the Croix de Saint André.[59] Hélène Dutrieu achieved recognition not only as a professional cyclist but also as a vaudeville performer and acrobat. In both Marseille and in London in 1903, she performed a circus act in which she 'looped the loop' with her bicycle on a specially constructed track. Dutrieu also performed on a motorcycle.[60] She was given the nickname 'The Human Arrow', after an act in which she rode at full speed and then jumped from a raised platform.[61] When this act no longer drew the public in the hoped-for numbers, Hélène Dutrieu decided to increase the spectacle value by doing the same act with an automobile. In Berlin, however, she ended up under the automobile and had to spend six months in a hospital. While there, her desire to become a pilot originated (see Figure 3). Coincidentally, the French company Clément-Bayard had just built a new model, the Demoiselle Santos-Dumont, and needed a light pilot to fly it. The constructor thought a female pilot would be ideal in this respect and also would generate more publicity than a male pilot. Dutrieu

Figure 3.   Hélène Dutrieu began as a bicycle racer, became an entertainer on stage with bicycle and automobile stunts, and then ventured into aviation sports. On 25 November 1910, she became the first Belgian woman to obtain a flying licence.
Source: Royal Museum of the Armed Forces and of Military History, Brussels, Belgium.

promptly signed the contract, which provided her a monthly salary of 2,000 francs, an automobile, and a mechanic.[62]

During her first real attempt, flying at the airfield of Issy-les-Moulineaux on 21 January 1910, Hélène Dutrieu came down brusquely after a jump in the air of 14 metres – because, it is said, she had not received any flying instructions. She came out unhurt but her Demoiselle was totally destroyed. After more unfortunate attempts, she decided to terminate her contract with Clément-Bayard and sought refuge with the French aviation pioneer René Sommer. He put his more stable biplane at her disposal, and she remained 20 minutes in the air on her first flight in Mouzon (French Ardennes). A couple of days later, she became the first woman to take a passenger aboard.[63]

The agreement between Hélène Dutrieu and René Sommer did not last long. When Dutrieu crashed her airplane into a chimney at a flying meeting in Odessa, Sommer refused to provide her a new one. The brothers Henri and Dick Farman wanted to help her out with an airplane but made two demands. First, Dutrieu had to provide the engine herself, and, second, she had to obtain a pilot's licence. She received an engine from Seghin, the director of Gnome, which was reputed to be the best engine manufacturer in France, and, on 23 August 1910, she passed the French examination for her pilot's licence. Because of confusion among the examiners, the Aéro-Club de France decided that she had to take the test again. However, that was impossible as she was awaited at a demonstration in Blankenberge on the Belgian coast.

In Blankenberge, her male colleagues/competitors strongly advised her not to fly because they were firmly convinced that women were not able to. However, she spurned them and so, on 2 September 1910, became the first woman in the world to undertake a long-distance flight (Blankenberge-Bruges-Blankenberge) and the first woman in the world who did this with a passenger, her mechanic, Edouard Béaud. Because of her striking performance, the Aéro-Club de Belgique issued her licence no. 27. As a result, she became the first Belgian female pilot and was among the first women in the world to earn a pilot's licence.[64]

Hence Hélène Dutrieu became a welcome guest at aviation meetings and gave many demonstrations in Belgium, France, the Netherlands and Great Britain. Due to her successful performances at air shows, she acquired the nickname 'The Girl Hawk'. On 31 December 1910, she won the first *Coupe Femina* in Étampes (France). The *Coupe Femina* was an award of 2,000 francs established by Pierre Lafitte, the publisher of the French women's magazine *Femina*, to honour women pilots. It was awarded to the woman who, on New Year's Eve, had made the longest flight, in time and distance.[65] Dutrieu was the first woman in the world to fly longer than one hour non-stop. A pithy detail: she objected strongly to the contest regulation that stipulated that it was safer for women to fly only above an airfield.[66]

In May 1911, Hélène Dutrieu beat her 14 male competitors (such as the French pilots Émile Védrines, Maurice Tabuteau and Eugène Renaux) during the *Copa del Rei* in Florence. In addition, in September of the same year, she went for the first time to the United States, where she took part in the Nassau Boulevard Aviation Meet on Long Island (New York). She also signed up for a cross-country race against Harriet Quimby, the first American woman to obtain a licence. However, Dutrieu did not appear at the start because her airplane was not ready in time. Two days later, when her airplane was completely finished, she broke the American duration record for women by staying aloft for 37 minutes and 22 seconds in a strong wind.[67] The prize money was nice, but still meagre in comparison to the men's prizes. While Harriet Quimby received $600 and Hélène Dutrieu $500, their male colleagues, Claude Grahame-White and Thomas Sopwith, received $4,200 and $4,800 respectively. In this context, Eileen Lebow observed that 'women's prizes were about what one would expect for a meet whose advertising featured male stars and women's events as curiosities.'[68] During an interview in the Knickerbocker Hotel in New York City where Dutrieu stayed during the exhibition, she gave her opinion about the gender issue: 'I think, as in aviation, the man has the steadier nerves, the firmer grip. But women have a finesse, and an inborn tact and sense of the fitness of things which men lack utterly – some men that is.'[69]

Back in France, Hélène Dutrieu won the *Coupe Femina* in Étampes for the second time, where she greatly improved her performance of the previous year with a distance of 254.8 km in 2 hours and 58 minutes. She was honoured several times for her achievements – she received the *Medaille d'Or* from the Aéro-Club de France, the *Grande Plaque* from the Aéro-Club de Belgique, and the *Médaille de l'Aviation* from the Sorbonne.[70] In February 1913, the French government awarded her the *Croix de Chevalier de la Légion d'Honneur*.[71] 'Of all the women who took to flying she is the only one who has, as it were, kept pace with the leading aviators, and has in many instances surpassed them in her achievements,' reported the *New York Times* on the occasion of this award.[72] In Belgium, she received the title of *Officier de l'Ordre de Léopold*.[73]

When all civilian air activities were suspended during the First World War, Hélène Dutrieu worked for five months as ambulance driver for the Red Cross in France, along the Marne.[74] Thereafter, she was placed in charge of the annex of the military hospital of Val-de-Grâce in Paris and volunteered for aerial observation work above Paris for the French Army. Because she could not be officially entered upon the army rolls, she worked on a private basis.[75] When she was asked what prompted her to volunteer for air scouting, she replied: 'Three things. I love France. I love adventure. I knew my business.'[76]

In June 1915, Hélène Dutrieu returned to the United States under the auspices of the French Red Cross to campaign for help. She stayed for a month in the Knickerbocker Hotel, where she gave lectures on the situation in Europe. In August 1915 she visited the Chalmers Motor Company with her interpreter and financial agent – a certain G.J. Kluyskens – and entered into an agreement to become the distributor of the American automobile manufacturer in France, whereupon she left for Paris with a fleet of Chalmers cars.[77] After the war, in 1922, Hélène Dutrieu married the renowned publicist Pierre Mortier and acquired French nationality. She took care of the administration of her husband's activities. After the death of her husband, Dutrieu dedicated herself to the promotion of women pilots in air travel. She did not consider herself as a feminist but stressed that women were not inferior to men, and that women could be equally competent pilots. Dutrieu became vice president of the women's section of the Aéro-Club de France and, from 1956 on, she awarded each year the *Coupe Franco-Belge Hélène Dutrieu-Mortier* to a woman pilot who had made the longest flight that year. Hélène Dutrieu died on 26 June 1961 in her home in Paris.[78]

Jan Olieslagers (1883–1942)

Jan Olieslagers was born on 14 May 1883 in Antwerp, the second son of Léonard Olieslagers and Jeanne-Catherine Coppens. Unlike his well-to-do Antwerp fellow,

Pierre de Caters, Jan Olieslagers was of modest origins. After the death of his father in 1894, he started to work for a carpenter at 0.5 francs per week. After the summer vacation, he did not return to school but went to work as an apprentice for a ship repairer and a bicycle maker. In 1897, Olieslagers offered his services to an agent of the French bicycle company Gladiator, who assigned him to the maintenance and repair of racing bicycles in the Zurenborg velodrome in Antwerp. After that, he worked for the professional cycling team of the Antwerp bicycle manufacturer Mercury Cycle and, in 1898, he moved to the newly founded Minerva bicycle factory of Sylvain de Jong & Co. His employer put a racing bicycle at his disposal, and his performance quickly attracted the attention of Émile de Beukelaer, the later chairman of the Union Cycliste Internationale (1900–22),[79] who registered him as a member of the Antwerp Bicycle Club.[80] He was very successful both on and next to the track. In 1900, as a 17-year-old, he was promoted to salesman for Minerva. In addition, that same year, he was also involved in the construction of a first motorcycle by mounting a Zürcher & Lüthi engine on a Minerva bicycle. He won the first Belgian motorcycle championship in the Antwerp velodrome and was given the nickname 'The Antwerp Devil'. When Minerva Motors Ltd. started to produce automobiles in 1904, Olieslagers did not make the athletic transition. He continued to swear by motorcycles and asked, after the formation of a Minerva subsidiary in Paris, to be able to try his luck as a salesman and motorcycle rider in the French capital. He immediately achieved success in the Paris-Bordeaux-Paris race of 1,200 kilometres divided into eight stages. As the youngest of 60 participants, he won with a lead of 28 minutes over his nearest competitor. After the thanks, invitations and rewards from the manufacturers of the various components of his Minerva motorcycle, there was another surprise for him: a fine because he had ridden from Paris to Bordeaux and back without a driver's licence. The case was settled amicably, however, because such a driver's licence did not exist yet in Belgium. As a result of this event, an official Belgian motorcycle riding licence was introduced on 24 February 1904, and Olieslagers was the first to receive it.[81]

Jan Olieslagers also made a name as pace-setter or stayer. Thus in 1904 he led the American Bobby Walthour to victory during the world championships in London. In the same year, he was the motorcycle star at the opening of the renewed Zurenborg velodrome. He received 1,300 francs for his *acte de présence*, one-tenth of the gross receipts. Olieslagers added motorcycle victories in Belgium and elsewhere to his list of awards. Even a stray bullet that pierced his head just under the ear during shooting practice on 4 May 1906 could not stop him. Two days later, against doctor's orders, he met the previously planned challenge from the Italian Alessandro Anzani. Ultimately, he lost in three rounds, after which he underwent surgery the next day. The small-calibre bullet, however, could not be removed and would remain in his head for the rest of his life. It did not seem to bother him very much. In 1906, he became the Belgian motorcycling champion for the third time and also won races in Turin, Paris, Berlin, Düsseldorf, Cologne, Leipzig and elsewhere. As 'ultimate champion in motorcycling' he broke many world records and accumulated a great deal of prize money. The fortune he acquired enabled him to venture higher in 1909: into aerial sport (see Figure 4).[82]

From his home in Levallois-Perret near Paris, Jan Olieslagers regularly visited the airfield of Issy-les-Moulineaux. He first ordered an airplane from Santos-Dumont for 7,500 francs but finally was persuaded by Louis Blériot to buy a Blériot XI for 12,500 francs. It was the same type as the one that the French aviation pioneer used

Figure 4.   Jan Olieslagers (on the motorcycle): a perfect model of upward social mobility via sports. He began as a bicycle racer, then raced motorcycles, and, when he had collected enough prize money, he bought an airplane and became a successful aviator. © Frans Mielants.

to cross the Channel from Calais to Dover for the first time on 25 July 1909. After Olieslagers had spent a week familiarising himself with the mechanics of the aircraft in Blériot's workshop in Paris, he began to practise on the airfield of Issy-les-Moulineaux. On 23 October 1909, he participated in the *Semaine d'Aviation d'Anvers*. On 1 November 1909, he made a successful flight that was observed by the Minister of Public Works, Auguste Delbeke. Because the winter weather did not permit him to train in Belgium, he left with his brother Max and his mechanic for Oran in Algeria. He there concluded an agreement with a certain Bouisse, who had the first aerodrome on African soil laid out for him. Olieslagers would not stay there very long as, after an accident on 20 January 1910, he went first to Paris for a new airplane and then to the flying school in Pau for further training.[83]

On 31 March 1910, the Aéro-Club de Belgique issued licence number 5 to Jan Olieslagers. In April 1910 he took part in the aviation shows of Seville and Nice and, in May, in those of Barcelona, Genoa and Bologna. The lucrative contracts piled up. Olieslagers's successes were also noticed by the *New York Times*: '[H]e flew to heights and made dips and turns with his tiny monoplane such as not even its inventor and the first man to fly across the English Channel [Louis Blériot] would attempt.'[84] On 7 July 1910, during the *Grande Semaine d'Aviation de la Champagne* at the airfield of Bétheny near Rheims, he outclassed all the great champions – more than 60 pilots had registered – and raised the world record in distance flying over a closed circuit to 225 kilometres (3 hours and 40 minutes) and three days later to 392 kilometres and 750 metres (5 hours and 3 minutes). Later that summer, Olieslagers captured most of the prizes during the *Meeting d'Aviation* in Stockel (Brussels), which brought him 40,000 francs, enough to purchase a third Blériot.[85] After Stockel, he went to the Netherlands in order to acquire fame in the flying shows in Groningen, Utrecht, Zwolle, Amsterdam, Leeuwarden, Rotterdam, Enschede, Nijmegen and The Hague.[86] The balance after one year of flying was, in any case, impressive: participation in meets and demonstrations in 22 cities over seven countries.[87]

Jan Olieslagers also began to give flying lessons. During the winter months, when his airplanes were stored in the hangars on the private airfield of Baron Pierre de

Caters, he taught his brother and mechanic, Max, to fly. On 25 May 1911, Max improved the Dutch duration record of 54 minutes – set by Jan – to an hour. His brother Jules had less success in the air. After a crash and a bad landing, he ceased flying. At the end of 1911, the Olieslagers trio worked on their own airplane after the example of Blériot. In the beginning of 1912, it was ready to fly. Since the Belgian Army was assembling an air fleet, Olieslagers offered the Ministry of War his self-made monoplane, but his offer was refused.[88] After he saw the French air acrobat Adolphe Pégoud make a loop at a meeting in Ghent,[89] Olieslagers took it as a new challenge. He displayed his skills in Paris, Antwerp and Amsterdam, and Blériot even gave him the airplane with which Pégoud had made the loop in Ghent.[90]

His last exploit before the commencement of the First World War was a confrontation with Roland Garros, who was very popular in France. The challenge took place on 9 June 1914 at the *Meeting d'Aviation* in Stockel and was to determine who was the best aerial acrobat. The result was a draw. Olieslagers was also invited for the first time to a show in Germany, but, because of the political situation at the time, Olieslagers sent a telegram saying that he could not leave Antwerp. On 1 August 1914 Olieslagers sent a letter and a telegram to Charles de Broqueville, Minister of War, offering his services and putting his equipment at the disposal of the government for the defence of Belgian territory.[91] His brothers Jules, Max and Albert also volunteered for the war. Jan was enlisted as *sapeur-aviateur* (pilot-sub-lieutenant) of the engineers under the leadership of Henri Crombez and began his military flying career with observation flights. On 12 September 1915, he was the first Belgian fighter pilot to bring down an enemy aircraft. He would quickly become one of the Belgian aces along with Willy Coppens, Edmond Thieffry, André De Meulemeester and Fernand Jacquet.[92]

After the war, Jan Olieslagers operated a Minerva garage in Antwerp. He also strongly supported the development of aviation in Antwerp. This resulted in the creation of the international airport in Deurne in 1923. On 3 November 1927, he was founding president of the Antwerp Aviation Club. In 1931, he was appointed member of the High Council for Aviation at the proposal of the Minister of Aviation Maurice Auguste Lippens. Three years later, he became a member of the board of directors of the National Committee for Aviation Propaganda. In 1934, he was a flag bearer at the funeral of King Albert I. On 21 July 1935 the absolute pinnacle followed when he was appointed Dean of Belgian Aeronautics by King Leopold III. Two years later, he was founding president of the aviation-veteran association, Vieilles Tiges. Jan Olieslagers passed away in 1942, during the Second World War.[93] On 14 May 1953, a monument in honour of Olieslagers was erected at the airport of Deurne.[94]

Interpretation

The three biographies above clearly show the transition from bicycle racing to (motorcycle racing and) automobile racing, and subsequently to aviation sport during the belle époque.[95] This phenomenon was more broadly reflected at the club level. Around 1896 members of cycling clubs became members of automobile clubs and around 1908 the same members became engaged in aviation clubs.[96] This shift could also be observed in several magazines' name changes. For example, *Le Véloce: Journal Quotidien de la Vélocipédie* became *Le Véloce: Quotidien du Cycle, de l'Automobile et de Tous les Sports* in 1896, and *Le Véloce et l'Automobile: Journal du*

Cycle, de l'Automobile et de Tous les Sports in 1899. *L'Automobile et le Véloce* became *Automobile-Véloce* and, subsequently, *Automobile-Aviation* in 1909. Likewise, the name of the first *Salon du Cycle* in Belgium, organised in 1892 by the Union et Véloce Club Bruxellois, turned into *Salon du Cycle et de l'Automobile* in 1896, and to *Salon de l'Automobile et du Cycle* in 1899.[97] The *Chambre Syndicale de l'Automobile et des Industries qui s'y Rapportent* (established in 1894 as the *Syndicat Belge du Commerce et de l'Industrie Vélocipédiques*) organised a competing *Salon du Cycle* from 1902 onwards. In 1913 it was called *Salon de l'Automobile, de l'Aéronautique et du Cycle*.[98]

There are at least three possible explanations for this shift. First, the aspects of 'adventure' and 'speed' were undoubtedly important driving forces behind the switch from cycling to motoring and aviation. Gijs Mom indicated that the adventurous character of the bicycle slowly disappeared, while its utilitarian character gained ground. The underlying factors included the improvement of road quality and bicycle construction (the replacement of the 'elevated' penny-farthing by the more practical safety bike), the expansion of bicycle club power and the reduction of bicycle prices.[99] Mom described automobilism as a 'civilized adventure' or 'a periurban touring adventure', which favoured speed, spatial exploration and functional challenges at the mechanical level of easily detectable and easily repairable defects. As such, this strand of automobilism was a continuation of the preceding bicycle culture.[100] Still, aviation sport was even more adventurous. In case of technical failure, the chances that the accident was fatal were far greater than in car racing. Therefore, aviation sport was more attractive than automobile sport for certain sporting members of the upper classes. In the programme-bulletin of the *Semaine d'Aviation d'Anvers*, this thrilling transition was accentuated:

> The rally racers are found among today's most prominent aviators. These intrepid drivers, observed by many when they sped up their cars to 100 kilometres an hour on famous race tracks, aspired to other forms of daredevilry. They switched the steering wheel for the controls of an airplane. As a result, they now take their machines up in the air where there are no obstacles and where unlimited routes open up for them.[101]

A second explanation for the switch in sports practice has to do with class distinction or 'social distinction'. This concept was introduced in academic circles by Pierre Bourdieu in 1979 with his work *La distinction. Critique sociale du jugement*, but nineteenth-century author Thorstein Veblen had already presented a similar explanation in 1899 with his concept of 'conspicuous consumption'.[102] In his book *The Theory of the Leisure Class*, he argued that all consumption goods and leisure time had a utilitarian as well as a symbolic value.[103] Hence, his view that the members of the 'leisure class' desired to impress and to distinguish themselves from lower classes through choosing particular types of leisure.[104] While the bicycle was a quite exclusive hobby horse of the rich bourgeoisie in the nineteenth century, it became more accessible around 1900. Between 1893 and 1908, the number of bicycles in Belgium rose from 20,000 to 340,000.[105] In her study on the belle époque, Gita Deneckere considered the bicycle – the 'new Pegasus' – to be the symbol of freedom and liberation for the period, an implement to be used also by the lower classes for travel from home to work.[106] For members of the upper classes, however, the bicycle lost its fashionableness and they stepped into more exclusive motorised vehicles.

The acquisition of a motorcycle, automobile or airplane required indeed a great deal of money. The average workman with a daily wage of 2.5 francs could not acquire an expensive Minerva (8 h.p.) for 3,275 francs let alone a Mors (40 h.p.) for 50,000 francs. As for planes, a Santos-Dumont Demoiselle (24 h.p.) cost 5,000 frank, a Farman Type 7 (70 h.p.) no less than 26,750 francs. Even the prize of a motorcycle ranged from 425 to 788 francs.[107] Automobiles and airplanes were luxury eye-catchers. The fact that most Belgian automobile races took place in the Ardennes (e.g. *Circuit des Ardennes, Meeting Automobile de Spa, Coupe de la Meuse, Coupe Pilette* and *Coupe de Liedekerke*) and at the Belgian coast (e.g. *Semaine Automobile d'Ostende* and *Meeting d'Ostende*) is not at all surprising, for that was where the Belgian *beau monde* had its country or coastal homes.[108] On the Belgian coast, too, several flying demonstrations took place, for the beach itself made a perfect landing strip.[109]

What is remarkable is that motor sport pioneers such as Hélène Dutrieu, Jan Olieslagers, Charles Van den Born, Arthur Duray, Jules Fischer, Lucien Hautvast[110] and Joseph Christiaens were of modest origins. Through their successes on the bicycle – and for some on the motorcycle later – they were able to acquire capital and a reputation as daredevils. As a result, they could also devote themselves to the expensive automobile and/or aviation sport. Motor sports were thus not only a professional occupation but also a prime opportunity for upward social mobility. For pilots of wealthy origins, too, the prize money was more than welcome to pay for their expensive hobby. In this sense, paradoxically, the expensive motorised sports were not as much socially stratified as one might expect. Hence, the dividing line between amateurs and professionals is not always easy to draw, neither is it clear whether motorised sports were seen as Olympic disciplines during the belle époque. Although automobile races were organised during the Olympic Games of 1900 in Paris, it is difficult to determine which events may be considered as being Olympic. Indeed, these games were organised as a part of the Paris World's Fair and the exposition's organisers spread the events over five months.[111] On the official programme of the games of 1908 in London there were motorboat races, and Rome, which had submitted its candidacy for the same games, was planning to organise automobile races.[112] The argument of Bill Mallon and other sport historians to consider automobile races as being non-Olympic is based on there being money prizes associated with them, which was in conflict with the amateur regulations. Nevertheless, this conclusion is also open to scrutiny. In several other events, prizes were also to be won, although it is not always clear whether they were given in the form of money (professionals) or art objects (amateurs). The fact that Olympic circles were not averse to motorised sports is also indicated by the awarding of the Olympic Diploma of Merit. Created during the Olympic Congress in Brussels in 1905, it was awarded to 'an individual with a general reputation for merit and integrity which has been active and efficient in the service of amateur sport and has contributed substantially to the development of the Olympic Movement'.[113] In 1905, Alberto Santos-Dumont, who had flown around the Eiffel Tower in 1901 with a motorised Zeppelin, was one of the laureates. Other winners during the belle époque were the German Count Ferdinand von Zeppelin (in 1909) and the French aviator Géo Chavez, who was the first to fly over the Alps (in 1910).[114]

Furthermore, the participants at the Olympic Congress in 1905 expressed the desire to found a Fédération Aéronautique Internationale. The following resolution was ultimately adopted: 'That an association be formed in each country to regulate aviation sport and that a universal federation then be formed consisting of all the national associations with a view to diverse events, the general regulations for the scientific and sportive popularisation of aviation.'[115] Four months later, on 14 October 1905, the Fédération Aéronautique Internationale was created in Paris by representatives from Belgium, France, Germany, Great Britain, Italy, Spain, Switzerland and the USA.[116]

The ways in which Hélène Dutrieu successfully navigated her way from the cycle racing to the aviation circuit can also be related to the second explanation regarding social distinction versus social mobility. Although their number was extremely small, some women were able to make their way into competitive sport activities prior to the First World War. It seems that most women involved in motorised sports were either affluent and therefore able to purchase a car or airplane (for example Great Britain's first aviator Hilda Hewlett and Amelie Beese, the first woman in Germany to earn a pilot's licence), or they started out their career as bicycle performers, acrobats or actors in vaudeville theatres. Relying on their expertise as 'performers' and driven by their desires for adventure, these last ones then made the shift to more dangerous activities, such as car racing and aviation when these disciplines gained in popularity. In this last category, for example, we find not only Hélène Dutrieu but also the French Raymonde de Laroche, the very first 'aviatrix'.[117] At the end of the nineteenth century, however, women's participation in competitive sport created much controversy.[118] In France, for example, cycling was the very first sport with competitions for women.[119] Richard Holt has described the cycling issue as 'a kind of prism in which the whole gamut of men's attitudes towards women was put on display'.[120] Men were afraid 'that women would either lose sex appeal or, conversely, that they as men would lose control of their wives and daughters'.[121] Furthermore, (pseudo) medical discussions arose on the potential dangers of cycling for the female anatomy and on the possibilities of the bicycle for sexual stimulation. Moreover, major road races were considered far too demanding for women.[122] Similar trends can be observed for women's participation in motorised sports. When the popularity of cars and airplanes amplified prior to the First World War and women became increasingly interested in driving and flying, much debate arose over women's 'proper' roles as automobile drivers and aviators. Although a small number of women succeeded in entering competitive sports and using them as a means for emancipation and upward social mobility, most women wanting to drive a car or fly an airplane met with much resistance from the male-controlled sporting circuits and industries. In the case of aviation, for example, women's airplane crashes were often explained in terms of women's alleged lesser intelligence and inferior biology. Many believed that most women were too nervous to be able to steer an aircraft and that they should certainly not fly during their menstrual periods.[123] Nevertheless, the few women making remarkable progress in cycle racing, auto sport and aviation prior to the First World War established exceptional feats and set the pace for a generation of enthusiastic sportswomen to come.

A third explanation for the shift in sports deals with industry, technology and its commercialisation. Although the automobile was invented in Germany and was also first commercialised there, France started automobile production on a massive scale at the end of the nineteenth century and remained the largest producer in the world until the USA took over the lead in 1906.[124] The success of the French automobile industry was soon followed in Belgium. In their French study Saunier et al. stressed the importance of Belgium in world automobile production: 'One can say that, from the origin of the modern times of the automobile, our neighbours and friends the Belgians were the companions of the French labour, [and] that their efforts have been among the most fruitful that our industry has seen.'[125]

In 1903, Belgium occupied the fourth place in world automobile production after France, England and Germany. One of the reasons for this international position was due to its prosperous iron and coal industry.[126] Thus the primary materials needed for the construction of automobiles were available. According to Kupélian et al., who studied the history of the automobile in Belgium, there were three more favourable elements: highly skilled manual labourers, dynamic entrepreneurs and an economic policy that favoured trade.[127] Around the turn of the century, Belgium, with its 7.6 million inhabitants, was not only the most densely populated but also the most industrialised country in the world,[128] so the industrial infrastructure required for the production of automobiles was already in place.

Furthermore, the invention of the inflatable rubber tyre by Dunlop had launched a lucrative industry in the Congo Free State, where rubber could be obtained cheaply on the back of the exploited local population. As a result, the tyre industry in Belgium flourished, with Englebert in Liège, Jenatzy in Brussels and Colonial Rubber in Ghent as the most important firms.[129] King Leopold II, who was their 'rubber supplier', was eager to promote the automobile infrastructure in Belgium: the creation of more infrastructure and the production of more cars would further expand the rubber market. As the first monarch to drive an automobile and patron of the Salon de l'Automobile in Brussels,[130] he planned to build motorways – aptly called Allées du Congo – between Brussels and other important cities such as Ostend, Antwerp, Luxemburg, and Paris.[131] He even interfered with the construction of automobiles. When he ordered a customised Panhard in 1902, the new body style was called 'Roi des Belges'.[132] The 'Roi des Belges' coachwork was synonymous with spacious, luxurious and expensive, and it was copied worldwide.

Alongside exclusive automobile constructors such as Miesse (Anderlecht, Brussels), Excelsior (Zaventem, Brussels), Pipe (Brussels) and Royal Star (Berchem, Antwerp); armaments manufacturers such as the Fabrique Nationale d'Armes de Guerre, or simply FN (Herstal, Liège), Saroléa (Liège), Nagant (Liège) and Pieper (Liège); bicycle manufacturers such as Minerva (Antwerp), Delin (Leuven), Belgica (Molenbeek, Brussels) and Linon (Ensival-lez-Verviers, Liège); machine manufacturers such as Snoeck (Ensival-lez-Verviers, Liège); and manufacturers of railway material such as Métallurgique (Tubize, Nivelles, La Sambre) and Germain (Monceau-sur-Sambre, Hainaut) also turned to producing automobiles.[133] In the Revue Mensuelle du Cycle et de l'Automobile, a certain Legrand stated in the year 1906 that it was typical that 'many factories that used to produce only bicycles, now focus almost exclusively on the manufacturing of motorcycles and cars'.[134] The transfer from the manufacturing of bicycles to the production of cars sometimes happened via the motorcycle. For the construction of a motorcycle little extra money and knowledge was needed. The motor blocks could be purchased and incorporated into the bicycle's wheel frame. If a bicycle constructor possessed the necessary financial resources and knowledge, he could attempt to also produce cars. Vincent van der Vinne pointed out in his publication on the Dutch (motor)cycle and car manufacturer Eysink, that a similar trend occurred in the Netherlands.[135] To promote their vehicles, manufacturers competed with each other in automobile races, and cups were created by sponsors to challenge engineers and constructors to innovate.

While Belgium had a flourishing automobile production sector in the belle époque, this was not the case for the construction of airplanes. The basic components of airplanes were wood and canvas,[136] so automobile constructors apparently did not feel drawn to build them.[137] The company Bollekens, which had a woodworking firm in Antwerp, first ventured to construct aircraft after de Caters had asked them to make emergency repairs to his airplane during the *Semaine d'Aviation d'Anvers* in 1909. In 1910, the brothers Eugeen, Isidoor and Jozef Bollekens officially formed the Société Jéro – after their deceased father Jérome – to make airplanes. The airplanes were improved versions of the original French Voisin as the Bollekens brothers had come up with the idea of using wood from the silver fir instead of poplar for the long components. This choice would later become the general standard in aircraft construction.[138]

In addition to the Société Jéro, two other airplane constructors were established in Belgium in 1910. On 17 February 1910, the French company Aviator, which started up in 1909, opened a branch in Belgium. Pierre de Caters's cousin, Maximiliaan de Caters, was among the founders. Their workshops were initially set up in Zeebrugge but were very soon moved to the private airfield of Pierre de Caters in Sint-Job-in-'t-Goor. Another important constructor was Aéroplanes Léon de Brouckère, also founded in 1910 with construction shops in Kiewit (near Hasselt) and Herstal. In contrast to other constructors, who used mostly wood and canvas for their designs, de Brouckère worked with metal, which was less common. It was also the first Belgian company to have a wind tunnel at its disposal.[139]

These constructors tried to convince the Belgian army to develop an aviation section by buying airplanes and training pilots. Already in March 1909, Pierre de Caters informed the Minister of War, Joseph Hellebaut, that the airfield that he had built was available to all officers who wanted to learn to fly, but his offer was not accepted. Yet military aviation rapidly picked up speed on 7 July 1910 when Hellebaut was invited for a flight during a visit to the airfield of Chevalier Jules de Laminne.[140] Jules de Laminne had obtained his pilot's licence in May 1910 at the French military base Camp de Châlons near Mourmelon-le-Grand with a Farman, the Belgian Charles Van den Born having been his instructor. Back in Belgium, de Laminne began to work as representative of Farman and had a small airfield laid out in Kiewit.[141] Hellebaut asked de Laminne to train military pilots, who immediately offered his services free of charge. With a possible order of Farman aircraft for the army in the offing, this was a strategic move that could provide generous returns. On 21 December 1910, Georges Nélis was the very first officer to obtain an official Belgian military certification. On 1 May 1911, the army opened its own airfield in Brasschaat and terminated the instruction contract with de Laminne, but he still delivered four Farman airplanes.[142]

In one last charm offensive, Pierre de Caters gave an Aviator airplane as a New Year gift to King Albert, who gave it in turn to the Brasschaat military flying school a while later.[143] The insolvent Aviator firm was taken over by Jéro, as was de Caters's flying school. When the Bollekens brothers joined up with Farman at the end of 1911 for the construction of Farman airplanes for Belgium and the Netherlands[144] – undoubtedly via de Laminne[145] – Jéro became the exclusive supplier for the Belgian army. However, the army inserted several conditions in the contract so that the company was de facto 'militarised'. Jéro had to provide for the construction, maintenance and repair of the army airplanes and also for the civilian training of the candidate pilots. Before one could obtain a military flying certificate, one first had to obtain a civilian licence.[146]

Jéro's exclusive contract with the Belgian army also meant a serious setback for de Brouckère, although he did not submit immediately to Jéro's dominant position. At the end of 1911, he entered into a licence contract with the French airplane constructor Deperdussin for the construction and sale of Deperdussin aircraft in Belgium. The company remained operational until it was taken over by Jéro in 1913. By August 1914, Jéro had built about 25 Farman aircraft for the Belgian army. On 4 October 1914, the Antwerp shops (personnel, machines, materials etc.) were evacuated by train to Ostend (in light of the approaching fall of Antwerp on 9 October 1914), and then ordered to travel on to France. There, Jéro settled finally in an empty factory in Calais in Northern France. A little later, in 1915, a technical service was established in Beaumarais near Calais by the Belgian army on the proposal of Captain Georges Nélis. Nélis had been assigned to the military airfield in Brasschaat, where he took care of the technical training of the pilots and the administration.[147] In 1917, the Belgian army unilaterally broke the contract with Jéro because it preferred its own workshop under the direction of Nélis.[148] Critics, among them Willy Coppens, the most successful Belgian flying ace during the First World War, faulted Nélis because, with this, all knowledge about airplane construction disappeared from Belgium. He accused Nélis of acting opportunistically because he wanted to become a constructor himself and thus wanted to eliminate his biggest competitor.[149]

In any case, Nélis later played a prominent role in post-war Belgian aviation as director of the Société Nationale pour l'Étude des Transports Aériens (SNETA, the National Society for the Study of Aviation Transport) and later also of the Société Anonyme Belge de Constructions Aéronautiques (SABCA, Belgian Aeronautics Constructions Ltd.) and the Société Anonyme Belge d'Exploitation de la Navigation Aérienne (SABENA, the Belgian Company for Air Navigation Ltd).[150] SNETA, which was founded on 31 March 1919, strived to create a national aeronautical construction industry, to organise air transport in the Congo and to organise air services in Belgium itself. On 16 December 1920, the first objective was realised with the founding of SABCA, which built airplanes under licence but made little effort to launch a Belgian airplane. Another objective was realised with the founding of the national aviation company SABENA on 23 May 1923.[151] While the banks had had little interest in aviation in pre-war Belgium, they certainly expressed interest after the First World War. The Banque d'Outremer, the Société Générale, the Banque de Bruxelles and the Banque de Paris et des Pays-Bas – the four most important banks active in Belgium – now became the largest shareholders in SABENA. According to Guy Vanthemsche, the parties that displayed interest in aviation had in common, primarily, their involvement in colonial affairs. The use of airplanes in the colony had been studied already before the First World War: on 25 February 1911 a commission to study the potential of air travel in the Congo had been established by the Ministry of Colonies by royal decree.[152] In this context, Fernand Lescarts made a few rather unsuccessful attempts to fly near Elisabethville at the end of 1912. King Albert I was one of the supporters of the project and also financed the airplane.[153]

The commission also concluded that seaplanes were the most suitable for colonial use. Seaplanes were tested extensively in Belgium and abroad. The Belgian Jules Fischer won the very first competition for seaplanes, which was held in Monaco in March 1912.[154] In the summer of 1912, Hélène Dutrieu tested seaplanes built by Henri Farman on Lac d'Enghien (France) and on Lac Léman (Switzerland/France).[155] From 7 to 16 September 1912, the Aéro-Club de Belgique organised a 'fluvial and colonial seaplane competition' on the Schelde river, where 'the size of the river and the current are much like those of most of the rivers of the Congo'.[156] The government was convinced of the economic opportuneness of these seaplanes and provided a prize of 20,000 francs. Major industrialists such as Edouard Empain and Ernest Solvay increased the amount to 45,000 francs.[157] The objective of the meeting was described as 'to demonstrate the qualities of seaplanes able to be used in the colonies and particularly in the Congo'.[158] Nevertheless, before the First World War, no seaplanes would fly in the Congo[159] and only in 1935 was the Belgium-Congo airline connection realised.[160]

SABENA took off and prospered until, finally, on 7 November 2001, in the aftermath of the attacks on 11 September 2001 and the resultant plummeting of the air-travel sector, it was declared bankrupt.[161] Minerva, the illustrious Belgian automobile brand, had already been declared bankrupt in 1958.[162] Nevertheless, foreign car manufacturers continued to assemble some of their car models in Belgian factories, so that the auto industry remained important.[163] Successful Belgian car racers had already left the circuit immediately after the introduction of the airplane.[164] Belgian cyclists, however, continued to dominate cycle races in the twentieth century; the democratisation and massification of the bicycle in Belgium certainly was one of the explanatory factors.[165] It was the start of this democratisation, as we have demonstrated, that had caused some 'prime movers' to distance themselves from the bicycle just before 1900 to be able to gain short-term successes in the new motorised sports. In only one of the motorised sports, motocross, did Belgians continue to gather titles. Since 1957, when the first world championships were organised by the Fédération Internationale Motocycliste (FIM, the International Motorcycling Federation), Belgian motocross riders have all together won more than 50 world titles. In the top ten of multiple-time winners, Belgians take up the first seven places. With ten world titles, Stefan Everts heads the list.[166]

Notes

1. Shared first authorship. The authors want to thank Frans Mielants, Roger Vanmeerbeek and Jozef Verckens for their support and archives. The foundation for our article was laid in 2006 with Bieke Gils's thesis and subsequent article in *Sportimonium* later in 2006. Donald Weber added to this particular line of research with his very solid doctoral dissertation on the history of automobilisation in Belgium and its subsequent publication in 2010. In this light, we had to update our article at the last moment before publication because it had already been accepted for publication in 2009. We would like to thank David Hassan and Andrew Riley for offering the opportunity to make these changes.
2. Ferdinand Verbiest was active in China as missionary and stayed at the Chinese court. He designed a motorised vehicle as a kind of toy. A copy of the vehicle has been built in the visitor's centre in Pittem (Verbiest's home town), which was opened in his memory in April 2010. However, debate exists over whether or not this 'toy' can be considered the first motorised vehicle. Also with regard to the internal combustion petrol engine, invented by Jean-Jospeh Etienne Lenoir, scepticism exists.
3. It needs to be noted that in the past some authors already drew attention to this transition. See for example the chapter on technological sports in Guttmann's *Sports: The First Five Millennia*; Hubscher *et al.*, *L'histoire en mouvements*, 300; Lebow, *Before Amelia*; Gils, 'Baanbrekers en hoogvlieger'; Donald Weber, 'Automobilisering en de overheid in België vóór 1940', 118.
4. Already on 22 July 1894, a trial was organised from Paris to Rouen. However, it was not a race as such, but a reliability competition. Hence not the fastest car but the most manageable and economic car was judged first in this 'race' (see Hospitalier, 'Voitures automobiles. Le concours du "Petit journal"', 9; Hospitalier, 'Voitures automobiles. Les lauréats du concours du "Petit journal"',198–9).
5. Kupélian *et al.*, *De geschiedenis van de Belgische auto*, 146; Weber, 'Automobilisering en de overheid in België vóór 1940', 121–30; Vincke and Delmer, *Voitures automobiles*.
6. For more information on the production of cars in Belgium, see, for instance, Boval, 'De geschiedenis van de Belgische autoindustrie'; Weber, 'Automobilisering en de overheid in België vóór 1940'.
7. Kupélian *et al.*, *De geschiedenis van de Belgische auto*, 146; den Hollander, *Sport in 't Stad*, 224; Saunier *et al.*, *Histoire de la locomotion terrestre*, 284–6; Dick, *Mercedes and Auto Racing in the Belle Époque*, 19–20; Dumont and Bernard, *Sportaffiches in België*, 106.
8. Lynch, *The Irish Gordon Bennett Cup Race*, 59.
9. For a more extensive overview, see Weber, 'Automobilisering en de overheid in België vóór 1940'; Weber, *De blijde intrede van de automobiel in België*.
10. See, for example, Robène *et al.*, 'Pau et l'invention de l'aviation "sportive"'.
11. Deneckere, *1900*; Van Cauwenberge, 'Ambivalente gevoelens'; Bairati *et al.*, *La Belle Époque*; Schoonbroodt, *Art nouveau kunstenaars in België*.
12. Deneckere, *1900*, 17.
13. In 1905, in the context of the 75th anniversary of the Belgian nation, a *Congrès International d'Expansion Économique Mondiale* was organised in order to triumph in a peaceful way in the conflict of the nations (with an important role for physical education and sport): see Ameye and Delheye, 'Expansionism, Physical Education and Olympism'; Delheye, 'Struggling for Gymnastics'.
14. Rearick, *Pleasures of the Belle Époque*, 28, 182.
15. In Weber, 'Gymnastics and Sport in Fin-de-Siècle France', 109.
16. Guttmann, *The Olympics*, 12–13.
17. *Bulletin du Comité International des Jeux Olympiques*, July 1894; de Coubertin, *Olympic Memoirs*, 8–11; Guttmann, The Olympics, 12–14; Young, *The Modern Olympics*, 87–92.

18. Mattheus, 'De interne geschiedenis van de Koninklijke Belgische Wielrijdersbond', 97, 151.
19. Ameye and Delheye, 'Expansionism, Physical Education and Olympism'.
20. For further clarification on the establishment of the Belgium Olympic Committee, and the constitution of a Belgian delegation and its participation in the 1906 Intercalated Games, see Ameye and Delheye, 'Expansionism, Physical Education and Olympism'; Ameye, 'Belgium'; Renson *et al., Enflammé par l'olympisme*, 35–7.
21. See Ameye and Delheye, 'Expansionism, Physical Education and Olympism' and Delheye, 'Fit for the Nation'.
22. Deneckere, *1900*.
23. See, for instance, Ranieri, *Léopold II, urbaniste*; Lombaerde and Gobyn, *Léopold II*; Catherine, *Bouwen met zwart geld*; Vangroenweghe, *Rood Rubber*; Hochschild, *King Leopold's Ghost*; Ameye and Delheye, 'Expansionism, Physical Education and Olympism'.
24. Translated from Dutch: Tollebeek, 'Degeneratie, moderniteit en culturele verandering', 300. See also Pick, *Faces of Degeneration*.
25. Deneckere, *1900*, 15, 208–9. See also Van Cauwenberge, 'Ambivalente gevoelens', i–ii, 114–25; Mom, 'Civilized Adventure as a Remedy', 158–9.
26. Guttmann, *The Olympics*, 12–14; Renson *et al., Enflammé par l'olympisme*, 20.
27. De Caters, *Baron de Caters*, 9; Gérard, 'Les débuts de l'aviation militaire en Belgique', 159.
28. Mandl and Wuyts, 'Baron Pierre de Caters', 3.
29. De Caters, *Baron de Caters*, 13; Goyens, 'L'histoire de notre club', 15; den Hollander, *Sport in 't Stad*, 224.
30. den Hollander, *Sport in 't Stad*, 227; Mandl and Wuyts, 'Baron Pierre de Caters', 2; de Caters, *Baron de Caters*, 13–19.
31. Kupélian *et al., De geschiedenis van de Belgische auto*, 167.
32. In 1865, with the Latin monetary union, Belgium, France, Italy and Switzerland concluded an agreement whereby the currency of these countries would be made equivalent with respect to each other. Since Belgian francs, French francs, Italian lire and Swiss francs had similar values during the belle époque, these monetary amounts are expressed in 'francs' throughout this article, regardless of the country (see Janssens, *De Belgische frank*, 87–115). However, for Germany and the United States, German marks and American dollars will be mentioned explicitly.
33. De Caters, *Baron de Caters*, 14–15; Mandl and Wuyts, 'Baron Pierre de Caters', 3.
34. In a 'flying kilometre' the automobile first got up to full speed after which the time and speed were measured over the distance of a kilometre.
35. On 15 May 1904 he would reach a new speed record of 156 km/h on the Ostend-Newport road at the Belgian coast (see, Hans Etzrodt, 'Grand Prix Winners 1895–1949', online at www.kolumbus.fi/leif.snellman/gpw1.htm; Gérard, 'Les débuts de l'aviation militaire en Belgique', 160–1; den Hollander, *Sport in 't Stad*, 227; de Caters, *Baron de Caters*, 36–43).
36. Lynch, *The Irish Gordon Bennett Cup Race*, 141–2.
37. René de Knyff gave up motor racing after losing the 1903 Gordon Bennett Cup race to Jenatzy. He continued, however, to be present for many years in the councils of the Automobile Club de France (see Court, *A History of Grand Prix Motor Racing*, 8).
38. 'Automobile Topics of Interest. Race for Bennett International Trophy a Victory for Belgian Racing Men and German Construction', *New York Times*, 5 July 1903.
39. Gérard, 'Les débuts de l'aviation militaire en Belgique', 162–3; de Caters, *Baron de Caters*, 36–43.
40. *Revue Mensuelle du Cycle et de l'Automobile*, Jan. 1906, 14.
41. Gérard, "Les débuts de l'aviation militaire en Belgique', 162–3; de Caters, *Baron de Caters*, 36–9, 42–3.
42. Pierre de Caters formed the link between an Italian group led by Alberto Manzi-Fé and the Liège firm Mécanique et moteurs, represented by Edmond Tart (see Kupélian *et al., De geschiedenis van de Belgische auto*, 180–1; Georgano, *The Beaulieu Encyclopedia of the Automobile*, 686).

43. In 1907 de Caters won the last *Circuit des Ardennes* – and his last auto race – in a car from Minerva, an Antwerp company: Goyens, 'L'Histoire de notre club', 17.
44. There is no consensus over whether the triplane was a design of de Caters himself based on a Goupy-Voisin or was an exact copy (see de Caters, "Baron Pierre de Caters, 1908', 4–6; de Caters, *Baron de Caters*, 50–3; Lelasseux and Marque, *L'aéroplane pour tous*, 118; Vanthomme, 'Eerste vliegtuig van Baron Pierre de Caters', 8–9). Nonetheless, in his publication entitled *Histoire de l'aviation* (235) Louis Turgan wrote: 'The de Caters-Voisin triplane is identical to that one [the Goupy-Voisin triplane] for which we have provided the characteristics' ('Le triplan de Caters-Voisin est identique à celui [le Goupy-Voisin triplane] dont nous venons de donner les caractéristiques').
45. Lampaert, *Van pionier tot luchtridder*, 8; Matthews, *Pioneer Aviators of the World*, 25–9. Nevertheless, the Montalvy brothers and Léon Druet constructed a biplane out of bamboo with which they made a jump into the air of a half a metre for a few seconds in the first half of 1906 at the military base in Etterbeek (see Mortier, "De Belgische luchtvaartindustrie', 1–2). On the corresponding website of the Brussels Air Museum Magazine (http://bamm.fotopic.net/), a photograph of this prototype can be found.
46. De Caters, *Baron de Caters*, 55.
47. Ibid., 59–67; Capron, *L'aviation belge et nos souverains*, 20; Vrancken, *De geschiedenis van de Belgische militaire vliegerij*, 20–1; den Hollander, *Sport in 't Stad*, 237–8.
48. Meerbergen, 'Sport of transport', 42; Zonderman, 'De geschiedenis van de sportluchtvaart in België', 38; Dhanens and De Decker, *Een eeuw luchtvaart boven Gent. Deel I*, 24–38.
49. 'Semaine d'Aviation d'Anvers 1909, Vliegweek van Antwerpen, 23 Oct., 2 Nov. 1909', Hendrik Conscience Library, Antwerp, c:lvd:361438; de Caters, *Baron de Caters*, 13, 59.
50. Gérard, 'Les débuts de l'aviation militaire en Belgique', 164–86; Guy de Caters, "Het ontstaan van de luchtvaart in België: Baron Pierre de Caters (tweede deel)", 7–10; Guy de Caters, 'Baron Pierre de Caters (derde deel)', 3–9; de Caters, *Baron de Caters*, 48–98; Vanthomme, 'Eerste vliegtuig van Baron Pierre de Caters', 7–9; Ghoos, *75 jaar luchtvaart Antwerpen*; 'Semaine d'Aviation d'Anvers 1909, Vliegweek van Antwerpen, 23 Oct., 2 Nov. 1909', Hendrik Conscience Library, Antwerp, c:lvd:361438; Van Belle, 'De penetratie van de luchtvaart in België', 127.
51. In contrast to what various authors contend (see, for example, Vrancken, *De geschiedenis van de Belgische militaire vliegerij*, 24; Mandl and Wuyts, 'Baron Pierre de Caters', 6) Aviator was not founded by Pierre de Caters. This has been demonstrated by the research of Konrad Mortier, who devoted a dissertation to the Belgian aviation industry (see Mortier, 'De Belgische luchtvaartindustrie', 8–12).
52. Ghoos, *75 jaar luchtvaart Antwerpen*, 25; de Caters, *Baron de Caters*, 117–37; van Hoorebeeck, *La conquête de l'air*, 88; Francis Bollekens, *Gebroeders Bollekens. Vliegtuigbouwers*, 25.
53. de Caters, *Baron de Caters*, 136–37.
54. He probably had a coordinating function. A letter dated 17 October 1916 indicates that then already he had not flown for several years (see 'Armée belge. Extrait de matricule. De Caters, Pierre, 1018', Archives of the Royal Museum of the Armed Forces and of Military History, Brussels).
55. 'Baron de Caters Arrives', *New York Times*, 5 July 1916; 'Four Liners Leave, Two of Them Armed'," *New York Times*, 29 Oct. 1916.
56. Correspondence shows that the French Minister of Commerce, Etienne Clémentel, had urged their leave and that the utility of this company for the Allies was an argument for granting it (see 'Armée belge. Extrait de matricule. De Caters, Pierre, 1018', Archives of the Royal Museum of the Armed Forces and of Military History, Brussels).
57. Matthews, *Pioneer Aviators of the World*, 29; Mathy, *Encyclopedie van de Belgische sportlui en sporten*, 60.
58. Alphonse Dumoulin and Robert Feuillen, 'Hélène Dutrieu 1877–1961: première aviatrice belge, pionnière de l'aviation féminine, membre d'honneur a titre posthume de la Société Royale les Vieilles Tiges de l'Aviation Belge', 2, online at www.vieillestiges.be; 'Hélène Dutrieu pionnier de l'aviation avait été recordwoman cycliste', Smithsonian Institution Archives (National Air and Space Museum, Washington, DC), CD-821000-01 Dutrieu Hélène; 'Hélène Dutrieu, première femme pilote belge et seconde femme

pilote au monde', *Les Vieilles Tiges*, www.vieillestiges.be; Lebow, *Before Amelia*, 21–2, 27–8.

59. Dumoulin and Feuillen, 'Hélène Dutrieu 1877–1961', 2; 'Hélène Dutrieu pionnier de l'aviation avait été recordwoman cycliste', Smithsonian Institution Archives; 'Hélène Dutrieu', *Les Vieilles Tiges*; Lebow, *Before Amelia*, 21-2, 27–8.

60. Apparently, prior to World War I, not more than five Belgian women rode a motorcycle (see Bosmans, 'De Belgische motorfietsen 1900–1965', 16).

61. Lebow, *Before Amelia*, 22.

62. Vanthomme, 'De "Demoiselle"', 7–11; Dumoulin and Feuillen, 'Hélène Dutrieu 1877–1961', 2; 'Hélène Dutrieu', *Les Vieilles Tiges*; Lebow, *Before Amelia*, 21–3, 27–8; 'Hélène Dutrieu pionnier de l'aviation avait été recordwoman cycliste', Smithsonian Institution Archives.

63. Lebow, *Before Amelia*, 23–4.

64. 'Autour du beffroi de Bruges', *L'Aérophile*, 1 Oct. 1910, 435; 'Helene Dutrieu, Aviator, is Dead', *New York Times*, 28 June 1961; van Hoorebeeck, *La conquête de l'air*, 85; Capron, *L'aviation belge et nos souverains*, 13.

65. Lebow, *Before Amelia*, 27–8; Berlanstein, 'Selling Modern Feminity', 623, 642. Pierre Lafitte was editor of numerous illustrated magazines: *La Vie au Grand Air, Revue Illustrée de Tous les Sports, Musica, Je Sais Tout, Fermes et Châteaux, Excelsior*. Moreover, he was member of the Automobile Club de France and the Aéro-Club de France (see Feyel, 'Naissance, constitution progressive et épanouissement', 28). *La Vie au Grand Air*, which was published between 1898 and 1914, and again after World War I until 1922, addresses many sport events held at the time in France (and abroad) and provided a considerable amount of media coverage for the Belgian sport performers, especially with regard to the cyclists, motorcycle and car racers as well as the aviators (for further reading, see Gils, 'Belgische sportlui door een Franse bril'; Gils, 'Baanbrekers en hoogvliegers').

66. According to Albert Morel, she raised the record a few days later to 2 hours 35 minutes and 167 kilometres 200 metres (see Morel, 'Hélène Dutrieu, la première aviatrice belge'). In an article in the *New York Times* a comparable performance was suggested: 'It was also a test as to who could support the biting cold longer – Mlle. Dutrieu, who flew for three long hours, or the timekeepers, who, with their usual male vanity, had imagined that it would all be over in five minutes' (see 'Aviatress Gets the Cross', *New York Times*, 23 March 1913).

67. 'Helene Dutrieu, Aviator, is Dead', *New York Times*, 28 June 1961; 'Hélène Dutrieu … retrouvée', Private archives of Roger Boin, Brussels, Nos silhouettes sportives, file 4, nr 51; 'Hélène Dutrieu pionnier de l'aviation avait été recordwoman cycliste', Smithsonian Institution Archives; Lebow, *Before Amelia*, 28–30.

68. Lebow, *Before Amelia*, 31.

69. 'Helene Dutrieu, Aviator, is Dead', *New York Times*, 28 June 1961.

70. Dumoulin and Feuillen, 'Hélène Dutrieu 1877–1961'; Lebow, *Before Amelia*, 31; 'Woman Flies 158 Miles. Mlle. Dutrieu Wins Femina Cup for Woman Making Longest Flights', *New York Times*, 1 Jan. 1912.

71. Dumoulin and Feuillen, 'Hélène Dutrieu 1877–1961', 3; 'Hélène Dutrieu', *Les Vieilles Tiges* ; Lebow, *Before Amelia*, 32; 'Hélène Dutrieu. Chevalier de la Légion d'Honneur', *La Conquête de l'Air*, 4 March 1913, 81.

72. 'Aviatress Gets the Cross', *New York Times*, 23 March 1913.

73. Dumoulin and Feuillen, 'Hélène Dutrieu 1877–1961', 3.

74. Ibid.; 'Hélène Dutrieu', *Les Vieilles Tiges*.

75. 'Helene Dutrieu, Aviator, is Dead', *New York Times*, 28 June 1961; Pfister, *Fliegen-Ihr Leben*, 82.

76. 'Tiny Woman Flier Dares German War Hawks for her Loved France and Prevents Air Raids on Paris', *Washington Post*, 27 June 1915; van Hoorebeeck, 'Hélène Dutrieu', 6.

77. 'News and Notes of the Automobile Trade', *New York Times*, 15 Aug. 1915; 'Aviatrice Now French Dealer', *Los Angeles Times*, 22 Aug. 1915; 'Chalmers Secure Feminine Aviator', *Hartford Courant*, 22 Aug. 1915.

78. Dumoulin and Feuillen, 'Hélène Dutrieu 1877–1961', 3; 'Hélène Dutrieu', *Les Vieilles Tiges*; Lebow, *Before Amelia*, 34; Helene Dutrieu, Aviator, is Dead', *New York Times*,

28 June 1961; Mathy, *Encyclopedie van de Belgische sportlui en sporten*, 89; Van Belle, 'De penetratie van de luchtvaart in België', 151.

79. Guido Wuyts and Jos Ghoos, 'Jan Olieslagers, "Den Antwerpschen Duvel" een der voornaamste figuren van de Belgische luchtvaart uit de periode van haar ontstaan, Medestichter en oud-voorzitter van de Vieilles Tiges', *Les Vieilles Tiges*, online at www.vieillestiges.be; Mathy, *Encyclopedie van de Belgische sportlui en sporten*, 56–7, 176; Willy Coppens de Houthulst, *Un homme volant: Jan Olieslagers*; Coppens de Houthulst, 'Jan Olieslagers'; Kupélian and Kupélian, *Minerva*, 9–18.

80. The contention that he drove under the pseudonym of John Max (see Buytaert and Dillen, *Jan Olieslagers*, 6; De Kinder, *De Antwerpsche Duivel*, 17; Coppens de Houthulst, *Un homme volant*, 26; *De geschiedenis van de luchtvaart*, 41) must be cast in doubt. In *La Presse*, the French-language sister newspaper of the *Gazet van Antwerpen* (see, for example, 17 Aug. 1906), the names of Jan Oliesagers and John Max appear in the same competition reports. Moreover, Frans Mielants received from Mady Olieslagers, the granddaughter of Jan Olieslagers, the confirmation that Jan's younger brother Max drove under this name.

81. Coppens de Houthulst, *Un homme volant*, 27–38, 50–6; De Kinder, *De Antwerpsche Duivel*, 16–31, 44–7; Kupélian *et al.*, *De geschiedenis van de Belgische auto*, 17.

82. 'Champion incontesté de la motocyclette': Coppens de Houthulst, *Un homme volant*, 27–38, 50–6; De Kinder, *De Antwerpsche Duivel*, 16–31, 44–7.

83. Den Hollander, *Sport in 't Stad*, 227–9, 241–2; Wuyts and Ghoos, 'Jan Olieslagers, "Den Antwerpschen Duvel"'. One of the most prominent figures of Belgian aviation in its early period, co-founder and former-chairman of the 'Vieilles Tiges', *Les Vieilles Tiges*, online at www.vieillestiges.be; Mathy, *Encyclopedie van de Belgische sportlui en sporten*, 176.

84. 'Who's Who in the Times New York-Chicago air Race', *New York Times*, 17 July 1910.

85. At the same meet, the Belgian aviation pioneer Nicolas Kinet died on 4 August 1910 after a crash while he was competing with Olieslagers for the *Schaal van de Koning* (Cup of the King), a prize for the longest distance flown. His brother Daniel was killed a few weeks before – on 15 September 1910 – during a meet in Ghent and thus became Belgium's first aviation casualty (see Coppens de Houthulst, *Un homme volant*, 115–22, 127, 131–45; Morel, 'Daniel et Nicolas Kinet'; Morel, 'Jan Olieslagers le "Démon Anversois"'; 'Aviation Victims Now Number 100', *New York Times*, 15 Oct. 1911; van Hoorebeeck, *La conquête de l'air*, 84–5; Dumas, *Les accidents d'aviation*, 8–9; 'La quinzaine de Stockel', *L'Expansion Belge*, Sept. 1910, 711).

86. Schoenmaker and Postma, *Aviateurs van het eerste uur*, 71. Nevertheless, Olieslagers was not the first pilot to fly in the Netherlands. This honour falls to Count Charles de Lambert. De Lambert was a Frenchman of Russian origin who lived in Liège (Belgium) and learned to fly from Wilbur Wright. He made a successful flight on 27 June 1909 with a Wright biplane above Etten-Leur (the Netherlands) (see Postma and Wesselink, *De vliegende Hollanders*, 10–11; Schoenmaker and Postma, *Aviateurs van het eerste uur*, 15–17).

87. Coppens de Houthulst, *Un homme volant*.

88. Ibid., 46–155; De Kinder, *De Antwerpsche Duivel*, 103–55; Vrancken, *De geschiedenis van de Belgische militaire vliegerij*, 48–9.

89. 'L'acrobatie aérienne. Chevillard & Pégoud', *L'Expansion Belge*, Dec. 1913, 801–5; Dhanens and De Decker, *Een eeuw luchtvaart boven Gent. Deel I*, 61–8.

90. Mathy, *Encyclopedie van de Belgische sportlui en sporten*, 176; Meerbergen, 'Sport of transport'; Wuyts and Ghoos, 'Jan Olieslagers'; 'Olieslagers', *La Conquête de l'Air*, 1 January 1914, 4.

91. Letter of Jan Olieslagers to Baron Charles de Broqueville, Minister of War, 1 aUG. 1914 from 'Armée belge. Extrait de matricule. Olieslagers, Jan. 3760, Archives of the Royal Museum of the Armed Forces and of Military History, Brussels.

92. After five officially recognised victories, a military pilot received the title of 'ace' (see 'Armée belge. Extrait de matricule. Olieslagers, Jan. 3760, Archives of the Royal Museum of the Armed Forces and of Military History, Brussels; Buytaert and Dillen, *Jan Olieslagers*, 15–17; Victor Boin, 'Jan Olieslagers "Doyen de l'aéronautique belge"', Les sports (Private archives of Roger Boin, Brussels, Nos silhouettes sportives, file 1,

no. 11, 1936); Coppens de Houthulst, 'Les notes d'un combattant', 2021; Houart, 'The Belgian Aces', 138–47; 'Jan Olieslagers. De crack met zes overwinningen').

93. Buytaert and Dillen, *Jan Olieslagers*, 18–20; Antwerp Aviation Club, 'Auto-Moto-Avion', 15 Jan. 1929; 'Historique des Vieilles Tiges de Belgique', 45.

94. Coppens de Houthulst, 'Jan Olieslagers, mon ancien', 480.

95. Also the famous flying Wright brothers were initially active in the cycling milieu (see Gaboriau, 'Les trois âges du vélo en France', 20).

96. See, for instance, den Hollander, *Sport in 't Stad*, 224–6, 346; Derwael, 'Sociale achtergrond van de Gentse sportverenigingen'.

97. Lauters, *Les débuts du cyclisme en Belgique*, 181–91; Verbauwhede, 'De Belgische pers en de automobiel', 380–3. In the memorial book of the Royal Touring Club de Belgique other data are mentioned concerning the changing name of the salon, respectively 1892, 1895 and 1901 (see Royal Touring Club de Belgique, *Mémorial du Royal Touring Club*, 35).

98. Lauters, *Les débuts du cyclisme en Belgique*, 188–92; 'Vue générale du XIIe Salon de l'Automobile, de l'Aéronautique et du Cycle', *La Conquête de l'Air*, 1 Feb. 1913, 32. For more examples of the transition from cycling to automobile sports see Weber, 'Automobilisering en de overheid in België vóór 1940', 118–20.

99. Mom, 'Civilized Adventure as a Remedy for Nervous Times', 161; Mom, *Geschiedenis van de auto van morgen*, 79–86; den Hollander, *Sport in 't Stad*, 346; Gaboriau, 'The Tour de France and Cycling's Belle Époque', 57.

100. Mom, 'Civilized Adventure as a Remedy for Nervous Times', 157.

101. 'Ce sont des automobilistes qu'on retrouve au premier rang des aviateurs. Ces conducteurs intrépides que nous avons vu lancer leurs machines à des vitesses de 100 km. à l'heure dans les circuits célèbres ont rêvé d'autres prouesses. Ils ont abandonnés le volant pour le gouvernail, et les voici qu'ils lancent leurs machines volantes dans l'espace où il n'y a pas d'obstacles et où les routes s'ouvrent devant et auteur d'eux, sans limites': 'Semaine d'Aviation d'Anvers 1909, Vliegweek van Antwerpen, 23 Nov., 2 Nov. 1909', Hendrik Conscience Library, Antwerp, c:lvd:361438.

102. Bourdieu, *La distinction: Critique sociale du Jugement*; Bourdieu, *Distinction: A Social Critique on the Judgement of Taste*.

103. Veblen, *The Theory of the Leisure Class*.

104. See also Goodale and Godbey, *The Evolution of Leisure*, 98.

105. Mattheus, 'De interne geschiedenis van de Koninklijke Belgische Wielrijdersbond', 47, 239–41; Delheye and Renson, 'Belgique', 122.

106. Deneckere, *1900*, 32. See also Gaboriau, 'Les trois âges du vélo en France', 20–2; Gaboriau, 'The Tour de France and Cycling's Belle Époque'.

107. Verbauwhede, 'De Belgische pers en de automobiel', 384–6; Hirschauer, *L'aviation de transport*, 77–89; Bosmans, 'De Belgische motorfietsen', 15.

108. Van Cauwenberge, 'Ambivalente gevoelens', 33; Vanhove, *Het Belgisch kusttoerisme vandaag en morgen*; Deneckere, *1900*, 24–9; Constandt, *Een eeuw vakantie*, 19–22; Thomas Ameye, 'Gejaagd door de wind', 51.

109. See, for instance, Major and Vanthomme, *Vleugels boven Oostende*.

110. Lucien Hautvast (Liège, 1865–1923) was the best Belgian road racer in 1890. He was second in October 1891 in the first large bicycle race that was organised in Belgium on the route Brussels-Antwerp-Aarschot-Leuven-Brussels. As automobile driver, he came in sixth in the Gordon Bennett Cup race of 1904 and second on the circuit of Hamburg in 1907 in his Pipe. He was the first winner of the Liedekerke Cup in 1905 in the touring car class. He won the Maas Cup in 1911 and the Grand Prize of Ostend in 1912 (see Yvens, *Hautvast. Sportsman, gentlemen-driver et tutoyeur de légendes*).

111. Bill Mallon used five criteria to test the Olympic status of the various events at these games: 1. the event should be international in scope, allowing entries from all nations; 2. handicap events should not be allowed; 3. the entries must be open for all competitors, meaning that limitations based on age, religion, national origin or competency, such as junior or novice events, should not be allowed; 4. no events based on motorised transport should be allowed; 5. the events should be restricted to amateurs (see Mallon, *The 1900 Olympic Games*, 8–13). The fourth criterion, however, he discarded. The IOC specification 'Sports, disciplines or events in which performance depends essentially on

mechanical propulsion are not acceptable' came, indeed, at a later date. However, it is noteworthy that this condition was still included in the Olympic Charter Version of 1 September 2004 (see www.youthsport.bg/docs/OlympicCharter.pdf) but that not one word about it appears about in the most recent Olympic Charter of 7 July 2007 (see http://multimedia.olympic.org/pdf/en_report_122.pdf).

112. Heijmans, 'Motorsport at the 1900 Paris Olympic Games', 31; Mallon and Buchanan, *The 1908 Olympic Games*, 200–4.
113. 'Candidatures for Olympic Awards for 1965', 61.
114. Lennartz and Renson, 'Natuursporten en de olympische beweging', 88–9.
115. 'Qu'il se forme dans chaque pays une association chargée de réglementer le sport aéronautique et qu'il soit formé ensuite une fédération universelle unissant toutes les associations nationales en vue de manifestations diverses, de règlements généraux pour la vulgarisation scientifique et sportive de l'aéronautique': Comité International Olympique, *Congrès international de Sport et d'Education physique*, 202.
116. See, for instance, www.fai.org/about/history
117. Lebow, *Before Amelia*, 1–4.
118. There is a considerable body of research on the history of female involvement in sport. See, for example, Mangan and Park, *From 'Fair Sex' to Feminism*; Vertinsky, *The Eternally Wounded Woman*; Costa and Guthrie, *Women and Sport*; Guttmann, *Women's Sports*; Arnaud and Terret, *Histoire du sport féminin. Tome 1*; Arnaud and Terret, *Histoire du sport féminin. Tome 2*. Specifically for cycling, see, among others, Holt, 'The Bicycle, the Bourgeoisie and the Discovery of Rural France'; Pasteur, *Les femmes à bicyclette* ; Hubscher *et al.*, *L'histoire en mouvements*, 299–300.
119. Holt, 'Women, Men and Sport in France', 124–6; Arnaud, 'Le genre ou le sexe?', 153; Mom, 'Civilized Adventure as a Remedy for Nervous Times', 160.
120. Holt, 'Women, Men and Sport in France', 125.
121. Ibid.
122. Ibid., 125–6.
123. For a more elaborate discussion of women and gender in aviation, see Corn, *The Winged Gospel*; Gils, 'Pioneers of Flight'.
124. See Robène, 'Naissance et structuration du vol sportif'; Boval, 'De geschiedenis van de Belgische autoindustrie', 15, 63.
125. 'On peut dire que dès l'origine des temps modernes de l'automobile nos voisins et amis les Belges furent les compagnons du labeur français, que leur effort a été un des plus féconds qu'ait vus notre industrie': Saunier *et al.*, *Histoire de la locomotion terrestre*, 361.
126. Boval, 'De geschiedenis van de Belgische autoindustrie', 63; 'Commerce mondial', *L'Expansion Belge*, March 1908, 115.
127. Kupélian *et al.*, *De geschiedenis van de Belgische auto*, 7.
128. Reynebeau, 'Economie zonder grenzen', 88.
129. Catherine, *Bouwen met zwart geld*, 167–8; Saunier *et al.*, *Histoire de la locomotion terrestre*, 361; Reynebeau, 'Economie zonder grenzen', 85, 88; Van Moorter, 'De zoektocht naar financiers', 30–1.
130. Van Moorter, 'De zoektocht naar financiers', 31.
131. It would take about half a century before they were realised. Catherine, *Bouwen met zwart geld*, 167–8; Couttenier, *Congo tentoongesteld*, 141.
132. It is, however, not very clear what the exact innovation was. According to David Burgess-Wise it was about the cars 'hand-beaten, tulip-shaped seats and graceful, inswept waist' (see his 'A Good Idea at That Time: Roi des Belges Body Style', online at www.telegraph.co.uk/motoring/4749364/A-good-idea-at-the--time-Roi-des-Belges-body-style.html). Lucas Catherine mentioned the passenger side-entrances of the car as originality. Prior to this new invention, passengers had to enter the car through a door at the rear (see Catherine, *Bouwen met zwart geld*, 169). David Gartman, finally, reported that the 'Roi des Belges' (or tulip phaeton) style car had a side-entrance tonneau body and that 'this elegant body had wide, bulging sides and a rear of double-reversed curves reminiscent of a tulip' (see Gartman, *Auto Opium*, 27).
133. Boval, 'De geschiedenis van de Belgische autoindustrie', 35–62; Kupélian *et al.*, *De geschiedenis van de Belgische auto*, 9; Geurts, *Adel in het zadel*; Weber, *Automobilisering en de overheid in België vóór 1940*.

134. '[N]ombre d'usines produisant uniquement, il y a quelques années, des bicyclettes, se sont consacrées aujourd'hui, presqu'exclusivement à la motocylette et l'automobile': 'La bicyclette', *Revue Mensuelle du Cycle et de l'Automobile*, Jan. 1906.
135. Van der Vinne, *Eysink*, 34–6.
136. 'Nouvelles diverses. Bois ou métal', *La Conquête de l'Air*, 15 July 1914, 219.
137. Konrad Mortier mentions 20 airplane designs in the 1905–1914 period. Four constructions also succeeded in flying. In 18 cases, they remained in the prototype stage (see Mortier, 'De Belgische luchtvaartindustrie', 5). Research by the members of BAHA (Belgian Aviation History Association, 1996) resulted in a provisional list of about a hundred pioneers (see Brackx *et al.*, *100 jaar luchtvaart in België*. Several of them are mentioned in the *Brussels Air Museum Magazine*.
138. Ghoos, *75 jaar luchtvaart Antwerpen*, 25–8; *60 jaar luchtvaart in Antwerpen: 1909–1969*; Bollekens, *Gebroeders Bollekens*, 25.
139. Mortier could not find a memorandum of association for the Ateliers Léon de Brouckère and thus could not provide a precise date of its establishment (see Mortier, 'Belgische luchtvaartindustrie', 13–25).
140. Gérard, 'Les débuts de l'aviation militaire en Belgique', 167; Vrancken, *De geschiedenis van de Belgische militaire vliegerij*, 18–19; de Caters, *Baron de Caters*, 117–18; Pacco, *Militaire luchtvaart*, 5. It is not clear whether the flight took place on 7 July or 8 July 1910. Jules de Laminne was, on 15 July 1910, also the first who gave a monarch, Czar Ferdinand I of Bulgaria, a maiden flight (see 'Le czar des Bulgares en Belgique', *L'Expansion Belge*, Sept. 1910, 703–4; van Hoorebeeck, *La conquête de l'air*, 85).
141. Vrancken, *De geschiedenis van de Belgische militaire vliegerij*, 20; No stated author, 'Le berceau de l'aviation belge 1910–1934 à Kiewit'; Morel, 'Le Chevalier Jules de Laminne'; Albert Morel, 'Charles Van den Born le "poète"'; Gérard, 'Les débuts de l'aviation militaire en Belgique', 198; Van Belle, 'De penetratie van de luchtvaart in België', 133–4. For more information on the history of aviation activities in Kiewit, see De Greeve, *Een eeuw luchtvaart boven Kiewit*.
142. Lampaert, *Van pionier tot luchtridder*, 10–11; Vrancken, *De geschiedenis van de Belgische militaire vliegerij*, 23–4, 33–4; Capron, *L'aviation belge et nos souverains*, 20.
143. Lampaert, *Van pionier tot luchtridder*, 11; Vrancken, *De geschiedenis van de Belgische militaire vliegerij*, 28–31.
144. A catalogue of the Société Jéro mentions the end of 1911 as when an agreement was concluded (see Prade, *Véritable histoire de l'aéroplane*, 5). Francis Bollekens, who compiled a catalogue for the exhibition 'Gebroeders Bollekens Vliegtuigbouwers 1909–1916' in 1999, however, gives 1 March 1912 as the date (see Bollekens, *Gebroeders Bollekens*, 27).
145. 'Aéronautique. Une visite aux ateliers de la société 'Jéro', à Anvers. (Aéroplanes Farman)', *L'Expansion Belge*, Jan. 1913, 50; Van Belle, 'De penetratie van de luchtvaart in België', 57.
146. This way, many military pilots learned to fly under Fernand Verschaeve, who was instructor at Jéro. On 8 April 1914, however, he was killed in a crash when he was testing the new Jéro/Farman HF20 in Sint-Job-in-'t-Goor. He was the sixth Belgian pilot who was killed in a crash and would be followed at Jéro by René Vertongen (see 'La mort de l'aviateur Verschaeve', *La Conquête de l'Air*, 1 April 1914, 122–3; 'Une visite à l'école d'aviation militaire de Brasschaet', *L'Expansion Belge*, Nov. 1912, 667–70; 'Aviation. Un grand disparu: Fernand Verschaeve', *L'Expansion Belge*, May 1914, 330–1; Van Belle, 'De penetratie van de luchtvaart in België', 109–210).
147. Vrancken, *De geschiedenis van de Belgische militaire vliegerij*, 28–31; Mortier, 'Belgische luchtvaartindustrie', 13–25; Bollekens, *Gebroeders Bollekens*, 35–8.
148. The Bollekens brothers launched a lawsuit in which the definitive judgement was finally pronounced only in December 1941. The state had to pay the brothers 3,000,000 francs. After the Armistice, the Bollekens brothers left aircraft construction completely. The carpentry shop restricted itself exclusively to making roll-down shutters, Venetian blinds and the like. It is striking that the company shifted in 1924 from woodworking to a bodywork company. The emphasis lay on the body work for trucks and delivery vans

(see Mortier, 'Belgische luchtvaartindustrie:', 13–25; Bollekens, *Gebroeders Bollekens*, 35–8; Van Engeland, *Duffel. 2006*, 131).

149. See Vanthemsche, 'The Birth of Commercial Air Transport in Belgium', 916.

150. The glamorous story that is told about Georges Nélis by a number of authors (see for example Van Belle, 'De penetratie van de luchtvaart in België', 28, 182–3; Bollekens, *Gebroeders Bollekens*, 38) and finds its origin in Nélis's publication *L'expansion belge par l'aviation* is toned down by Guy Vanthemsche. For more information on post-war Belgian aviation, see Vanthemsche, 'The Birth of Commercial Air Transport in Belgium'.

151. Vanthemsche, 'The Birth of Commercial Air Transport in Belgium', 919–35; *Les Belges à la conquête de l'air*, 105–108.

152. Vanthemsche, 'The Birth of Commercial Air Transport in Belgium', 915–19; Boin, 'België-Congo 1925–1935–1985', 8–9; Van Hoorebeeck, 'Belgische vleugels in Afrika', 3–5; *Les Belges à la conquête de l'air*, 11–14.

153. 'Automobiles et aéroplanes du Katanga', *L'Expansion Belge*, July 1914, 458–60; Van Belle, 'De penetratie van de luchtvaart in België', 176; Capron, *L'aviation belge et nos souverains*, 22.

154. Jules Fischer was first a track and road racer and then an automobile driver. After that, he turned to aviation sport. He was also 'chief pilot for Farman' (see 'Le premier concours d'hydro-aéroplanes à Monaco', *L'Expansion Belge*, May 1912, 299).

155. Lebow, *Before Amelia*, 32.

156. '[C]oncours d'hydro-aéroplanes fluviaux et coloniaux … la largeur du fleuve et le courant ont beaucoup d'analogie avec la plupart des rivières du Congo': 'Le concours d'hydro-aéroplanes de l'aéroclub de Belgique', *L'Expansion Belge*, July 1912, 479.

157. This 'patriotic work' was possibly also sponsored by companies with colonial interests, such as the Société du Kasai and the Société Commerciale et Financière Africaine (see 'Le concours d'hydro-aéroplanes de l'aéroclub de Belgique', *L'Expansion Belge*, July 1912, 479; Verstraeten, *Vleugels boven Klein-Brabant*, 8).

158. 'Mettre en évidence les qualités des hydro-aéroplanes pouvant être utilisés aux colonies et particulièrement au Congo': 'Le concours d'hydro-aéroplanes de Tamise', *L'Expansion Belge*, Septe. 1912, xxx–xxxii.

159. This was first the case when in 1916, during World War I, seaplanes were used to destroy the German dominance of Lake Tanganika. Its size made Lake Tanganyika an interesting frontier area and an outstanding transport route. From November 1914 on, the Germans had achieved sole dominance of Lake Tanganyika from their colony, German East Africa. The success of the Belgian seaplanes launched the allied conquest (see Behaeghe, *Aimé Behaeghe (1890–1916)*, 7–20; Behaeghe, 'Aimé Behaeghe. First Pilot', 3–22; Vanthemsche, 'The Birth of Commercial Air Transport in Belgium', 917–18; Pacco, *Militaire luchtvaart*, 14–15).

160. Boin, 'België-Congo 1925–1935–1985', 14.

161. Guy Vanthemsche, *La SABENA*, 301–2. Several Belgian companies still actively contribute (delivery of supplies) to the development of the highly sophisticated space/aeronautics industry.

162. Georgano, *The Beaulieu Encyclopedia of the Automobile*, 751.

163. Recently this sector is dwindling too (e.g. closure of Renault Vilvoorde in 1997 and virtual closure of Opel Antwerp).

164. Jacky Ickx and Thierry Boutsen are among the exceptions during the past one hundred years.

165. The Research Centre for the History of Sport and Kinesiology at K.U. Leuven has recently started a research project aiming at assessing the 'national' impact of the bicycle in Belgium.

166. It is to be noted, however, that the FIM World Championships are a predominantly European affair, next to the AMA (American Motorcyclist Association) Motocross Championships in the United States of America. Still, with 14 titles, Belgium is one of the most successful countries in the Motocross of Nations, the annual motocross race event considered the world championship for national teams and staged since 1947. Great Britain dominated the early years (16 titles), whereas the United States total 21 victories.

References

60 jaar luchtvaart in Antwerpen: 1909–1969. Antwerp: Jeugd en Luchtvaart, 1969.

Ameye, Thomas. 'Belgium'. *Journal of Olympic History* 14, no. 3 (2006): 20–9.

Ameye, Thomas. 'Gejaagd door de wind. 110 jaar strandzeilen in De Panne (1898–2008)'. *Sportimonium* 3–4 (2007): 50–66.

Ameye, Thomas, and Delheye Pascal. 'Expansionism, Physical Education and Olympism: Common Interests of King Leopold II of Belgium, Cyrille Van Overbergh and Pierre de Coubertin'. *Olympika. The International Journal of Olympic Studies*, forthcoming.

Arnaud, Pierre. 'Le genre ou le sexe? Sport féminin et changement social (XIXe–XXe siècle)', in *Histoire du sport féminin. Tome 2. Sport masculin-sport féminin: éducation et société*, eds. Pierre Arnaud and Thierry Terret. Paris: L'Harmattan, 1996, 147–83.

Arnaud, Pierre and Thierry Terret, eds. *Histoire du sport féminin. Tome 1. Le sport au féminin: histoire et identité*. Paris: L'Harmattan, 1996.

Arnaud, Pierre and Thierry Terret, eds. *Histoire du sport féminin. Tome 2. Sport masculin-sport féminin: éducation et société*. Paris: L'Harmattan, 1996.

Bairati, Eleonora, Julian Philippe, Falkus Malcolm, Monelli Paolo, Riesz Janos, and Vigezzi Brunello. *La Belle Époque. Fifteen Euphoric Years of European History*. New York: William Morrow and Company, 1978.

Behaeghe, Tillo. *Aimé Behaeghe (1890–1916) de eerste piloot in Centraal Afrika*. Ghent: Tillo Behaeghe, 2008.

Behaeghe, Tillo. 'Aimé Behaeghe. First Pilot in Central Africa'. *Cross & Cockade International* 39, no. 1 (2008): 3–22.

Berlanstein, Lenard R. 'Selling Modern Feminity: Femina, a Forgotten Feminist Publishing Success in Belle Époque France'. *French Historical Studies* 30, no. 4 (2007): 623–49.

Boin, Victor. 'België-Congo 1925–1935–1985'. *Brussels Air Museum Magazine XV*, no. 45 (1985): 8–13.

Bollekens, Francis. *Gebroeders Bollekens. Vliegtuigbouwers: 1909–1916* (tentoonstellingscatalogus). Sint-Katelijne-Waver: Erf en Heem, 1999.

Bosmans, Bert. 'De Belgische motorfietsen 1900–1965: een studie van de techniek, de sociologie, de wetgeving en de economie van de motorfiets en zijn berijder'. Unpublished diss., K.U. Leuven, 1996.

Bourdieu, Pierre. *La distinction: Critique sociale du jugement*. Paris: Ed. de Minuit, 1979.

Bourdieu, Pierre. *Distinction: A Social Critique on the Judgement of Taste*. London: Routledge and Kegan Paul, 1984.

Boval, Philippe. 'De geschiedenis van de Belgische autoindustrie: ontstaan, ontwikkeling en verdwijning'. Unpublished diss., University of Antwerp, 1985.

Brackx, Daniel, Pierre Cryns, Yves Duwelz, Jean-Louis Roba, Peter Taghon and Frans Van Humbeek. *100 jaar luchtvaart in België: het album van de Belgian Aviation History Association*. Tielt: Lannoo, 2002.

Buytaert, D. and J. Dillen. *Jan Olieslagers: 1883–1942*. Antwerp: Royal Antwerp Aviation Club, 1992.

'Candidatures for Olympic Awards for 1965'. *Olympic Review* 90 (May 1965).

Capron, Freddy. *L'Aviation belge et nos souverains*. Brussels: J.M. Collet, 1988.

Catherine, Lucas. *Bouwen met zwart geld. De grootheidswaanzin van Leopold II*. Antwerp: Houtekiet, 2002.

Comité International Olympique, *Congrès International de Sport et d'Education Physique*. Auxerre: Editions de la Revue Olympique, 1905.

Constandt, Marc. *Een eeuw vakantie. 100 jaar toerisme in West-Vlaanderen*. Tielt: Lannoo, 1986.

Coppens de Houthulst, Willy. *Un homme volant: Jan Olieslagers*. Brussels: Les Éditions Rex, 1935.

Coppens de Houthulst, Willy. 'Les notes d'un combattant – Jan Olieslagers, homme volant'. *Le Courrier de l'Armée* 23 (15 May 1936): 2021–2.

Coppens de Houthulst, Willy. 'Jan Olieslagers. Un pionnier de l'aviation belge'. *La Gazette du Soldat* 3, no. 19 (1947).

Coppens de Houthulst, Willy. 'Jan Olieslagers, mon ancien'. *Le Flambeau* (July–August 1956): 469–81.

Corn, Joseph. *The Winged Gospel. America's Romance with Aviation, 1900–1950*. New York: Oxford University Press, 1983.

Costa, D. Margaret and Sharon R. Guthrie, eds. *Women and Sport. Interdisciplinary Perspectives*. Champaign, IL: Human Kinetics, 1994.

Court, William. *A History of Grand Prix Motor Racing 1906–1951. Power and Glory*. London: Macdonald, 1966.

Couttenier, Maarten. *Congo tentoongesteld. Een geschiedenis van de Belgische antropologie en het museum van Tervuren (1882–1925)*. Leuven: Acco, 2005.

de Caters, Guy. 'Baron Pierre de Caters, 1908: het ontstaan van de luchtvaart in België'. *Periodiek Bulletin van de V.Z.W. Vrienden van het Lucht- en Ruimtevaartmuseum* 21 (1978): 3–6.

de Caters, Guy. 'Het ontstaan van de luchtvaart in België: Baron Pierre de Caters (tweede deel)'. *Periodiek Bulletin van de V.Z.W. Vrienden van het Lucht- en Ruimtevaartmuseum* 22 (1979): 7–10.

de Caters, Guy. 'Baron Pierre de Caters (derde deel)'. *Periodiek Bulletin van de V.Z.W. Vrienden van het Lucht- en Ruimtevaartmuseum* 23 (1979): 6–9.

de Caters, Guy. *Baron de Caters: 1875–1944. Een leven vol beweging*. 's-Gravenwezel: Heemkring De Drie Rozen, 2008.

de Coubertin, Pierre. *Olympic Memoirs*. Lausanne: International Olympic Committee, 1989 (orig. pub. 1931).

De geschiedenis van de luchtvaart. Beroemde luchtvaart-pioniers. 1980. Rotterdam: Lekturama, 1980.

De Greeve, Karin. *Een eeuw luchtvaart boven Kiewit*. Erembodegem: Flying Pencil, 2009.

De Kinder, Constant. *De Antwerpsche Duivel. Uit het sportieve en oorlogsverleden van Jan Olieslagers*. Antwerp: L. Opdebeek, 1936.

Delheye, Pascal. 'Struggling for Gymnastics. The Scientisation and Institutionalisation of Physical Education in Belgium (1830–1914)'. Unpublished doctoral diss., K.U. Leuven, 2005.

Delheye, Pascal. 'Fit for the Nation: A Utopian View on Physical Education in Belgium (1900–1914)', in *Utopianism and the Sciences, 1880–1930*, eds. Mary Kemperink, and Leonieke Vermeer. Louvain/Paris/Walpole (MA): Peeters, 2010, 157–168.

Delheye, Pascal and Renson Roland. 'Belgique', in *Histoire du sport en Europe*, eds. James Riordan, Arnd Krüger and Thierry Terret, Paris/Budapest/Trina: L'Harmattan, 2004, 113–145.

Deneckere, Gita. *1900. België op het breukvlak van twee eeuwen*. Tielt: Lannoo, 2006.

den Hollander, Marijke. *Sport in 't Stad. Antwerpen 1830–1914*. Leuven: Universitaire Pers Leuven, 2006.

Derwael, Joachim. 'Sociale achtergrond van de Gentse sportverenigingen en hun bestuurders op het einde van de negentiende en het begin van de twintigste eeuw (1890–1914)', Unpublished disse., University of Ghent, 2001.

Dhanens, Piet and Cynrik De Decker. *Een eeuw luchtvaart boven Gent. Deel I*. Erembodegem: Flying Pencil, 2008.

Dick, Robert. *Mercedes and Auto Racing in the Belle Époque: 1895–1915*. Jefferson, NC: McFarland & Company, 2005.

Dumas, Alexandre. *Les accidents d'aviation. Étude générale de leurs causes. Recherche des moyens propres à en diminuer la fréquence*. Paris: Librairie aéronautique, 1914.

Dumont, Fabienne and Bernard Marie Laurence. *Sportaffiches in België 1890–1916*. Brussels: Gemeentekrediet, 1981.

Feyel, Gilles. 'Naissance, constitution progressive et épanouissement d'un genre de presse aux limites floues: le magazine'. *Réseaux* 105, no. 1 (2001): 19–51.

Gaboriau, Philippe. 'Les trois âges du vélo en France'. *Vingtième Siècle* 29, no. 1 (1991): 17–34.

Gaboriau, Philippe. 'The Tour de France and Cycling's Belle Époque'. *International Journal of the History of Sport* 20, no. 2 (2003): 57–78.

Gartman, David. *Auto Opium. A Social History of American Automobile Design*. New York: Routledge, 1994.

Georgano, Nick. *The Beaulieu Encyclopedia of the Automobile*. Chicago: Fitzroy Dearborn, 2000.

Gérard, Hervé. 'Les débuts de l'aviation militaire en Belgique (1910–août 1914) et Pierre de Caters, premier aviateur belge', Unpublished diss., K.U. Leuven, 1977.

Geurts, Frans. *Adel in het zadel. 100 jaar motorsport in België en Nederland van A tot Z.* Zaltbommel: Europese Bibliotheek, 2001, 2002, 2004.

Ghoos, Jos. *75 jaar luchtvaart Antwerpen.* Antwerp: n.v. de Vlijt, 1984.

Gils, Bieke. 'Belgische sportlui door een Franse Bril: een analyse van het tijdschrift *La Vie au Grand Air (1898–1914)'*. Unpublished diss., K.U. Leuven, 2006.

Gils, Bieke. 'Baanbrekers en hoogvliegers: Belgische pioniers in het rallyrijden en de vliegerij tijdens de Belle Époque'. *Sportimonium* 3–4 (2006): 74–81.

Gils, Bieke. 'Pioneers of Flight: An Analysis of Gender Issues in United States Civilian (Sport) and Commercial Aviation 1920–1940', Unpublished diss., University of Windsor, Ontario, 2009.

Goodale, Thomas and Godbey Geoffrey. *The Evolution of Leisure: Historical and Philosophical Perspectives.* Oxford: Venture Publishing, 1988.

Goyens, Henri. 'L'histoire de notre club, anniversaire 1898–1948, Royal Automobile Club Anversois. *Speed. Le Bulletin Officiel du Royal Automobile Club Anversois* (1948): 15–23. (in Hendrik Conscience Library, Antwerp: 593783).

Guttmann, Allen. *Women's Sports: A History.* New York: Columbia University Press, 1991.

Guttmann, Allen. *The Olympics: A History of the Modern Games.* Urbana: University of Illinois Press, 1992.

Guttmann, Allen. *Sports: The First Five Millennia.* Amherst, MA: University of Massachusetts Press, 2005.

Heijmans, Jeroen. 'Motorsport at the 1900 Paris Olympic Games'. *Olympic Review* 3 (Sept. 2002): 30–5.

Hirschauer, L. *L'aviation de transport. L'évolution de la construction de 1907 à 1919 et la réalisation des avions de transport. L'utilisation économique des appareils.* Paris: Dunod, 1920.

'Historique des Vieilles Tiges de Belgique'. *Brussels Air Museum Magazine* XX, no. 67 (1990): 45–8.

Hochschild, Adam. *King Leopold's Ghost. A Story of Greed, Terror and Heroism in Colonial Africa.* Boston, MA: Houghton Mifflin, 1998.

Holt, Richard. 'The Bicycle, the Bourgeoisie and the Discovery of Rural France 1880–1914'. *British Journal of Sports History* 2 (1985): 127–39.

Holt, Richard. 'Women, Men and Sport in France, c.1870–1914: An Introductory Survey'. *Journal of Sport History* 18, no. 1 (1991): 121–34.

Hospitalier, E. 'Voitures automobiles. Le concours du 'Petit Journal''. *La Nature*, 28 July 1894: 129–31.

Hospitalier, E. 'Voitures automobiles. Les lauréats du concours du 'Petit Journal''. *La Nature*, 25 Aug. 1894: 129–31.

Houart, Victor. 'The Belgian Aces'. In *Air Aces of the War 1914–1918*, ed. Bruce Roberston, Letchworth: The Garden City Press Limited, 1959, 32–147.

Hubscher, Ronald, Jean Durry, and Bernard Jeu. *L'histoire en mouvements. Le sport dans la société française (XIVe–XXe siècle).* Paris: Armand Colin, 1992.

'Jan Olieslagers. De crack met zes overwinningen'. *In Vogelvlucht* 12 (1958): 2–4.

Janssens, Valéry. *De Belgische frank: anderhalve eeuw geldgeschiedenis.* Antwerp: Standaard, 1976.

Kupélian, Yvette, Jacques Kupélain and Jacques Sirtaine. *De geschiedenis van de Belgische auto. Het fabelachtige verhaal van meer dan honderd automobielmerken.* Tielt: Lannoo, 1980.

Kupélian, Yvette, and Kupélian. Jacques. *Minerva.* Overijse: Yvette & Jacques Kupélian, 1985.

Lampaert, Roger. *Van pionier tot luchtridder. De geschiedenis van het Belgisch militair vliegwezen voor en tijdens de Eerste Wereldoorlog.* Erpe: De Krijger, 1997.

Lauters, Francis. *Les débuts du cyclisme en Belgique: souvenirs d'un vétéran.* Brussels: Office de Publicité, 1936.

'Le berceau de l'aviation belge 1910–1934 à Kiewit'. *L'Aviation Illustrée III*, no. 12 (1934).

Lebow, Eileen. *Before Amelia Women Pilots in the Early Days of Aviation.* Washington DC: Brassey's Inc., 2002.

Lelasseux, Louis, and René Marque. *L'aéroplane pour tous*. Paris: Librairie aéronautique, 1909.

Lennartz, Karl, and Roland Renson. 'Natuursporten en de olympische beweging'. *Sportimonium* 3–4 (2006): 82–90.

Les Belges à la conquête de l'air. Brussels: Hayez, 1976.

Lombaerde, Piet and Ronny Gobyn. *Léopold II. Roi-bâtisseur*. Ghent: Pandora, 1995.

Lynch, Brendan. *The Irish Gordon Bennett Cup Race 1903. Triumph of the Red Devil*. Dublin: Portobello, 2002.

Major, Walter and Vanthomme Norbert. *Vleugels boven Oostende 1909–1919*. Erembodegem: Flying Pencil, 2009.

Mallon, Bill. *The 1900 Olympic Games. Results for All Competitors in All Events, with Commentary*. Jefferson, NC and London: McFarland & Company, 1998.

Mallon, Bill and Ian Buchanan. *The 1908 Olympic Games. Results for All Competitors in All Events, with Commentary*. Jefferson, NC and London: McFarland & Company, 2000.

Mandl, Michel and Guido Wuyts. 'Baron Pierre de Caters: premier aviateur et avionneur belge, membre-fondateur des Vieilles Tiges de l'aviation belge'. *Les Vieilles Tiges* (www.vieillestiges.be).

Mangan J.A. and Roberta J. Park, eds. *From 'Fair Sex' to Feminism. Sport and the Socialization of Women in the Industrial and Post-Industrial Eras*. London: Routledge, 1987.

Mathy, Theo. *Encyclopedie van de Belgische sportlui en sporten*. Brussels: Legrain, 1983.

Mattheus, Ruben. 'De interne geschiedenis van de Koninklijke Belgische Wielrijdersbond, de Union Cycliste Internationale en hun Belgische voorzitters (1882–1922)'. Unpublished diss., University of Ghent, 2005.

Matthews, Hart. *Pioneer Aviators of the World. A Biographical Dictionary of the First Pilots of 100 Countries. Jefferson*, NC: McFarland & Company, 2003.

Meerbergen, Johan. 'Sport of transport: de luchtvaart in België 1900–1918. Bijdrage tot het Archief voor de Moderne Sport'. Unpublished diss., K.U. Leuven, 1991.

Mom, Gijs. *Geschiedenis van de auto van morgen*. Deventer: Kluwer, 1997.

Mom, Gijs. 'Civilized Adventure as a Remedy for Nervous Times: Early Automobilism and Fin-de-siècle Culture'. *History of Technology* 23 (2001): 157–90.

Morel, Albert. 'Charles Van den Born le "poète"'. *L'Aviation Illustrée* IX, no. 84 (1941).

Morel, Albert. 'Daniel et Nicolas Kinet. Premières victimes de l'aviation en Belgique'. *L'Aviation Illustrée IX*, no. 92 (1941).

Morel, Albert. 'Hélène Dutrieu, la première aviatrice belge'. *L'Aviation Illustrée* IX, no. 85 (1941).

Morel, Albert. 'Jan Olieslagers le 'Démon Anversois''. *L'Aviation Illustrée* IX, no. 83 (1941).

Morel, Albert. 'Le Chevalier Jules de Laminne'. *L'Aviation Illustrée* IX, no. 82 (1941).

Mortier, Konrad. 'De Belgische luchtvaartindustrie: 1905–1940. Een analyse'. Unpublished diss., University of Ghent, 1983.

Nélis, George. *L'expansion belge par l'aviation*. Brussels: L'Expansion Belge, 1919.

Pacco, John. *Militaire luchtvaart. Aviation militaire (1910–1929)*. Aartselaar: J.P. Publications, 2000.

Pasteur, Claude. *Les femmes à bicyclette à la Belle Époque*. Paris: France-Empire, 1986.

Pfister, Gertrud. *Fliegen-ihr Leben. Die ersten Pilotinnen*. Berlijn: Orlanda Frauen, 1989.

Pick, Daniel. *Faces of Degeneration: A European Disorder, c.1848–c.1918* ('Ideas in Context' 15). Cambridge: Cambridge University Press, 1989.

Postma, Thijs, and Wesselink. Theo. *De vliegende Hollanders. De geschiedenis van de Nederlandse luchtvaart vanaf de eerste vlucht in 1909 tot heden*. Dieren: De Bataafsche Leeuw, 1984.

Prade, Georges. *Véritable histoire de l'aéroplane* (Catalogue de la Société 'Jéro'). Antwerp: H. & M. Farman.

Ranieri, Liane. *Léopold II, urbaniste*. Brussels: Hayez, 1973.

Rearick, Charles. *Pleasures of the Belle Époque. Entertainment & Festivity in Turn-of-the-Century France*. New Haven, CT and London: Yale University Press, 1985.

Renson, Roland, Ameye Thomas, Maes Marc, Lien Vandermeersch and Roger Vanmeerbeek. *Enflammé par l'olympisme: cent ans de Comité Olympique et Interfédéral Belge: 1906–2006*. Roeselare: Roularta, 2006.

Reynebeau, Mark. 'Economie zonder grenzen (1900–1914)'. *De Standaard* (March 2005): 88.

Robène, Luc. 'Naissance et structuration du vol sportif: le rôle du comte H. de la Vaulx (1870–1930)'. *Sport History Review* 32 (2001): 126–39.

Robène, Luc, Domique Bodin, and Stéphane Héas. 'Pau et l'invention de l'aviation 'sportive' (1908–1910). Des enjeux technologiques aux plaisirs mondains: naissance d'un loisir et nouveaux pouvoirs du corps'. *Revue Internationale des Sciences du Sport et de l'Education Physique* 87 (2010): 13–31.

Royal Touring Club de Belgique, *Mémorial du Royal Touring Club de Belgique: 1895–1955*. Brussels: Henri Wauters, 1955.

Saunier, Baudry de, Charles Dollfus, and Edgar de Geoffroy. *Histoire de la locomotion terrestre: la locomotion naturelle, l'attelage, la voiture, le cyclisme, la locomotion mécanique, l'automobile*. Paris: L'Illustration, 1942.

Schoenmaker, Wim, and Postma Thijs. *Aviateurs van het eerste uur. De Nederlandse luchtvaart tot de Eerste Wereldoorlog*. Weesp: Romen luchtvaart, 1984.

Schoonbroodt, Benoît. *Art nouveau kunstenaars in België. 1890–1914*. Tielt: Lannoo, 2008.

Tollebeek, Jo. 'Degeneratie, moderniteit en culturele verandering: een Belgisch perspectief'. In *Degeneratie in België 1860–1940. Een geschiedenis van ideeën en praktijken*, eds. Jo Tollebeek, Geert Vanpaemel and Kaat Wils. Leuven: Universitaire Pers, 2003, 299–319.

Turgan, Louis. *Histoire de l'aviation*. Paris: L. Geisler, 1909.

Van Belle, Franck. 'De penetratie van de luchtvaart in België: 1904–1914'. Unpublished diss., University of Ghent, 1978.

Van Cauwenberge, Sabine. 'Ambivalente gevoelens. Het geïllustreerde familieblad en de burgerlijke leefwereld in Fin-de-Siècle en Belle Époque'. Unpublished diss., K.U. Leuven, 1992.

van der Vinne, Vincent. *Eysink. Van fiets tot motorfiets: ondernemen tijdens de opkomst van het gemotoriseerd verkeer*. Amsterdam: De Bataafsche Leeuw, 2001.

Van Engeland, Dirk. *Duffel. Dorp van orgels, koetswerk en chocolade. De saga van drie families en hun bedrijven: Stevens, Bollekens en Renaux*. Duffel: Den Grooten Duffelaar, 2006.

Vangroenweghe, Daniel. *Rood Rubber. Leopold II en zijn Kongo*. Brussels/Amsterdam: Elsevier, 1985.

van Hoorebeeck, Albert. *La conquête de l'air. Chronologie de l'aérostation, de l'aviation et de l'astronautique, des précurseurs aux cosmonautes*. Verviers: Gérard & Co, 1967.

van Hoorebeeck, Albert. 'Belgische vleugels in Afrika'. *Periodiek Bulletin van de V.Z.W. Vrienden van het Lucht- en Ruimtevaartmuseum* 24 (1980): 3–5.

van Hoorebeeck, Albert. 'Hélène Dutrieu'. *Bulletin Périodique de l'A.S.B.L. Amis du Musée de l'Air et de l'Espace* I, no. 2 (1970): 5–6.

Vanhove, Norbert. *Het Belgisch kusttoerisme vandaag en morgen*. Bruges: Westvlaams ekonomisch studiebureau, 1973.

Van Moorter, Joost. 'De zoektocht naar financiers van de automobiel door middel van de kapitaalvorming in een aantal Belgische automobielbedrijven (1895–1914)'. Unpublished diss., University of Ghent, 2002.

Vanthemsche, Guy. 'The Birth of Commercial Air Transport in Belgium (1919–1923)'. *Revue Belge de Philologie et d'Histoire-Belgisch Tijdschrift voor Filologie en Geschiedenis*, 78 (2000): 913–44.

Vanthemsche, Guy. *La SABENA. L'aviation commerciale belge. 1923–2001*. Brussels: De Boeck, 2002.

Vanthomme, Norbert. 'De 'Demoiselle.' De eerste ultralichte sportkist uit de luchtvaartgeschiedenis'. *Cahier voor Luchtvaartgeschiedenis* 3 (Nov 1977).

Vanthomme, Norbert. 'Eerste vliegtuig van Baron Pierre de Caters'. *Periodiek Bulletin van de V.Z.W. Vrienden van het Lucht- en Ruimtevaartmuseum* IX, 21 (1979): 7–9.

Veblen, Thorstein. *The Theory of the Leisure Class: An Economic Study of Institutions*. New York: Mentor books, 1953.

Verbauwhede, Geert. 'De Belgische pers en de automobiel (1890–1914) (eerste deel)'. Unpublished diss., University of Ghent, 1990.

Verbauwhede, Geert. 'De Belgische pers en de automobiel (1890–1914) (tweede deel)'. Unpublished diss., University of Ghent, 1990.

Verstraeten, Walter. *Vleugels boven Klein-Brabant. 100 jaar luchtvaartgeschiedenis tussen Schelde en Rupel.* Bornem: Vereniging voor Heemkunde in Klein-Brabant v.z.w., 1999.

Vertinsky, Patricia. *The Eternally Wounded Woman. Women, Doctors and Exercise in the Late Nineteenth Century.* Manchester: Manchester University Press, 1990.

Vincke, Nicolas and Louis Delmer. *Voitures automobiles, bateaux, moteurs, etc. Catalogue pour 1896,* 1895.

Vrancken, Ludo. *De geschiedenis van de Belgische militaire vliegerij: 1910–1918.* Brussels: Koninklijk Legermuseum, 1999.

Weber, Donald. 'Automobilisering en de overheid in België vóór 1940. Besluitvormingsprocessen bij de ontwikkeling van een conflictbeheersingssysteem'. Unpublished diss., University of Ghent, 2008.

Weber, Donald. *De blijde intrede van de automobiel in België. 1895–1940.* Ghent: Academia Press, 2010.

Weber, Eugen. 'Gymnastics and sport in fin-de-siècle France'. *Olympic Review* 53–54 (Feb.–March 1972): 102–14.

Young, David C. *The Modern Olympics. A Struggle for Revival.* Baltimore, MD, and London: The Johns Hopkins University Press, 1996.

Yvens, Claude. *Lucien Hautvast. Sportsman, gentlemen-driver et tutoyeur de légendes.* Neufchâteau: Weyrich Edition, 2005.

Zonderman, Geert. 'De geschiedenis van de sportluchtvaart in België 1918–1995: bijdrage tot het archief voor Moderne Sport (MOSAR)'. Unpublished diss., K.U. Leuven, 1995.

From Dictatorship to Democracy in Spain: The Iconography of Motorcyclist Angel Nieto

Teresa González Aja

Polytechnic University of Madrid, Madrid, Spain

Motorcycling in Spain was a minority sport from its very inception. However, the emergence of certain personalities, especially Angel Nieto, and their subsequent successes attracted the attention of high-ranking government officials who began to take an interest in it. Relatively quickly they identified the sport as a convenient method of advancing propaganda for the regime. The iconography associated with a sports hero, someone who began with nothing only to overcome great suffering and attain fame and recognition through sheer willpower, carried considerable symbolic resonance. Such sporting stars represented a set of values that state departments considered useful, and for which they did not hesitate to use both the press and even educational institutions to advance a relationship, as they saw it, between success in motor sport and the well-being of the nation. The subsequent emergence of a democratic system of government in Spain brought with it considerable levels of freedom, which in turn would have a profound impact on sport, including motorcycle racing. It would allow circuits to be built, foreign bikes to be imported into the country and a new type of sports star to emerge, one who now owed his/her success not alone to his/her own efforts but also to the considerable sporting infrastructures that existed in the 'new' Spain.

An Early History of Motorcycling in Spain

The early history of motorcycling in Spain can be traced back to 1899 when on 19 December that year the first motorcycle race took place over a total distance of four kilometres in Barcelona, alongside the first automobile and cycling races, all of which were promoted by the prominent newspaper *Los Deportes*.[1] This initial race was followed by several others, including a similar event staged on 13 April 1904, but the first major race, the Sportsmen's Club Cup, did not take place until 1906 and was jointly sponsored by the *Club Fotográfico Deportivo* (Sports Photography Club) and the *Unión Velocipédica Española* (UVE – Spanish Velocipede Union).[2] The UVE had evolved out of the Society of Velocipedists founded in 1891, which was an organisation that had a strong interest in the sport of motorcycling from the outset.

However it was not until February 1923 that the by-laws of the Spanish Motorcycling Federation were established and approved.[3] They subdivided Spanish motorcycling into three zones: Zone A – Galicia/Asturias/Santander/the Basque country/Navarre; Zone B – Catalonia/Aragon/the Balearic Islands/Valencia; and Zone C – The rest of Spain. The rules decreed that this division could not be modified for the following two years, and that if it were it would be solely for sporting expediency and never for geographic reasons. Responsibility for Zones B and C fell to the Royal Motor Clubs of Catalonia and Spain, respectively, but no single organisation was made responsible for Zone A. Finally this designation fell to the *Peña Motorista Vizcaya* (the Biscayan Motorist Group) in 1927, following its establishment over the preceding year.

It is useful to examine the workings of the motorcycling federation within three distinct time frames: from its creation in 1923 until the Spanish Civil War of 1936; from the end of the Civil War and the establishment of Franco's regime in 1939 until 1985; and thereafter its experiences under a democratic government, including up to the present day. In the initial stage, the existence of the federation was limited to the work of its directors' committee, composed of representatives from the three clubs which at that time controlled each of the aforementioned zones, and which shared the various positions with the general secretariat based in Barcelona. The latter was the region in which the majority of motorcycling activities took place throughout this early period. Indeed it was in the Catalonian region where the first Spanish Motorcycling Championship was staged in 1909, the race being held at the Sitges-Baix Penedes (Barcelona) circuit. The Spanish Motorcycling Championship consisted of seven laps of the circuit, over a total distance of 196 kilometres, and was considered by competitors to be the most gruelling endurance race imaginable.

The lack of a fully fledged federation at that time – as previously established, one was not created until 1923 – meant that this first attempt to organise a motorcycling championship of Spain was not realised until 1912. This was the same year in which Madrid and Catalonia, the two main development regions for motorcycling at this time, agreed to stage the first Motorcycling Championship of Spain in the Velodrome at Ciudad Lineal, Madrid. This was to be the last time the race would be staged on an established track until 1919. For financial reasons the Motorcycling Championship of Spain was not held in 1913 or 1914. Instead the second championship was postponed until 1915; on this occasion the event was organised by the Sports Club of Bilbao[4] and held over a distance of 335km. The championship continued to take place annually, although with some interruptions (1918, 1920–3, 1927–9) until 1935, when following the outbreak of the Civil War in 1936 this first era of motorcycling drew to a close.

The second stage would begin after the end of the Spanish Civil War (1936–9). The dispute pitted the values of two very different ways of life against each other. At all levels it was a terrible episode from which Spain did not easily recover.[5] The new era, which began at its close – not counting the actual war years during which a part of Spain had already effectively fallen under Franco's control – lasted more than 36 years, and was characterised by a homogeneity not readily apparent in the preceding period; a homogeneity that was defined both by the evolving continuity of the system and by the permanency of one man who almost singularly took charge of Spain's destiny.

Franco's Regime

As Jose Luis Comellas has stated, 'the period during which General Franco was the head of state should be studied as a unique chapter in our contemporary history. It is not a parenthesis, but a differential singularity, whose historical transcendence can only be judged after continuous and serious research'.[6] Sport, a mirror and reflection of the society in which it develops, was naturally affected by the events which derived from this war and came to form part of just this 'historical singularity'.

The study of post-Civil War sport in Spain should be considered from two points of view, as were the sports policies during this era: within the domestic and the international spheres. Internationally the aim was to project a confident and determined image of Franco's Spain; in the domestic sphere there was a programme designed to inculcate the values considered central to the new regime. It is necessary therefore to examine the ideologies underpinning sport during the Franco era in order to understand the specific world of motorcycling at this time. This period was defined by the omnipotence of Franco in all aspects of political and cultural life as everything revolved around his personage. Franco considered that the liberalism of the nineteenth century had been the root cause of Spain's decline and that political self-interest during this era was responsible for the anarchy which, in his opinion, was rife throughout Spain. Changes of government during this period were practically non-existent. Instead, Franco's ideas and his personal beliefs decisively influenced the life of Spanish men and women for almost four decades.

Until his death in November 1975, General Franco continued to be, as proclaimed on the coins printed in his honour, 'Leader of Spain by the Grace of God' and answerable, according to his apologists, only to God and history. Although in his final years he distanced himself from direct intervention in day-to-day politics, the truth is that no important decision was taken without his consent. Up until his last moments, as a result of what was called the 'Francoist Constitution', he retained the right to designate and dismiss ministers, a power that he was willing to utilise whenever he considered it appropriate to do so.

He believed that 'troops, when they are well commanded, obey; if they don't they should be punished for mutiny. Subjects, well governed, obey; if they don't they should suffer the consequences of their sedition'.[7] He therefore carried out a systematic purge of men and ideas that were counter to his own. The regime of freedoms, which characterised the preceding system, was replaced by one in which it was necessary to secure permission to undertake any form of organised or public activity. Furthermore, the media and the education systems were used to inculcate ideas and values that would ensure an unquestioning attitude towards the new regime. The only values that were taken into account were religious and patriotic ones, and the Falange and the Church were incorporated into the educational task to adequately instil them among the new generations. It seems totally logical, given these set of circumstances, that sport too would be recruited to serve as an extension of François politics.

Sport in Franco's Spain

From a political perspective there was, loosely speaking, an attempt to follow the approach advanced by Nazi Germany. That said, Franco was never willing to build a single-party totalitarian state on the Italian or German model and indeed, after the defeat of the Axis powers, he accepted the need to abandon the fascist image associated with his regime. In contrast to either Hitler or Mussolini, Franco was never prepared to spend money on sport and failed to appreciate the value of doing so. Nevertheless, once the Spanish Civil War had ended, and after a resulting parenthesis of inactivity, a decree signed on 22 February 1941 created the *Delegación Nacional de Deportes de Falange Tradicionalista y de las JONS* (National Sports Delegation of the Traditionalist Falange and of the National Syndicalist Offensive Juntas). This decree charged the Falange with 'the direction and promotion of Spanish sport'.

The Falange had been founded in 1933 by Jose Antonio Primo de Rivera. The party's ideology borrowed many concepts from Fascist Italy: the defence of Christian values against the dangers of Marxism; the establishment of a totalitarian state that would create a classless society promoting the interests of workers; and the expression of imperialism at the expense of the weaker races. In April 1937 Franco incorporated this thinking into the ambiguous *Movimiento* (national movement) and as mentioned, made it responsible for sport, by in turn creating the *Delegación Nacional de Deportes* (DND – National Sports Delegation). This body was presided over by the National Delegate of Physical Education and Sport, who was also President of the Spanish Olympic Committee (clearly contravening the rules of the IOC, which state that the different national committees should be strictly non-political) and responsible for sports medicine, legal affairs, transport, press and propaganda, and the Departments of Military Sports and Sports in the National Movement; he was also the head of the Department of National Federations. His control over the different federations was absolute, including the motorcycling one. The DND not only designated the presidents and vice presidents of the different Spanish federations, but also the members of the directors' committees and, in addition, the presidents and vice presidents of all the regional branches of these federations. As if this were not enough, article 4 of the decree afforded a right to the DND to veto any federation's decision that was not to its liking. As Cazorla Prieto makes clear, 'All social organisation of sport was subject, if not to an absolute nationalisation or para-nationalisation, then to rigid discipline on the part of the public authorities practically stifling any whiff of social protagonism'.[8]

The new organism was destined to be an agency of the General Secretariat of the National Movement, the only political party permitted, and an uncomfortable alliance of Falangists, monarchists and Carlists. Its mission was to use the international sports arena to vaunt Spanish virility and fury, as the German and Italian regimes had successfully achieved in the decade from 1930 to 1940. Therefore, from the very beginning, any possibility of sport having a degree of independence from the new political power was dismissed. The National Sports Delegation was an institution where the majority of its members were Falangists. However, the first National Sports Delegate was an army general, General Moscardó, the hero of the siege of the Alcázar in Toledo in 1936, whose relationship to sport was limited and only extended to his being a horse riding and clay pigeon shooting enthusiast. He introduced a series of Falangist symbols and customs to the sporting realm, for example changing the usual red shirts of the national football team to blue and including the fascist salute by the sportsmen and women at the beginning of international competitions. His reign ended with his death in 1955, after which he was succeeded by José Antonio Elola Olaso, a voluntary Falangist officer during the Civil War, who had served since 1940 as the head of the Falange Youth Groups. In 1966 he was relieved of his post by the Minister Secretary José Solís, officially for health reasons, although it was thought to be due to Spain's continual under-achievement in international competitions. He was succeeded by José Antonio Samaranch, who became a popular figure in Spanish sport and was identified at the

DND as a 'good Falangist'. However he was subsequently dismissed in 1970, an event that was generally received with surprise and sadness. This dismissal occurred a month after Solís also lost his post as Minister Secretary. His replacement, Torcuato Fernández Miranda, a Falangist 'old shirt'[9] put his good friend Gich at the head of the DND, but when José Solís was reinstated to his job, he in turn was dismissed and replaced by Tomás Pelayo Ros, who remained in post until 1976.

Thus the position of National Delegate (for sport) was largely occupied by war heroes, Falangists and rising politicians. It is not surprising therefore that the DND failed at almost everything it set out to achieve. It certainly failed in its attempt to make Spain a nation of sportsmen and -women, in spite of the advertising slogan 'Practise sport and improve the race', within the 'Sport for All' campaign that was launched in the 1960s; it similarly failed in its attempt to achieve glory for Falangist Spain in international competitions – the few Spanish sports achievements recorded, especially those of Real Madrid, were the product of the mass importation of foreign stars, mostly recognised as such abroad. Finally, it failed to win the respect of either sportsmen and -women or the general public, as demonstrated by the widespread rejection of the DND, which became apparent when censorship was repealed in 1976.

Franco's regime was largely to blame for this depressing situation. One of the reasons for the failure of the DND clearly emerged from the failed system used to appoint the delegates, which meant that the post was occupied by people whose capacity for sports management (with the exception of Samaranch) left much to be desired but who remained totally trustworthy in the eyes of the regime. This system of selection not only affected the post of delegate and sport more broadly; it also spread to the civil servants working in the delegation. The other main reason to explain its failure was the scant investment Franco considered appropriate for sport, which meant that the DND had to exist on a meagre budget mainly drawn from proceeds generated from the football pools.

It is, however, important to highlight that under Franco's regime sport performed somewhat different functions depending upon the particular era one chooses to study. Franco's reign lasted almost 40 years (1939–75) and amid the domestic situation, as well as relationships with the exterior, things continued to evolve as this period elapsed. According to Evaristo Acevedo, during the Franco era Spain can be classified into three distinct eras or generations. Firstly, 'the politicised generation', the generation that fought in the war and from 1946 onwards, given the pressure from abroad, began to depoliticise. Secondly, 'the football generation', which began from c.1947, when a nationwide fascination with association football took hold, to 1967, in which the relaxing of media restrictions under the Press Law produced the first symptoms of a gradual 'defootballisation'; and thirdly 'the protest generation'.[10] These stages become apparent also in the sport of motorcycling with an initial period of penury, a second phase coinciding with the launch of the motor racing industry, which brought about a certain level of development, and the third phase which constituted the moment at which motorcycling achieved widespread acceptance, due in no small part to the considerable personal achievements of Angel Nieto.

At the beginning of the Franco era, due to the ostracism[11] to which Spain was condemned during the 1940s, the opportunity to compete abroad was almost non-existent. Motorcycling, which during the 1930s had attained a more than negligible level of development in the country, with names such as Fernando Aranda and

Miguel Simó,[12] was practically abandoned after the Civil War. Fifty years were to pass before a Spaniard took part in international competitions, such as the Isle of Man Tourist Trophy (TT), for example.[13] Not even in football, the most important sport during Franco's regime, were there international matches, as the national team could rarely secure countries to play against. On the domestic scene sport was used as a vehicle to promote fascist attitudes and propaganda and was an important element in the hands of the newly established regime. A good example of this is the image of the two football teams Seville and Racing Club de Ferrol which, in 1939, contested the inaugural final of the Generalissimo's Cup. Both teams lined up before the start of the match with their right arms raised, making the fascist salute, and enthusiastically sang 'Cara al Sol' ('Facing the sun'), the Falangist battle hymn. In so doing they were imitated by the crowd which filled the stadium, standing and singing with their arms similarly raised.

During this period fascist concepts began to be widely applied to sport. The Falange, which, as mentioned, was put in charge of sport, considered it an excellent means of mobilising the masses under its flag, to reflect the traditional Hispanic masculine 'virile and impetuous' values, and, above all, to show the world the impressive power and potential of the 'new Spain'. Its purpose was to create a Spain in which everyone practised one sport or another, while the country's best sportsmen and -women demonstrated their talents at international competitions, especially the Olympic Games, and gained the admiration of the world. Again sport would be the place where the Hispanic masculine values which the Falange spoke so much and so often about – virility, impetuosity and fury[14] – would become fully incarnate.

However, in the starving Spain of the 1940s, the grand ideas of the Falange were inevitably destined to fail miserably. This was not only in regard to the practice of sport by ordinary people, but also with respect to the international competitions it participated in such as the Olympic Games, in which the results obtained were disastrous. During 1940, in spite of the outbreak of the Second World War, the Spanish motorcycling championships began to be staged once more. The second edition of the Madrid Grand Prix[15] was held in May 1945, at the circuit in the Casa de Campo. For some incomprehensible reason the title of first Madrid Grand Prix was utilised once again even though it was organised by the same Royal Motor Club of Spain which had staged the previous race. Although not on an annual basis, this competition would continue to be held for some time after. Barcelona, for its part, could count on a viable circuit for motorcycling which the Universal Exhibition of 1929 had left in Montjuic.[16] In the 1930s several editions of the Grand Prix of Catalonia were held there, but after the Civil War it would be 1946 before the fifth edition was staged and again not until 1949 before the records set in 1936 were broken.

In 1948 the Grand Prix of Guipuzcoa was born; in 1949 those of Bilbao and Malaga were similarly conceived. They would be followed later by a number of other Spanish cities – Saragossa, Alicante, Lugo, Seville and Leon – although being city circuits they were considered somewhat unsafe. During this decade, with the birth of the Soriano, Montesa and Lube makes, the national championships were enlarged to include less powerful motorcycles. The 1950s and 1960s coincided with what could be considered the second period of Franco's regime in relation to sport, the moment when the enormous interest in football took hold. Franco understood that to break free from ostracism the regime needed to evolve its image, which would necessarily mean the elimination of many of the Falangist symbols of fascist origin. For example, they no longer promoted the salute and hymn before games. However, at the structural level, the Falangist influence would still take many more years to lose its appeal in the sports domain. For example the rule that there had to be two Falangists present on the board of directors of any sports club was retained until 1967, at which point what has been referred to as the 'third period' began. During the second period Spain became a country in which a great deal of importance was afforded to sport, but not in the manner in which the Falange would have liked. Indeed the few athletics tracks and other facilities which did exist at that time were very seldom used.

In 1950, the championships were organised in four races, each of which scored points: Alicante, Valencia, Salamanca and Gijón. However at this point there were no permanent motorcycle tracks. The nearest thing to an established circuit was the one at Montjuic, which in 1955 hosted the first Grand Prix of Spain, an event that also counted towards the World Championship. It was generally regarded as a circuit for the riders not the machines, as the former had to know how to regulate the power of their engines and the manoeuvrability and braking ability of their motorcycles. This circuit continued to be the venue for the Grand Prix of Spain until 1968, the same year in which motorcycles made their debut at the Jarama circuit.[17]

However, the beginning of the 1950s saw the birth of the Spanish motorcycle industry as a new generation of riders began to emerge and in so doing brought about an important renewal for the sport with names such as the very young Juan Beltrand from Montesa or Juan Atorrasagasti from MV Avelló in Asturias. Where it was more challenging to enact any further improvement was in the more powerful motorcycle categories, which wouldn't fully arrive until 1955 and even then almost exclusively at the hands of the Valencian Paco Gonzalez.[18] The dawn of the 1960s witnessed the emergence of two factors that would have a profound impact on the sport of motorcycling in Spain. The first was the abandonment of racing by MV Avello, following the guidelines of MV Agusta in Italy. Although this could have sounded the death knell for speed racing in Spain, it coincided with another very important factor, the birth of Bultaco. This Spanish company, which belonged to Paco Bultó, was to have a tremendous impact upon motor sport in the country, not least as it also heralded the arrival of a host of new riders. These included César García, José M. Busquets, Pedrito Álvarez, José Medrana, Ramiro Blanco, Salvador Cañellas, Santiago Herrero and Ramón Torras, the latter regarded as one of the great names of Spanish motorcycling.[19]

Other sports were also beginning to assume an added significance within the 'new' Spain at this time and the viewing public responded with enthusiasm. For example, large crowds were amassing in the impressive new football stadiums, built by private clubs with very little assistance from the DND. Indeed football would be especially useful for the regime when improving its image abroad. This was recognised by José Solís, who as Minister Secretary of the Movement told the players of the famed Real Madrid:

> You have done much more than many embassies scattered afar in God's countries. People who used to hate us now understand us, thanks to you, because you have broken down many walls... Your victories constitute a legitimate cause for pride for all Spaniards, both within our homeland and abroad. When you go back to the changing rooms, at the end of each match, know that all Spaniards are supporting you

and are with you, proud of your triumphs, which have kept the Spanish flag flying so high.[20]

Real Madrid is considered as the team that most helped the regime to improve the poor image that Franco's Spain held in various countries throughout the world:

> Real Madrid has proclaimed all over the [European] continent the importance of a country which was evolving, albeit with an inevitable and forced delay, in comparison with all things European. This underdevelopment found an exception in Real Madrid something which permitted Spaniards to go abroad with 'their heads held high'.[21]

To conclude from the words of Santiago Bernabeu (president of the club from 1943 until his death in 1978), when responding to a congratulatory speech from José Antonio Elola Olaso upon a visit made to Franco in El Pardo in 1960, it seems that Real Madrid was conscious of its role as ambassador for the regime and for the country (they were considered one and the same, both within Spain and beyond its frontiers) and was proud of this responsibility:

> Excellency, the kind words of our national sports delegate fill us with satisfaction, because although humble, our club carries, as we all carry, our affection for, and our duty to, our homeland near to our hearts, and in our consciousness is ingrained the idea of seeking and finding, under any pretext, something which will be effective for the glory and prestige of Spain.[22]

It is certainly true that during this era, with the exception of football, sports success, which the press reported upon with great vigour, was limited only to a few insignificant international victories, in sports such as clay pigeon shooting or roller hockey. For example, in the six Olympic Games that Spain participated in during the Franco years, it only won one gold medal, two silver medals and two bronze medals. It represents a miserable record, worse than that of small countries like Finland, New Zealand or Ireland, and some considerable way from emulating the venerable sports successes of the old fascist Italy and Germany.

However, it would be unfair to state that football was the only sport that helped to improve the image of Franco's Spain abroad. The bullfights (leaving aside the controversy of whether they can be referred to as a sport or not) were a powerful tourist attraction. There was also a small group of individual sportsmen who contributed to improving the image of Francoism abroad, during this and the ensuing period. The 1950s produced the cyclist Bahamontes[23] and the gymnast Blume[24] and in the 1960s the tennis player Santana grew to national prominence. He is someone who represents one of the great sports stories of the Franco era: his humble origins, his determination to overcome obstacles in his path and his triumphs in a sport that was practically unrecognisable in Spain at that time all pay testimony to his remarkable achievements. His trajectory was similar to that of the most prominent sports figure of the 1970s, the motorcyclist Angel Nieto. His importance as an ambassador for his country was evident in the words of Jaime Alguersuari, president of the Alesport Group[25] when he said that he was 'one of the first international ambassadors'[26] or José Antonio Camacho when he claimed that 'He [Nieto] made everyone feel more proud to be Spanish'.[27] Indeed, barely had the third period begun, starting in 1967 with the lifting of censorship in the Press Law, than Angel Nieto,[28] one of the most emblematic figures in the history of Spanish sport, came to public prominence.

His sports career began in 1968 when he competed with the official Derbi team in the Isle of Man TT, riding in the 50cc category, where he fell after skidding on a bend at 150km/h. He also competed in the same category in the Jarama circuit, although with a very different result, as this time he emerged victorious. Unfortunately the number of spectators present was extremely small; the masses simply preferred football, crowding the stadiums specifically to see the great stars imported from abroad, Puskas, Kubala and Di Stefano, and didn't seem to feel the least bit interested in other forms of sporting excellence, including that demonstrated by Nieto. Nevertheless these sporting heroes who emerged from outside Spain fulfilled a very specific role in Franco's propaganda system: they represented proof of the ability of the country to welcome political refugees, and of the kindness of the regime towards these individuals when compared to other foreign regimes.[29] The experiences of sportsmen and women born in Spain[30] was completely different; even in the case of footballers such as Gento,[31] who were able to demonstrate how, despite coming from the most deprived upbringings (something which the majority of the country could relate to) they could attain fame and wealth.

This was essentially the story of Angel Nieto.[32] He was destined to become one of the sportsmen who would attract thousands of followers to see him compete, would secure a record of achievement to be revered and would be seen to enter the collective imagination of a nation. His story was that of a young man from the humblest of origins who following great sacrifice, effort and tenacity, managed to scale the heights of sporting success and enter into the most exclusive of social spheres:

> His initial training has been eclipsed by his autodidacticism which arose in the circuits of the world, in the executives' offices where he negotiated with his person as a means of advertising, and in the salons where he rubbed shoulders with the jet set. In spite of everything, Angel Nieto has not lost that air of Vallecas which always accompanies him, in offices, salons or discotheques. He is almost a type of guarantee of not forgetting one's origins, a man of very humble origins who moves, thanks to his fame and fortune, in the most exclusive circles of the country.[33]

This type of sporting iconography was extremely popular in Franco's Spain. Spanish films at that time were defined by stories told in a similar vein:[34] a boy from very humble origins, rebellious 'but with a heart of gold',[35] who leaves school and begins to work after finding his vocation at a very young age. In this case, Angel Nieto[36] came from the district of Vallecas, one of the most depressed areas of Madrid, and began to work aged 11 in a motorcycle repair shop, struggling from that moment onwards to retain his engagement with motorcycles. As a boy, he went alone to Barcelona, where at that time the motorcycle industry offered considerably more promise. His aim was to compete in motorcycling races, but he was obliged to work as a mechanic and to sleep wherever he could, often in deplorable conditions.[37] Finally at the age of 14 he began to train as a motorcycle racer in the Derbi factory where by now he was employed as a mechanic.

Derbi was a make which, in the 1950s, was not particularly well established in Spanish motorcycling, but by the 1960s it was more successful and better known. However by 1967, thanks to the personal achievements of Angel Nieto, it claimed the national championships in both the 50cc and 125cc categories. The victory in the 250cc category went to Santiago Herrero[38] riding with OSSA. This result was repeated the following year, except for the absence of the 50cc championship, where the minimum number of events required under race regulations was not achieved.

In 1971 and 1972 Derbi harvested three victories (50cc, 125cc, 250cc) solely thanks to the personal talents of Nieto, who also secured the world championship during these two seasons. His first victory in the world championships of 1968 had relatively few repercussions, although it did mean that he was received by Franco himself in one of the audiences that he gave at that time in El Pardo. However, thanks to this triumph, and from this moment on, participation in the world motorcycling championships received state subsidy through the offices of the Higher Sports Council.

His consecration as a mythical sporting figure occurred in 1971,[39] when on his own, it seemed, he managed to attract an attendance of 65,000 spectators to the Jarama circuit. He had already been world champion in the 50cc category and runner-up in the 125cc race. He was expected to win again but in the 50cc race he was thrown from his bike and in so doing lost the world championship. The spectators, convinced that he would not be able to race in the following event, began to abandon the circuit, but Nieto, after being attended to by the doctors (who sutured his leg), asked them to stay over the loudspeakers and lined up for the 125cc race. He duly won the Grand Prix and with it the world championship. This feat cast him into the role of an authentic hero. From then on people began to talk about motorcycling and it would cease to be a minority sport. Angel Nieto continued to race and won the world championships on no fewer than 13 occasions or, as he preferred to refer to it, 12+1 times.[40]

Angel Nieto constitutes the prototype of the sports hero during the Franco era. He incarnates the dream of thousands of adolescents who see in his sporting success, reached only after terrible trials, the possibility of being successful due in large part to individual will power. The press of the era promoted this model to an expectant nation. 'The idea was to create an emotive mythology for the middle classes that would act as a screen to hide conflictive aspects and transform reality into an image of Unity, Order and Hierarchy.' [41] The mythology applied to sport by the press continued to be of a fascist origin. The tone adopted by the media was vigorously patriotic, triumphalist and moralistic. It should be borne in mind that until 1978 freedom of expression and the right to information was not recognised. During the Franco period 'The Spanish press suffered rigorous control ... and journalism was subject to a discipline which made it the slave of political power'.[42] Given this premise, the transmission of models, or even more of values, on the part of the press could not be considered to have occurred independently of the established regime.

Conclusion

Franco died in 1975, and Juan Carlos I was proclaimed King of Spain. The death of Franco made way for the political transition that lasted until the definitive passing of the Constitution in 1978, laying the foundations of a new system of governance. The transition was followed by the constitutional governments of the Unión de Centro Democrático (UCD) between 1978 and 1982, during which the forms of the State of Autonomies were firmly established. In 1982 the Socialist Party won the elections, and from this moment on it would alternate in power with the Popular Party.

To summarise, the model of democracy that was typical of the most advanced Western countries, and which had never ceased to be defended by numerous groups of Spaniards in preceding eras, came to receive majority support. Spain changed, and with this sport in Spain also changed. Of course football continued (and still continues) to be the national passion, but the transformation in a range of other sports has been more radical. By way of example it is possible to point to the staging in Barcelona, in 1992, of the Olympic Games, and the organisational and sporting success for which it is renowned.[43]

Motorcycling also changed and at the end of the 1970s as well as the Yamaha TD and TZ 250/350, the Morbidelli 125, Yamaha OW31 and even the Suzuki RG-500 could be seen on the starting grids beside Spanish motorcycles: new and authentic Spanish racing motorcycles thanks to a series of genuine supporters such as Antonio Cobas,[44] among others – a whole movement which would herald the appearance of new riders, including the generation of the 1980s: Alfonso 'Sito' Pons, Carlos Cardús and Jorge Martínez Aspar. With them began a new era for Spanish motorcycling, a period in which new world championships were won and the riders continued to serve as models for many young people to imitate. However, the critical point in all of this was recognition that this was not a model that was imposed by the establishment but a model that emerged organically from within a free society.

Notes

1. This newspaper appeared for the first time on 1 November 1897. On page 2 it declared itself to be the official organ of the Royal Regatta Club, the Velocipedic Club and the Catalonian Gymnastics Association. The purpose of not creating a local journal meant that contributions could be included from other parts of Spain. Initially it came out every two weeks, but later would change to appearing weekly. In March 1899 it took over *Barcelona Sport*, which had been founded two years before in Barcelona. Also in 1899 the 'Los Deportes' company was created to take advantage of the journal and to organise events and promote sport: *Los Deportes* 401 (28 April 1906), 30. This publication apart from having participated in a large number of initiatives, is worthy of being remembered for the rigour of its contents and its work in defending sporting values.
2. It has been considered the deacon of the Spanish national sports federations. Cf. Rodríguez, *Compendio histórico de la actividad física y el deporte*, 722.
3. Herreros and Aznar: *Historia del motociclismo en España*, 34.
4. The Motorcycling Championship of Spain would be held in a different city every year.
5. On the economic situation and the previous period and its development, see Carr, *España 1808–1975*, 374ff.
6. Comellas, *Historia de España Contemporánea*, 482.
7. Carr, *España 1808–1975*, 663.
8. Cazorla Prieto, *Deporte y Estado*, 198.
9. Someone who was a Falangist even before the Civil War.
10. Acevedo, *Carta a los celtíberos esposados*, 190–1.
11. After the defeat of the Axis Powers in 1945, Spain was mostly considered by the outside world as a bastion of fascism and therefore subjected to a diplomatic and economic boycott by the United Nations.
12. All of them participated in the British Tourist Trophy, as well as Naure, Bejarano, Cantó Macaya and Faura.
13. Paco Bulto took part in 1951 with Montesa. In 1956, Marcelo Cama, Paco Gonzalez and Enrique Sirera also took part with Montesa and won second, third and fourth place in the 125 cc.
14. The last of these values was the easiest to apply to football as the myth of 'Spanish fury' had existed in the football world since the 1920 Olympic Games.
15. The first one had been held 14 years before on 5 April 1931 in the Camporreal circuit.
16. Cf. Arco de Izco: Montjuïc, *40 años de historia*.
17. In 1967 the Madrid Grand Prix for Formula Two cars was held there.

18. Francisco Gonzalez Sanchis, known as Paco Gonzalez was ten times motorcycling champion of Spain. He began to race regularly at the age of 36 in 1949, achieving in a little over a decade seven Spanish championships in 500cc, two in 350cc and one in 125cc. He began competing with a Norton; later on he rode legendary motorbikes such as the BSA, AJS, MV, Montesa or Bultaco. He was the first rider to race abroad. Together with the rider John Grace from Gibraltar he formed the first pair of professional motorcyclists in Spain which would be the origin of the Bultaco team.

19. He died in 1965 in a speed race on an urban circuit. He is still today one of the mythical names, figuring on many pages on the Internet which invite comments.

20. From the *Boletín del Real Madrid CF* 112 (Nov. 1959).

21. Botines, *La gran estafa del fútbol español*, 71.

22. *Boletín del Real Madrid CF* 128 (Jan. 1961).

23. Federico Martin Bahamontes, called 'The eagle of Toledo', was a professional cyclist between 1954 and 1956. During this time he won 74 victories.

24. Joaquin Blume was proclaimed senior gymnastics champion of Spain, a title which he held for ten years running. He died in 1959 when the plane he was travelling in crashed. He was awarded posthumously the ICO award for the best sportsman in the world.

25. Alesport is made up of five companies specialising in the organisation of sports events, in the publication of magazines and in worldwide services to large companies, in the production of images, in travel and in insurance. http://www.alesport.com/

26. *Ángel Nieto: 12+1*, minute 11.

27. Ibid., minute 12:18.

28. Records: he mounted the podium the following number of times in Grand Prix races: 85 (125cc), 2 (80cc), 52 (50cc). Number of victories in Grand Prix races: 62 (125cc), 1 (80cc), 27 (50cc);. Number of world championships: 7 (125cc) and 6 (50cc).

29. Cf. Gonzalez Aja, 'Le football ... ambassadeur du franquisme'.

30. Cf.:Gonzalez Aja, 'Fussball Und Regionale Identitat in Der Zeit Der Franco-Diktatur'.

31. He played for Real Madrid, the team with which he won 12 national league championships and two cups, as well as six European Cups (1956, 1957, 1958, 1959, 1960 and 1966) and one Intercontinental one (1960). He was considered the fastest outside left of all times.

32. 'His first contact with motorbikes was when he worked in a small motorcycle repair shop. In a few years he became the king of the small cylinder bikes, and one of the best riders in the world': Ignacio Lewin, *El País*, 23 May 1982.

33. Ibid.

34. In this sense the scripts of the films of the child star Marisol are totally representative of the Franco era. In the case of the lives of the footballers who were 'welcomed' by the regime, such as Kubala or Di Stefano, the films picked up their stories from the moment when they arrived in Spain as adults.

35. *Ángel Nieto: 12+1*, minute 2:30.

36. Born on 25 January 1947 in Zamora, his family went to Madrid when he was very small, so that traditionally he is called a 'Vallecano' (man from Vallecas).

37. *Ángel Nieto: 12+1*, minute 3:43.

38. Santiago Herrero was born on 9 May 1943 and died on 8 June 1970. In 1969 he began to compete in world championships in 250cc with Ossa, and came in seventh. He died from injuries at the Isle of Man circuit when he collided with Stanley Woods. His loss affected the Ossa company so much that it abandoned racing.

39. This year, 1971, a short film called *Ángel Nieto campeón del mundo* was made by Juan Cobos.

40. Due to the fact that he was and is superstitious he always talks about '12+1' to avoid 13, a number traditionally associated with bad luck.

41. Gonzalez Aja, 'Fascist and Christians!', 139.

42. Sinova: *La censura de Prensa durante el franquismo*, 11.

43. Cf. Moragas and Botella, *Las Claves del Éxito*.

44. In 1978 he created his first motorcycle before designing the chassis and motorcycles of several world champions, among them the Spaniards Sito Pons and Alex Criville who, with a JJ Cobas, won their first world championship and first Grand Prix in 125cc, in 1989.

References

Acevedo, E. *Carta a los celtíberos esposados*. Madrid: Magisterio Espanol, 1969.

Ángel Nieto 12 + 1. Directed by Alvaro Fernandez Armero, 2005.

Arco de Izco, J. *40 años de historia del automovilismo en el Circuito de Montjuïc – Montjuïc* ['40 years of motor racing history at the park circuit']. Barcelona: Reial Automobil Club de Catalunya, 2000.

Botines, A.J. *La gran estafa del fútbol español*. Barcelona: Amaika, 1975.

Carr, R. *España 1808–1975*. Barcelona: Ariel, 1979.

Cazorla Prieto, L.M. *Deporte y Estado*. Barcelona: Labor, 1979.

Comellas, J.L. *Historia de España Contemporánea*, Madrid: Rialp, 1996.

Gonzalez Aja, T. 'Le football ... ambassadeur du franquisme', in *Sport as Symbol, Symbols in Sport*, ed. Floris van der Merwe. Cape Town: Academia, 1996, 95–104.

Gonzalez Aja, T. Fussball Und Regionale Identitat in Der Zeit Der Franco-Diktatur', in *Fubball Und Region in Europa*, ed. Siegfried Gehrmann. Munster: Lit Verlag, 1997, 129–46.

Gonzalez Aja, T. 'Fascist and Christians! In the Spanish Martial Tradition of the Soldier-Monk'. *The International Journal of the History of Sport* 16, no. 4 (1999): 119–44.

Herreros, F. and J.L. Aznar. *Historia del motociclismo en España*. Barcelona: Real Automovil Club de Catalunya, 1998.

Moragas, M. de and M. Botella, eds. *Las Claves del Éxito. Impactos sociales, deportivos, económicos y comunicativos de Barcelona '92*. Barcelona: Centro de Estudios Olímpicos y del Deporte, 1996.

Rodríguez Rodríguez, L.P., ed. *Compendio histórico de la actividad física y el deporte*. Espana: Elsevier, 2003.

Sinova, J. *La censura de Prensa durante el franquismo*. Madrid: Espasa Calpe, 1989.

Before Fittipaldi, Piquet and Senna: The Beginning of Motor Racing in Brazil (1908–1954)

Victor Andrade de Melo

Federal University of Rio de Janeiro, Praia de Botafogo, 472/810, Botafogo, Rio de Janeiro, Brazil

Brazilian drivers have dominated the history of Formula One racing and therefore hold a prominent place in the international pantheon of the sport. Brazil is by no means a wealthy country, nor is it as socially advanced as a great deal of others, and therefore such a significant role in international motor sport may at first appear unlikely. This article unpacks the relationship between Brazil and the sport of motor racing, something that is strongly connected to the role played by the automobile since its arrival in Brazil. The main purpose of this article, however, is to discuss the history of Brazilian motor racing from the first structured auto races (São Paulo, 1908, and Rio de Janeiro, 1909) until the dawn of the Rio de Janeiro Grand Prix, staged at the famous Gávea Circuit, which represents the critical point at which Brazilian motor racing entered the highest echelons of world motor sport.

Introduction

By reflecting upon Formula One, one of the most important and prestigious categories in motor car racing, it should be sufficient to conclude that Brazilian drivers hold a prominent place in the long and distinguished history of this sport. The victories of Fittipaldi (1972 and 1974), Nélson Piquet (1982, 1983, 1987) and Ayrton Senna (1988, 1990 and 1991) place Brazil, together with Argentina, as the only two countries in Latin America to have secured world titles in this category.

Some more relevant data also serve to underpin the full extent of this achievement by Brazilian drivers. Argentina's five titles were won by one single driver, the legendary Juan Manuel Fangio, in the early years of Formula One, while the Brazilian victories were shared by three different drivers. Indeed Brazil has achieved more victories in Formula One championships than any other country – eight – followed by Germany (all won by Michael Schumacher) and England, with seven titles each. Brazilian drivers have also achieved eight second places (alongside the drivers named above the achievements of Rubens Barrichello and Felipe Massa should be recalled) and five third places. Furthermore, Brazil has already been represented by two manufacturers in Formula One racing: Chico Landi's *Escuderia Bandeirantes,*[1] and *Copersucar,*[2] managed by the Fittipaldis. No fewer than 29

Brazilian drivers have taken part in F1 racing to date, while several others, regularly securing good results, have been involved in other motor sport categories, including some not directly linked to the Fédération Internationale de l'Automobile (FIA), such as North American Indycar racing.[3]

Considering that Brazil remains comparatively underdeveloped in economic terms and the fact that motor racing is an expensive sport which demands high investments, such a record of achievement on the world level is clearly worthy of closer inspection. Without attempting to answer a question that appears to be constantly posed in sport reportage and in the motor racing world more generally (why is it that Brazil produce so many good drivers?), the aim of this article is to understand the relationship between Brazil as a nation and the history of motor sport, something that is strongly linked to the role the automobile has played since its arrival into the country.

Thus, to provide a little more detail, the main purpose of this work is to discuss Brazilian motor racing from the first structured auto races (staged at the Itaperica Circuit, in São Paulo, 1908; and the São Gonçalo Circuit, in Rio de Janeiro, 1909) until the inaugural hosting of the Rio de Janeiro Grand Prix, held at the Gávea Circuit (1933–54), when it could be legitimately said that Brazil had 'arrived' on the global sporting stage.[4] This investigation is centred upon the cities of Rio de Janeiro and São Paulo, due to their centrality in the national psyche during this era. At that point Rio de Janeiro was the country's federal capital, the city that best incorporated the pretensions of modernity; in contrast the second city was São Paulo, which although being one of the fastest growing industrial cities in the country, was comparatively underdeveloped. In both cases the genesis of Brazilian auto racing can be identified and mapped through a focused examination of these two urban centres.

However, before the national heroes of motor sport came to the fore – Fittipaldi, Piquet and Senna – other early proponents, with their automobiles, charted new pathways throughout the country, faced challenges and filled the popular imagination. Who were they? What does the sport of motor racing reveal about some of the new modernist perspectives emerging in the country at that time and their impact on Brazil? It is these two questions that will be addressed over the course of the next section.

The Desire to be Modern

The influence and impact of new inventions is one of the defining characteristics of the early part of the nineteenth century, especially in Europe and in the United States. It was not very long before these issues took hold in other countries, including Brazil. These new initiatives, perhaps more so than incidents of an economic nature, contributed to the restructuring of life generally, not only because they made the everyday existence of citizens more straightforward (even if initially only members of an advantaged elite had access to them), but also because they appeared to symbolise the emergence of a new way of life. Ideas closely linked to modernity were themselves tied to these new inventions, which in turn give rise to a set of new practices that cohered around them, including science, progress, velocity, fugacity and mobility.

The process of transition from a somewhat outdated regime to industrial capitalism, in which the nation state occupied an increasingly relevant space, unleashed a desire to explore international markets, promoting a strong traffic of cultural interchange, where what emerged from the leading, developed nations exercised a major influence and impact on those at the periphery. As Eric Hobsbawm states, 'The world was divided between a smaller part, where "progress" was born, and others, much larger, where they would arrive as foreign conquerors, aided by minorities of local collaborators'.[5]

In the last years of the nineteenth century this set of ideas, including those surrounding the development of the automobile, began to exercise a telling influence upon Brazil, even if the full extent of this would not be felt until the beginning of the 1900s. The English influence in particular became apparent around the time of Brazilian industrialisation, but from a cultural point of view, the impact of the Parisian urban reforms headed by Baron Haussmann, during the government of Napoleon III, were also significant.

Rio de Janeiro, the Brazilian capital at that time, incorporated the role of the metropolis, the political heartland of the country and the cultural centre, and was generally regarded as the focus of the country's development, spreading new habits and customs. In this city a process of seeking out public space as a locus of social life and of leisure activities, with evident peculiarities and differences from the European reality, can be clearly recognised.

In São Paulo, which assumed the role of an economic leader in the country, a similar process could be identified. Although the process of industrialisation was more intense than in the capital and although, to some extent, the political centre had shifted to the city in the last decade of the nineteenth century, São Paulo was still to undergo greater changes than Rio de Janeiro, not least from a cultural perspective. In both cities, a desire 'to be modern' began to take hold, as well as to site the country as being internationally relevant during the final years of the nineteenth century. Industrialism, urban reforms, health and hygienic concerns, new habits, control and the demeaning of 'old habits' alongside the importation of goods were all central to the speeches and the actions of those who held power within Brazilian society at this time.

Indeed in the *fin de siècle* it is clear that the structuring of a range of other sports – athletics, swimming, football and cycling – was also consistent with this new era. Those sports began to be perceived as 'international', fit for those who wished to be regarded as modern, central to the development of new habits, and in the forging of a new relationship with the body, hygiene and health.[6] The beginning of motor racing in Brazil fits neatly within this agenda, recognised as it was as a significant departure in the history of Brazil's comparative underdevelopment up until this point.

The First Races[7]

The idea of organising a more structured car race in Brazil appears to have been the work of a prominent political figure at that time, Washington Luis, then a government secretary in the state of São Paulo.[8] As one of his hobbies was driving his car around the outskirts of the town, he identified a route that seemed appropriate for a race and presented the idea to a group from the local elite, the same individuals who would soon create the São Paulo Auto Club.[9] Unbeknown to the assembled enthusiasts this simple proposal marked the beginning of the Itapecerica circuit.

In Europe at this time some of the major car manufacturers were reluctant to become engaged in the motor racing industry. But competitions similar to those emerging in Brazil at this time increased the prestige and publicity around racing and served as a great advertisement for the sport. 'The races were dangerous, but sold cars like bicycles had once been sold. The competition between manufacturers – they were in larger numbers in the *fin de siècle* France than in any other country – made advertising crucial.' [10] In Brazil, the process was different. There were some concerns over safety, but there still wasn't necessarily a market for the sale of the motor car, since few could afford the high costs of importing a vehicle. What really mattered to the first wave of car owners in Brazil was the European example, which they interpreted as a way of identifying with the 'modern' and 'civilised' continent overseas.

The organising committee formed by members of the São Paulo Auto Club established the rules for the circuit. It was to be a rally-style race (competitors starting at different intervals, with the time difference discounted at the end of the race), there would be five categories (divided according to the potency of the vehicles); a subscription fee of 100,000 réis for cars and 50,000 réis for motorcycles would be charged and 'professionals' were not permitted to take part (i.e. workers such as mechanics could not participate). In keeping with other sports in Brazil at this time, notably rowing, a set of rules for strict control of motor racing had been agreed and were designed to prevent members of others social classes from taking part in activities considered suitable only for the bourgeoisie. [11]

The opening race was initially scheduled for 14 July 1908 but following a request from Miguel Calmon, the Brazilian Minister of Industry, Transportation and Public Works, Mediated by Aarão Reis, President of the Automobile Club of Brazil, [12] the event was temporarily postponed. However on 26 July, with three motorcycles and 16 cars enrolled, the Itapecerica race was launched and became widely acknowledged as the first 'official' Brazilian motor race. [13] The competitors departed the city of Itapecerica da Serra en route to São Paulo city, a journey of approximately 75 kilometres. A large crowd gathered at the start of the race and at the end, which was in São Paulo's *Parque Antartica* (Antartica Park), an entertainment complex that has staged a vast array of events since the beginning of the twentieth century.

The spectators enthusiastically followed the race along its course. Indeed a short film produced about the event and released in 1908, reveals more about the audience:

An astounding effect of the powerful machines in great speed to the victory of the prize, the daring fearless 'chauffeurs', gentlemen of the noble city, ladies, many beautiful wealthy ladies with their most distinct families, as well as members of the automobile and other sport clubs from Rio and São Paulo. An interesting conversation between Congressman Carlos de Carvalho, Dr. Aarão Reis and the São Paulo Chief of Police in the stands of the *Antártica* stands out. [14]

Of the competing cars, 11 were French (Delage, Peugeot, Sizaire-Naudin, Renault, Berliet, Clément-Bayard, Lorraine-Dietrich, Herald and Brasier), three were Italian (Fiat), one was English (Brow) and one was German (Nag). They all used Pirelli tires. The three motorcycles were from the French manufacturer Griffon. The drivers were members of the São Paulo elites, such as Antônio Prado Júnior, [15] others were *cariocas* (people from the city of Rio de Janeiro) such as Gastão de Almeida, while others were foreigners, such as the experienced Frenchman Jordano Laport. Indeed it is possible to identify a strong French influence around the founding years of motor racing in Brazil. There were a number of reasons for this close association. There was a historic cultural relationship with France, which dated back to the nineteenth century and that continued to prove very strong throughout the early part of the twentieth century. There is also the fact that the Brazilian elite was constantly influenced by the cultural practices of the French nation, and absorbing a great deal of the latter's mores and values. Finally, it is in France and north central Europe of course that we find the genesis of motor car racing, as well as the mass popularisation of the automobile industry.

The leading driver at the time was the famous Count Lesdain.[16] The most potent car was Jorge Haentjens's 60 hp Lorraine-Dietrich, which had such an advantage over other cars that it had to be entered in a category of its own. But the major competition was the one between the *carioca* Gastão de Almeida, already renowned for his driving expertise, and Sylvio Álvares Penteado,[17] who eventually won the race in his Fiat, which enthralled and delighted the large Italian diaspora present at the race. However his win was somewhat fortuitous as de Almeida's car broke down near the finish line when he was comfortably ahead and almost certain to claim victory.

In the following year, 1909, inspired by its experience in São Paulo, the Brazilian Auto Club promoted its first structured race, staged at the São Gonçalo Circuit. The original idea was to have the race at *Alto da Boa Vista* (in the city of Rio de Janeiro), but the mayor, Souza Aguiar, forbade it, causing its transfer to the neighbouring city of Niterói.

It was practically the same style of race as the one staged in São Paulo the previous year. The 72-kilometre event was staged on 19 September 1909, after which the famous Gastão de Almeida, driving a Berliet, was proclaimed as the winner. He was followed in second place by João Borges Júnior, driving a Fiat. Emerging manufacturers at the time, including Isotta-Frascchini, Panhard and Itala, took part in the race.

As in São Paulo, the event had national and even international significance. On the day of the race, the newspaper *Jornal do Comércio* stated:

> Today, in the São Gonçalo circuit, we can see the auto racing that has aroused considerable interest in the graceful world of Rio de Janeiro and where the genuine sportsmen will enthusiastically follow the tricks and adventures of the daring drivers. The Brazilian Auto Club organised a party that has aroused people's curiosity and that will be fully appreciated. The first cars will leave from Neves – the starting point – at 1 p.m. sharp. Yesterday, the tickets for the stands and the area reserved for the cars were already eagerly sought. There will be a big competition and the fine society that so willingly impels this new entertainment will be chosen.[18]

A short film entitled *The São Gonçalo Circuit* was also produced at this time. The presence of auto racing on the screens is not particularly surprising. On the one hand, between 1907 and 1911 there was a considerable expansion in Brazilian cinematography, with many projection rooms opening and magazines published dealing with cinema, including one entitled 'The Belle Époque of Brazilian Cinema' by Araujo.[19] On the other hand, automobiles and cinema, two symbols of modernity, share a new form of representation as images presented in a fragmented, fast and provisional way. With the advent of the two circuits there was the beginning of regular car races in Brazil, something that would become more popular and attractive for its growing body of fans, and prove indicative of the nation's development more generally.

The Roads to Establishment

In the 1910s and 1920s, the automobile began to occupy a greater role in the lives of the middle classes, symbolising as it did success and upward mobility.[20] Cars also began to play an important role in economic terms, playing a significant part in advancing Brazil's emerging national economy. In 1919 a Ford subsidiary was established in Brazil and later under the banner of General Motors in 1925. Both factories were located in São Paulo, itself becoming increasingly industrialised at this point in history. The implementation of the production line and the manufacturing of certain parts on site helped lower the associated production costs and also served to diversify their consumer market. Among the latter it is possible to discern the emergence of local mechanics and car garages; indeed many of the early drivers and race cars emerged out of these garages.

The arrival of two major companies, Ford and General Motors, in Brazil was considered highly symbolic. The names Henry Ford and Alfred Sloan (from General Motors) served to diversify the market for, and the popularity of, the automobile. Similarly, their involvement also increased a move towards the standardisation of motor cars and the reduction of previously isolated ventures. As sections of the Brazilian people became accustomed to the concept of using a car for personal and domestic use, so it is possible to observe the emergence of Fordist/Sloanist control.[21] The articulation of the spectacle-consumption symbiosis becomes apparent:

> Fordism was characterised, in the American standard, by what has been conventionally called mass production. The strategy has led to the lowering of prices of an identical and standardised product that came from the huge modern industries. However, Henry Ford was not the great creator of the main characteristic of the industrial standard. ... It would be the 'Sloanism' of General Motors that would create the victorious strategy of new markets, offering diversity to mass production to generalise consumption, transforming it into a mass consumption, and therefore reaching enormous social segments that hadn't been incorporated into consumer society until then.[22]

These decades were also marked by an increase in North American influence over Latin America, from a cultural as well as an economic point of view (and increasingly from a political perspective as well). The cinema and the automobile are important products in this creeping Americanisation. Fordism, Americanism and velocity began to be commonly associated with each other.[23] This was not a linear process of imposition, but one of negotiation between perspectives from differing cultural matrices. In Brazil, due to local peculiarities, this process had many shades,[24] not least the fact that what was popular in the United States, for example the Ford model T, was increasingly viewed in Brazil as a symbol of distinction.

In the Brazil of the early twentieth century the sport of car racing was growing in popularity on an almost annual basis. The decade from 1910 to 1920 was marked by a large number of races, with different formats, in different states, even between cities and countries (the latter involving occasional international contests featuring Argentina and Uruguay). Again a growing number of fans were becoming attracted to these ever faster machines, admiring them and expressing their fascination with the cars as it was clear that an infatuation with the automobile was growing.

Although it was only in the 1950s that the Brazilian automobile industry was established in real terms, since the beginning of the twentieth century there were many attempts to build a Brazilian race car to compete in the F1 series. A discernible approach is established, which involves the manipulation of standardised road cars for the purposes of competition; thus was born a new industry surrounding the production of hybrid cars. Ever since the early races held in the 1910s and 1920s and more perceptibly in the 1930s and 1940s, many low-budget competitors, having little or no financial support to import cars from abroad, assembled their own automobiles, and adapted many parts from different manufacturers and technology generations in the process.[25]

In the 1920s a series of international automobile expositions took place – the equivalent of modern-day trade shows – in the cities of both Rio de Janeiro and São Paulo. This development served as a further move in the expanding role played by Brazil in the automobile industry. Among several events that may be highlighted, the *Quinzena Automobilística* ('Fortnight Auto Race') in Rio de Janeiro in 1926 was particularly significant as it attracted financial support from the government of the day. Many important figures of the racing industry took part in these events, included among them Irineu Correa[26] and Primo Fioresi.[27] It is important also to remember that at this time Washington Luis had become the Brazilian president and Antonio Prado Júnior was the mayor of Rio de Janeiro; both of these men were particularly supportive of motor racing and so the sport receive special dispensation when viewed against other sports of the day. In the same year the Brazilian Auto Club became affiliated to the FIA, which served as another landmark in the advancement of the automobile industry in the country.

In 1932, another important competition would link the actions of Prado Júnior and Washington Luis to motor racing: the *Subida da Montanha* ('Mountain Slope') was staged over the recently opened Rio-Petrópolis road, won by one of the best drivers in the world in that modality: the German Hans Von Stuck, who had come to Brazil at the invitation of Manuel de Teffé. The latter was himself one of the first Brazilian drivers to compete in European tracks.[28] It is important to remember that if the names of Prado Júnior and Washington Luis were symbolically linked to the mountain race because the road (Rio-Petrópolis) was built at their behest, in reality they were separated because of the Civil War in 1932.[29] Equally, the global economic crisis of 1929 had a more significant impact in São Paulo, the biggest industrial site in South America at the time, than many comparable cities throughout the world. Even if this city maintained some of its importance, the axis of sport development would nevertheless shift to Rio de Janeiro from the beginning of the 1930s.

Motor racing in Brazil was already important by the dawn of the 1930s but it developed significantly during this decade and remained extremely popular. At that time, motor sport was covered extensively in the major newspapers and magazines as well as in an emerging and dedicated sports press. These included *Auto Sport*, a fortnightly magazine covering motor racing, sport, fashion, arts and information, *Auto Magazine*, a Brazilian monthly motor racing publication, and *The Automobile*, all of which were published in Rio de Janeiro, alongside *Motor Racing*, which was published in São Paulo. Alongside this, several mainstream writers began to make reference to the automobile in their writings: Paulo Barreto, in the vanguard of Brazil's rise to international respectability, incorporated it in many of his works, usually with great aplomb. For example, it has a central role in the novels *A profissão de Jacques Pedreira* ('The Profession of Jacques Pedreira') and in the chronicle *A era do automóvel* ('The Automobile Era'), both published in 1911. As the author states:

> For the consolidation of the automobile era the transfiguration of the city was necessary. And the transfiguration was made as in the joyful holidays, at the sound of Satan's tam-tam. Streets were devastated, new avenues appeared, customs taxes fell, and triumphal and insolent the automobile came, dragging a torrent of automobiles. Now we live the positive moments of the automobile, in which a *chauffeur* is a king, a sovereign, a tyrant.[30]

Lima Barreto is less enthusiastic and considerably more critical. In the tale 'Um e outro' ('One and the Other'), for instance, the automobile is presented as a symbol of awe:

> The automobile, that magnificent machine, strolling down the streets as a conqueror, was the beauty of the man who was driving it; and, when she had him in her arms, it was not quite him who she hugged, it was the beauty of that machine that would create the inebriation, the dream and the unique joy of speed. On Saturdays, when she laid back on the big cushions, she would cruise the city streets, and concentrated the sights and everyone envied the car more than her, the power it had and the way the *chauffeur* drove it. The life of hundreds of wretched, sad and begging individuals who walked on foot, were waiting for a simple and imperceptible drive; and the driver, who she kissed and caressed, was like a God that used the humble beings of this sad and wretched planet.[31]

As far as the São Paulo writers were concerned, the connection was also quite strong and not surprising at all. If we consider their proximity to the Futurists (they were even called the 'Futurists from São Paulo') and the connection of the Italian movement to the automobile, it is possible to witness the intrinsic nature of the relationship.[32] *Klaxon*, the magazine most closely aligned to the emerging modernist movement, published initially in 1922, adopted the sound of a car horn as its title in a move not without significance.[33]

Finally, considering the symbolism associated with motor cars in Brazil's march towards modernity, the automobile and motor racing in general were constantly represented in the cinema, in fictional scenes, in newsreels and in documentaries.[34] The sport was evolving at a great pace but it still lacked the realisation of a much cherished dream – the establishment of an international race under the auspices of the FIA, something that Brazil had sought consistently since the 1910s.

Brazil in the International Auto Racing Calendar

The year was 1934. Soares[35] recalls how Nicolau Tuma, from São Paulo, one of the first radio commentators in Brazil, went to the country's capital (Rio de Janeiro) to broadcast for the Mayrink Veiga station (the nation's leading station of the time) the second running of the Gávea Circuit, which had captured the attention of the whole country during the previous year. The radio had already secured an important place in the lives of ordinary Brazilians with the creation, in 1923, of the Radio Club of Rio de Janeiro. As the Radio Club had purchased the broadcasting rights, Tuma was prevented from broadcasting the race 'live' by the host federation. Undeterred, however, Tuma located 12 transmission spots around the circuit, citing three people at each, and from the studio, without watching a single lap, broadcast the race with exacting detail for over five hours, celebrating the victory of the Brazilian Irineu Correa, driving a Ford. As Tuma said,

> Only a club that organises a race, in a circuit of its property, can stop broadcasting of this sort. Every sport practised in the street gives the public the right to watch, observe and criticise aloud. So the exciting highlights of the race will be transmitted to the friendly listener through PRA-9, the station that doesn't promise, but accomplishes.[36]

This episode represents a good example of auto racing's importance in the socio-cultural context of 1930s Brazil. The growing popularity of the sport was increasingly evident. The public attended the races in large numbers while others followed them through radio coverage and newspapers, which provided a thorough review of the events as they unfolded. A new glamour was becoming apparent even if the organisers still had to deal with the old peculiarities of a country that was attempting to emerge from a period of relative obscurity but that recognised nevertheless the widespread benefits of doing so.

Thus the 1930s are regarded as the initial phase of motor racing in Brazil on the international stage, in the shape of the Rio de Janeiro Grand Prix, also known as the Gávea Circuit. This aspiration was fully realised in 1933, with the support of President Getúlio Vargas, as well as the recognition of the FIA. The race was staged up until 1954, albeit with a break between 1942 and 1946. The Gávea Circuit, with a track just less than 12 kilometres in circumference, was designed by Manoel de Teffé and Primo Fioresi with the help of the Brazilian Auto Club, led by Carlos Guinle, a leading figure within Rio de Janeiro at that time and who was deeply involved with different sports. The circuit was perfect for forging heroes: it was impressive in its beauty and design. It had many curves, hills and dips, moved from pavements to cement, sand to paving stone and when combined proved extremely demanding for even the most skilled of drivers. There were few overtaking points on the circuit, while any carelessness could lead to a serious accident at a time when safety conditions were scarce.

It was not easy to consolidate the race and therefore to ensure its ongoing presence within the racing calendar. Initially, there was a need to overcome significant levels of internal resistance: doubts remained about the safety of the public attending the race and of the drivers participating in it. Another problem was convincing European competitors to race in a country that had little tradition in the sport: Brazil wasn't well known in the international sporting calendar and didn't have good transport links for those visiting from abroad.

From the 1936 race onwards it is clear that the circuit was attracting an international field of competitors and well-known constructors and leading drivers were by now taking part in the event. In that year, for example, Ferrari brought two of their best drivers, including the future Brazilian idol Carlos Pintacuda, to take part in the race. The highlight of the 1936 event was the presence of the Frenchwoman Mariette Hélène Delangle, better known as Hellé-Nice, one of the first women in the world to become involved in competitive motor racing.[37] Aside from her participation in the race, the Frenchwoman, a former model and dancer, attracted considerable attention by virtue of her often questionable practices such as smoking in public (at that time considered socially unacceptable) and going to the beach wearing a two-piece swimsuit.[38] This same year, taking advantage of the presence of many international drivers attending the major race in Rio de Janeiro, the inaugural São Paulo Grand Prix was staged. The winners were the Ferrari drivers, including Pintacuda, but the race became infamous on account of the accident involving Hellé-Nice, which injured many spectators. More than ever, the unsafe conditions of this kind of circuit were brought into the public domain.

Accidents were not uncommon in Rio de Janeiro either. In 1935, the Brazilian Irineu Costa lost control of his car and died after falling into a canal which ran parallel to the racecourse. In other races, two Italians also died, Nino Crespi and Dante de Palombo, and a Frenchman named Jean Acchar. Rather remarkably, Palombo died driving the same car as Correa, in 1938, while Jose Bernardo, in the following year, had a serious accident with the same vehicle, which was then nicknamed 'The Assassin'. In a similar vein and on account of its high difficulty level, the Gávea Circuit was internationally known as 'The Devil's Trampoline'.

In Rio de Janeiro, in spite of many criticisms concerning the safety of the track, these incidents only served to add to the legendary status of the race. In some ways this element of danger served as an exciting point of attraction for spectators and competitors alike and stood in stark contrast to the increasingly sanitised nature of many European circuits. It was possible to improve the safety conditions associated with the event, especially for the viewing public, but the drivers had be to aware of how to compete in the face of possible serious harm to them and to their fellow competitors, and this in turn serves to feed into the mythology of events such as those that unfolded at the Gávea Circuit.

In São Paulo, the events of 1936 gave rise to an argument for the banning of motor racing from the streets, which led to the races being staged in a number of rural towns (mainly Campinas, Piracicaba and Araraquara). In order that the race would be staged once more in the capital of the state, the first Brazilian race track was opened in 1940 – the world-renowned Interlagos Circuit. However, for all its many advantages the track could not stand comparison with the Gávea Circuit for notoriety and mystique. It was only when this Grand Prix ended that Interlagos became fully regarded as the new home and centre of Brazilian motor racing. Among many other events, the latter also hosted what would be for a long time regarded as the most prestigious Brazilian motor racing competition: the 'Thousand Miles' event first held in 1956, with Wilson Fittipaldi being principally responsible for its staging.[39]

The notoriety of the circuit grew very quickly over a short period of time and leading drivers began to participate more often. Alberto Ascari, for example, future two-times Formula One champion in 1952 and 1953, took part in the 1949 race. Juan Manuel Fangio, at the time already a champion in the same category, competed in 1952 behind the wheel of his Ferrari. It is interesting to note, however, that despite being considered as favourites, neither of these drivers managed to achieve any success. Instead it was the Brazilian drivers who were the ones that made history and achieved heroic status among their fellow Brazilians: Manuel de Teffé, Irineu Correa, Nascimento Junior, Rubem Abrunhosa, Henrique Casini and the legendary Chico Landi, the greatest name on the Gávea Circuit, and widely revered as the first Brazilian motor racing hero. He took part in 15 of the 16 scheduled races, winning in 1941, 1947 and 1948. He was in second place in 1938, 1940 and 1949, and third in 1954. His performances led to several invitations to drive in Europe, where he drove for Ferrari, among other teams, and managed to win the Bari Grand Prix, in Italy, twice (1948 and 1952). Considered one of the great drivers of his generation, his career was not successful from a financial perspective in spite of his considerable achievements on the track. Landi was perfect for what the Brazilians expected of their racing pedigree, a hero, an idol, one whose image was often connected to the Brazilian 'new state'.[40]

It is interesting to note how several national and international geopolitical influences are apparent in the events that unfolded in Rio de Janeiro. For example, in 1937, as another strategy in the propaganda of the supposed superiority of the Nazi regime, the German team Auto Union entered the competition with a car that could achieved a maximum output of 550 horsepower. The driver was already known as one of the world's greats, Hans Stuck. Victory – an almost certain occurrence – did not come, though. Instead the German entry was eclipsed by the first great idol of the circuit, the Italian Carlos Pintacuda, who, after winning in 1938, became known as the 'Gávea Hero'.[41]

But the connection of Italian teams and drivers with the Fascist regime of Mussolini is apparent within motor racing, having already been evident in other sports.[42] Following the 1933 race, Manuel da Teffé received a telegram from the Italian dictator, who felt very proud of the international victory of one of the Italian constructors, Alfa Romeo, in the event. It is also not surprising that the race had been interrupted between 1942 and 1946, due to the Second World War.[43] The internal political situation in Brazil was also a determinant factor for the event. The majority of the races, including the most important ones, took place during the governments of Getúlio Vargas. In this regard the first period of the Gávea Circuit is strongly tied not only to the government's economic intentions (the quest for the development of the country's industrial sector), but also to the role of sport in the Vargas's government. As Drumond remarks,

> Therefore, we can see that sport was also an important factor in the making of the image of the new nation. This, legitimated by the spectators in the stadiums, by the readers of the sport pages or even by the radio listeners, who cheered for the colours of their country ... suggested a new identity that could be commonly shared.[44]

It is also necessary to consider the use of the symbolic capital generated around sport, especially in relation to public events, as a way of advertising the good deeds and the successes of the government: 'Getúlio also knew how to use sport ... as an instrument of political propaganda of the regime. The public use of sports centres was one of Vargas's main strategies of symbolic approximation between his government and sport.'[45] Certainly, the support for the Gávea Circuit was related to Vargas's interest in the national and international standing of the race, something that had grown considerably over a relatively short period of time. Internally, it associated his name with the idea of progress; abroad, it forged the image of a new country.

Vargas was overthrown in 1945. The race resumed following the Second World War in 1947, with Eurico Gaspar Dutra as president. Dutra rose to power in Brazil as a new and energetic leader, but for the most part it meant a continuation of the previous era (Dutra was Vargas's Minister of War, and was supported by the former president in the presidential campaign). Vargas returned to the presidency, in a proper democratic manner and by direct elections, in 1951. In 1952 one of the most important races in the event's history took place, featuring as it did the Argentinian hero Fangio in a central role. Finally, in 1954, the final year of the circuit, President Vargas was present and so sure was he of a home victory that he had prepared a gift for Chico Landi, which to his great disappointment failed to materialise.

Landi always denied the rumour that Vargas had an active role in the purchase of the Ferrari which he drove for several seasons in Europe during the early 1950s (when the *Bandeirantes* team was created). Landi said he despised the relationship between sport and politics and showed indignation when called a fascist for having driven for Ferrari during the period before the Second World War. On the other hand, he never denied being close to the president or to his politics.

It is not surprising that with the abrupt ending of the Vargas government the race was itself brought to a sudden halt. At the same time, in Argentina, Juan Perón explicitly supported Fangio's career.[46] Argentina would then solely organise the most important race in South America. The centre of the sport in the continent was thus moved, under the flag of another authoritarian regime with distinctive characteristics, at the behest of President Juan Perón. With it came an end to an important chapter in Brazilian motor racing.

Conclusion

The loss of its 'official' race and the definitive shift of the focal point of racing in South America to Argentina had a big impact in Brazil. But it didn't mean the end of auto races: the sport was already popular and its presence still remained in many different formats. By the mid-1950s and in the 1960s, street races continued to take place, but slowly the race tracks, especially Interlagos, began centralising the most important races and motor racing took place in more sanitised surroundings. Just a few Brazilians competed abroad (Landi and Hernando da Silva Ramos among them), albeit primarily in Argentina, without achieving any degree of success.

Beyond the maintenance of the passion for motor racing, the fascination for the automobile continued to grow within Brazilian society. Still in the Vargas era, a commission was established to consider the further development of the national automobile industry. Under the Juscelino Kubitschek government, those efforts became more effective and 1957 is considered to be the beginning of the mass production of automobiles within Brazil. Some 12 car companies were set up in Brazil, including one entirely nationalised corporation, the National Engines Factory.

Because of the development of the Brazilian industrial sector, the material conditions, the supply of products and the demands of the population changed: the objects that make everyday life easier (blenders, driers, refrigerators, television sets etc.) became more accessible and valued. Among those, the automobile continued being the major middle-class consumer dream. The urban network itself reflected this set of values. Roads were built and/or repaired, homes were projected with garages, and traffic laws improved. Soon cars would be progressively used in more leisure activities, such as driving around the major cities or travelling to other large conurbations. Tourism was improved and in the 1960s the now traditional *Guia 4 Rodas* magazine was published with tips for road travellers.[47]

These many accomplishments and the continuous interest in motor sport prepared the scene for the 1970s, when Brazilian drivers really began to establish themselves in the international motor sport scene. But before Fittipaldi, Piquet and Senna, many other Brazilians, among whom were Landi, Teffé, Correa, Nascimento Junior, the pioneers Almeida, Penteado and Fioresi, and many anonymous ones, created, maintained and consolidated Brazilian motor racing, a practice that has always been closely tied to the making of the nation – from an economic point of view, in terms of increased industrialisation, or from a political point of view by providing a platform for many national groups, and especially from a cultural point of view. In the latter case Brazil was entering a period of increased modernity and its symbols needed to be read and interpreted according to these peculiarities.

The pioneer competitions and the first racers were essential in consolidating the widespread attraction for motor racing among the national populace. Their deeds generated expectations and gave birth to stories and legends that echoed from generation to generation, not only among the population, but also among those who intended to face adventures in the tracks. Their names, principally Chico Landi's, are recalled with fondness to the present day. There is no doubt that, among other factors presented in this article, they were also responsible for the deeply passionate relationship between Brazilians and automobiles, especially in those races where human beings merge with their fast machines, defying time and space, risking their own lives: true myths in a society where the idea of public excitation is seemingly inexhaustible.

Notes

1. After the Second World War, Chico Landi bought a Ferrari, painted it green and yellow and started the squad, a short lived team that didn't achieve good results.
2. The official name was *Escuderia Fittipaldi*. Created in 1975, it took part in 104 Grands Prix. It achieved some good results, but in the end it didn't stand out.
3. Emerson Fittipaldi was the champion in 1989, Gil de Ferran in 2000 and 2001 and Cristiano da Matta in 2002.
4. For more information about auto racing before those circuits, see Melo, *O automóvel*.
5. Hobsbawm, *A era dos impérios*, 35.
6. See Melo, *Cidade sportiva*.
7. This study uses the works of: Gonçalves, *Automóveis no Brasil*; Gonçalves, *A primeira corrida*; Correa, *Fórmula 1*; Talock, *El automóvil en América del Sur*; Leme, *História do automobilismo brasileiro*; Scali, *Circuito da Gávea*; and Scali, *Circuitos de rua*.
8. Washington Luis would later become the president of Brazil. One of his administration's motto was '*Governar é construir estradas*' ('Governing is building roads').
9. See Melo, *O automóvel*.
10. Weber, *França Fin de Siècle*, 252.
11. See Melo, *Cidade sportiva*.
12. This club was created in 1907. For more information, see Melo, *O automóvel*.
13. It is considered to have been an official race mainly because of the representation of the Auto Club involved in its organisation, despite its non-recognition by the FIA. Nevertheless, it is interesting to note that even in international result sites, this is the first Brazilian race to be mentioned.
14. *Circuito de Itapecerica* was produced by Antonio Leal for Photo-Cinematographia Brasileira, one of the pioneers of the national cinema. The synopsis was consulted in the database of Brazilian Cinematheque (www.cinemateca.com.br).
15. One of the most important names in São Paulo politics. After returning from a short period in Europe, he brought back with him the fascination for the automobile and the need to consolidate its presence in the country. Actually, Prado Junior was already involved with cycling, football, athletics and tennis, having been one of the most important names in sports in Sao Paulo and in Brazil until the 1930s. He was also involved in the creation of the National Olympic Committee and was a member of the International Olympic Committee.

16. Still in the year 1908, the Frenchman was famous for starring in the first automobile adventure in Brazil, doing the Rio-Sao Paulo trip by car. For more information, see Melo, *O automóvel*.
17. Member of a traditional family from Sao Paulo which was involved with the city's modernisation movements. Sylvio was among the first car owners and was a frequent race driver.
18. *Jornal do Comércio* (Rio de Janeiro), 19 Sept. 2008.
19. Araujo, *A bela época*.
20. See Sevcenko, *Orfeu extático*.
21. While the innovations of Fordism are mostly related with the production process, Sloanism is more closely related with internal organisation, marketing and distribution.
22. Goncalves and Goncalves, 'Da aldeia rural', 22.
23. See Bardense, "Individualism, Technology, and Sport'.
24. For more information about this process in other countries, see Kopytoff, 'The Cultural Biography of Things'.
25. Hybrid cars, called *carreteras*, were traditional in many other countries in South America, especially in Argentina, which severely influenced Brazil.
26. One of the first and more victorious drivers of the early Brazilian racing. Won a race in Cheste Fair, in the United States, in 1920.
27. Fioresi was one of the longest-lasting drivers of national motor racing. He ran in an important race, the 'One thousand miles from Interlagos', in 1956, when he was already 73 years old.
28. Teffe won a mountain race, the Coppa Galenga, in Italy, in 1927.
29. The Constitutionalist Revolution of 1932 was marked by polarisation between the allies of Getulio Vargas, ruling the country at the time after a military coup in 1930, and the Paulistas, who disagreed over the direction of national politics. This led to a short armed conflict with a big symbolic impact.
30. Barreto, *Vida vertiginosa*, 58.
31. Translated by Mauricio Drumond. Available at http://www.cce.ufsc.br/~nupill/literatura/umeoutro.html.
32. See Melo, 'Esporte, Futurismo e modernidade'.
33. For a deeper view of the presence of the automobile in the national literature, see Giucci, *A vida cultural*.
34. Two films can be highlighted. One is *Rio de Janeiro, aspectos da cidade, o movimento das ruas* ('Rio de Janeiro, aspects of the city, the movement of the streets') of 1923; the other is *São Paulo, a Sinfonia da Metrópole* ('Sao Paulo, the Symphony of the Metropolis') of 1929, produced by Rodolpho Rex Lustig and Adalberto Kemeny.
35. Soares, Bola no ar.
36. In ibid., 36.
37. It must be noticed that in spite of the presence of the Frenchwoman, a Brazilian woman had already pioneered as a race car driver in the 1920s: Dulce Barreiros, from Sao Paulo. The race of Rio de Janeiro would later have another female presence, the Frenchwoman Danielle Foufonis, in 1954.
38. For a discussion about the feminine presence and participation in motor racing, see Thacker, 'Traffic, Gender, Modernism'.
39. The trajectory of the Fittipaldi family is one of the most interesting ones in national motor racing. For more information, see Martins, *A saga*.
40. State of exception, a military dictatorship ruled by Getulio Vargas between the years 1937 and 1945. With totalitarian characteristics, the regime was often compared to the Nazi and Fascist experiences.
41. As a synonym for daring, the name Pintacuda was incorporated into popular language, including a song ('Marcha do Gago', by Armando Cavalcanti and Klecius Caldas, interpreted by Oscarito in the movie *Carnaval de Fogo*, 1949).

42. For more information, see Agostino, *Vencer ou Morrer*; and Morse, 'The Dark Side'.
43. See Koshar, 'Cars and Nations'.
44. Drumond, *Nações em jogo*, 118.
45. Ibid., 119.
46. See Drumond, *Nações em jogo*.
47. For more information, see Dias, *Urbanidades da natureza*.

References

Agostino, G. *Vencer ou morrer: futebol, geopolítica e identidade nacional*. Rio de Janeiro: Mauad/Faperj, 2002.
Araújo, V.P. *A bela época do cinema brasileiro*. São Paulo: Editora Perspectiva, 196.
Barreto, P. *Vida vertiginosa*. Rio de Janeiro: H. Garnier, 1911.
Correa, E. *Fórmula 1: Pela glória e pela pátria*. São Paulo: Globo, 1994.
Dias, C.A. *Urbanidades da natureza: Os esportes e a cidade do Rio de Janeiro*. Rio de Janeiro: UFRJ, 2008.
Drumond, M.S. *Nações em jogo: Esporte e propaganda política nos governos de Vargas (1930–1945) e Perón (1946–1955)*. Rio de Janeiro: UFRJ, 2008.
Giucci, G. *A vida cultural do automóvel*. Rio de Janeiro: Civilização Brasileira, 2004.
Gonçalves, J.S., and C.D. Gonçalves. 'Da aldeia rural à aldeia global: uma reflexão sobre a relação entre o avanço da comunicação e o desenvolvimento capitalista'. *Agricultura em São Paulo* 42 (1995): 17–25.
Gonçalves, V.C. *Automóveis no Brasil – 1893–1966*. São Paulo: Editora do Automóvel, 1966.
Gonçalves, V.C. *A primeira corrida na América do Sul*. São Paulo: Empresa das Arte, 1988.
Hobsbawm, E. *A era dos impérios*. São Paulo: Paz e Terra, 1988.
Kopytoff, I. 'The Cultural Biography of Things: Commodization as Process', in *The Social Life of Things*, ed. Arjun Appadurai. Cambridge: Cambridge University Press, 2001.
Koshar, R. 'Cars and Nations: Anglo-German Perspectives on Automobility Between the World Wars'. *Theory, Culture & Society* 21 (2004): 121–44.
Leme, R. *História do automobilismo brasileiro*. Rio de Janeiro: Sextante, 1999.
Martins, L. *A saga dos Fittipaldi*. São Paulo: Panda Books, 2004.
Melo, V.A. *Cidade sportiva: primórdios do esporte no Rio de Janeiro*. Rio de Janeiro: Relume Dumará/Faperj, 2001.
Melo, V.A. 'Esporte, Futurismo e modernidade'. *Revista de História da Unesp* 26 (2007): 201–25.
Melo, V.A. *O automóvel, o automobilismo e a modernidade no Brasil (1891–1908)*. Rio de Janeiro: PPGHC, 2008.
Morse, K. 'The Dark Side of Automobilism, 1900–30: Violence and the Motor Car. *Journal of Transport History* 24 (2003): 238–58.
Scali, P. *Circuito da Gávea*. São Paulo: Tempo & Memória, 2001.
Scali, P. *Circuitos de rua – 1908–1958*. Porto Alegre: Imagens da Terra, 2004.
Sevcenko, N. *Orfeu extático na Metrópole*. São Paulo: Companhia das Letras, 1992.
Soares, E. *Bola no ar: O rádio esportivo em São Paulo*. São Paulo: Summus, 1994.
Talock, A.C. *El automóvil en América del Sur: Orígenes – Argentina, Brasil, Paraguay, Uruguay*. Montevideu: Ediciones de la Banda Oriental, 1996.
Thacker, A. 'Traffic, Gender, Modernism'. *The Sociological Review* 54 (2006): 175–89.
Weber, E. *França Fin de Siècle*. Soã Paulo: Companhia das Letras, 1988.

The Great Race Across the Sahara: A History of the Paris to Dakar Rally and Its Impact on the Development of Corporate Social Responsibility Within Motor Sport

David Hassan and Philip O'Kane

University of Ulster, UK

This article provides a history of the Paris to Dakar Rally and its significance in terms of world motor sport. The criticisms of the race are examined together with the organising body's reaction to these within, among other considerations, the context of the fledgling emergence of corporate social responsibility within world motor sport. In developing this theme the essay also considers the future for the rally in light of a range of issues ranging from sustainability to global terrorism, which in a variety of different ways threaten the ongoing existence of one of motor sport's most iconic events.

Introduction: The History of the Rally and Its Significance as a Global Motor Sport Event

The Paris to Dakar rally is one of the most dangerous and challenging motor races in the world. The event is an off-road endurance event that has been held annually since 1978 from Paris, France to Dakar, Senegal, and takes place across the Sahara Desert over extreme off-road conditions. As a spectacle and a driving experience it has captured the imagination of the motor sport fraternity for three decades and more. Exotic-sounding destinations such as Timbuktu add to the aura and mystique of the race. It has been described as the most dangerous race in the world and for many drivers merely completing it is considered an achievement. Around 80% of the rally's participants are amateurs driving in one of three classes, car, motorcycle and truck, with the remaining entrants being professional racing drivers. Both the amateurs and the professional entrants require a great deal of financial backing and high levels of physical fitness in order to complete this most extreme of endurance races. It is the challenge and allure of the Dakar rally that attracts many competitors as for most the race is the adventure of a lifetime and one of the most anticipated motor sport events of the year. The fact that so few drivers finish it each year lends weight to the argument that it is the world's toughest and most dangerous motor race. The event takes place over a two-week period with stages of up to 900 km a day not uncommon and a total race distance of over 10,000 km. The race travels over some of the most inhospitable terrain on the planet and passes through Morocco, Western Sahara, Mauritania, Mali and Senegal and has on occasions also included Libya, Tunisia, South Africa, Angola and Egypt. Former World Rally Champion and four times Dakar rally winner Ari Vatanen is on record as saying 'it is impossible to overestimate the difficulty of this event'.[1]

The race was the brainchild of French racing driver Thierry Sabine, who in 1977 had become lost in the Libyan Sahara Desert while competing in the Abidjan, Ivory Coast, to Nice, France, rally.[2] This unfortunate event led to the idea of a Paris to Dakar rally across the Sahara desert, which he envisaged would represent the challenge of a lifetime for motor racing enthusiasts. Sabine, a successful racing driver in his own right who had won over 30 national races in France, the 1974 French GT Championship and had three starts in the Le Mans 24-hour endurance race,[3] set to work at once organising the rally and on 26 December 1978 over 170 entrants lined up at Le Trocadero in the shadow of the Eiffel Tower for the inaugural Paris to Dakar event.[4] Following this largely symbolic opening stage, the vehicles and drivers were transported to Marseille and then on by boat to Algiers for the start of the rally proper. In that first year there was just one class, with motorcycles clearly having an advantage as the first three race finishers were all competitors in this class. The race was just as tough as Sabine had envisaged it would be and on the 230 km stage from Arlite to Agades in Northern Niger over a quarter of the field were forced to withdraw due to the harsh and difficult conditions.[5] Many cars and drivers were not properly prepared for the conditions they would encounter and from this point forward the legend of the Dakar Rally was born. The Sahara Desert covers nearly a third of the African continent and is twice the size of Europe. Only a quarter of it is covered in sand dunes; the rest is rock and gravel, while the Sahara desert represents one of the most formidable climates on earth. Temperatures soar during the day but plummet to below freezing at night.[6]

Just finishing the race became the goal for many early competitors and the fact that so many participants remain incapable of completing the event each year again merely serves to embellish its mystique and allure. On 14 January 1979 Frenchman Cyril Neveu reached the iconic finishing line on the beach at Dakar to become the first winner of the race.[7] The rally grew over the next few years as adventurers from around the world subscribed to pit their skills against the vast Sahara desert with its diverse landscape and harsh terrain. Media coverage of the Dakar Rally was instrumental in promoting the race in these early years as the images of spectacular scenery and the nomadic civilisations of the region captured the imagination of many people and encouraged a desire to be part of the race.

Following the early years of the Dakar rally the event was eventually divided into three classes, motorbike, car and truck, in order to make the race more competitive by having three races within one.[8] The rally very quickly gained cult status among racing drivers as it became evident that the Paris to Dakar Rally was unlike any other motor race as the fastest driver was not necessarily the one who stood the best chance of winning. Instead there are many requirements needed to win the Dakar Rally. Navigational ability is extremely important: being able to correctly plot a course across the Sahara Desert in order to find fuel points and stage finishes can be the difference between winning and losing the event and, in some cases, between life and death. Drivers are also required to be somewhat mechanically minded, adaptable and ingenious, as they will be forced to repair damaged vehicles with minimal equipment and tools. In some cases competitors must even salvage spare parts from other vehicles that have been discarded by drivers who have dropped out of the race following crashes and mechanical failures.[9] Two drivers famed for their adaptability and navigational prowess were the Marreau brothers, Bernard and Claude, who earned themselves the nickname 'the desert foxes' because of their ability to finish ahead of much faster and better equipped drivers. After coming close to victory on a few occasions the Marreau brothers finally won the rally in 1982.[10]

There have been many famous drivers in the history of the race and none more so than five-times winner Cyril Neveu and three-times winner Hubert Auriol. These two men famously battled side by side in a memorable race staged in 1987. The two drivers were neck and neck throughout the rally until the penultimate stage when Auriol crashed his motorcycle, sustaining two broken ankles. Remarkably he got back on his bike and completed the remaining 20 km of the stage before retiring from the race.[11] This incident highlights the determination and toughness of Dakar Rally participants. Auriol went on to become the first driver to win the rally on both a motorbike (1981 and 1983) and in a rally car (1992). Five-times winner Cyril Neveu is another legend of the Dakar event, winning the inaugural race in 1979 and also triumphing in 1980, 1983, 1986 and 1987. The most successful driver in the history of the race, however, is another Frenchman, Stephane Peterhansel, who has won the Paris to Dakar Rally a record nine times. He has proved to be victorious no less than six times on a motorcycle (1991, 1992, 1993, 1995, 1997 and 1998) and three times in a rally car (2004, 2005 and 2007). Female drivers have also been notable in the history of the Dakar Rally, with the first woman to compete in the race, Michelle de Corteauz, finishing 18th in 1979. However it would be 2001 before a female driver was to win the race, when German woman Jutta Kleinschmidt claimed the car class driving a Mitsubishi rally car.

The Paris to Dakar Rally is famous for its challenging topography, which includes race stages through some of the most inhospitable terrain on earth. Some stages in the rally have become legendary because of their difficulty. In 1983 the race organisers decided to run a stage through a region of the Sahara Desert known as the Ténéré, which stretches from north-eastern Niger into western Chad. The Ténéré is very arid with an extremely hot and dry climate and virtually no plant life. During the stage through the Ténéré in 1983 a fierce sandstorm led to many competitors becoming lost; four drivers were reported missing for over 72 hours. Two of these drivers eventually walked over 60 km to Agades in Niger while the other two drivers were found and saved by a nomadic people known as the Tuareg, who are the principle inhabitants of the Saharan interior.[12] Other examples of extreme stages in the Dakar Rally include the one undertaken through the Mauritanian sand dunes in 1987, which only six out of 111 cars and trucks managed to successfully navigate,[13] or the stage across the Algerian desert in 1988 when 163 entries were eliminated in one fell swoop.[14] In 1994 the same thing happened when most of the field were again eliminated during a new stage from Atar to Nouhadibou in Mauritania, when difficult driving conditions, again through sand dunes, forced many competitors to withdraw.[15] These extreme conditions and stages once more highlight the difficulty of competing in the Dakar Rally and reaffirms the view that winning the race requires much more than merely being a fast racing driver. Again the rally thrives on its reputation for having some near impossible stages, which are made more difficult by changeable weather conditions. This is why the rally has been defined as being a blend of 'race and adventure'. The fact that the Paris to Dakar event has generated a legend far greater than its short lifespan is primarily as a result of the incidents and controversy surrounding it.[16]

Over the years there have been many incidents during the Dakar Rally that have captured media attention worldwide and none more so than during the 1982 race when Mark Thatcher, the son of then British Prime Minister Margaret Thatcher, went missing while competing in the rally. Thatcher, his co-driver and mechanic were eventually found unharmed after being missing for six days in the Sahara Desert.[17] In 1988 another incident during the event again made the headlines: Finnish rally driver Ari Vatanen was leading the event when his Peugeot 405 went missing overnight in Bamako, Mali. Peugeot team director Jean Todt (later to find fame as Ferrari Formula One team principal) claimed he received a phone call demanding a 27-million-franc ransom for the safe return of the car. The car was recovered without the ransom being paid but Vatanen failed to make the start of the following stage on time and was disqualified[18] and exactly who was behind the incident still remains a mystery.

The organisation, staging and coordination of the rally is an immense undertaking, yet the race is undoubtedly one of the best organised sporting events in the world. From 1978 until 1994 the rally was privately managed by an autonomous organising committee. However in 1994 the Amaury Sports Organisation (ASO) assumed responsibility for running the event. The ASO, which also organises the Tour de France cycle race, set about modernising the Dakar Rally and introduced new technology to enable a safer and more efficient staging of the race.[19] The coordinating of the event through many different countries presents a great logistical challenge and so the ASO introduced cutting-edge technology to ensure the safe and smooth passage of competitors over the course of the various stages. Each vehicle is numbered and is equipped with an alert system consisting of three buttons. Drivers are asked to press a blue button if they wish to speak to race headquarters, a green button if they have witnessed an accident or a red button if they have been involved in an accident. All competitors are now equipped with detailed maps and have a global positioning system installed in their vehicle.[20] Safety is of paramount importance and a speed limit of 31 mph is imposed through villages, with motorcycles and trucks limited to a 93 mph speed limit outside villages. Ironically financial and time penalties are imposed for speeding, once again highlighting that the Dakar Rally is an endurance race and is not simply about speed or who is the most fearless driver.

The Paris headquarters of ASO monitors the progress of all drivers and if a competitor's car has been stationary for a prolonged period of time then they contact the driver to ensure they have not been involved in an accident. These technological advances have made the race much safer over the years since the late 1970s and 1980s. In the interests of safety drivers are also required to observe mandatory rest periods at refuelling points. The scale of running the Dakar Rally represents an astonishing feat of organisation. This fact was highlighted during the so called 'air lift' incident of 2000. During the 2000 race there was a terrorist threat issued against the rally in Nigeria that led to the organisers deciding to airlift all vehicles, materials and drivers between Niamey in Chad and Sabha airport in Southern Libya. This represented a mammoth logistical undertaking and involved ASO chartering three huge Antonov 124 aircraft to successfully execute the airlift, which took over five days to complete.[21] The rally then resumed in Libya following the unscheduled stop. This episode illustrates just what a feat of organisation the Dakar rally presents, as such an airlift is an undertaking few other sporting organisations would have had the ability to successfully complete.

Criticisms of the Impact of the Rally

There is little question therefore concerning the status of the Paris-Dakar rally as one of the world's greatest motor sport events. However, as with all forms of motor sport, the dangers of entering the race are manifest. A total of 26 competitors have been killed in the history of the Paris-Dakar rally.[22] Many of these fatalities have involved privateer or amateur drivers who die in accidents or after becoming stranded in the desert. On occasion however, professional drivers have been killed such as two-time race winner Fabrizio Meoni, who died as a result of a crash in 2005, or noted Australian motorcyclist Andy Caldecott, who was killed during the 2006 race.[23] The highest-profile casualty of the rally was event organiser Thierry Sabine, who lost his life in a helicopter crash in Mali in 1986 whilst overseeing the race.[24] While these deaths are tragic, many commentators argue that the competitors appreciate the risks involved in entering the race and should be prepared for any eventuality that may arise. Rather it is the deaths of locals during the course of the rally that are considered to be most unacceptable. Many African non-competitors, including numerous children, have been killed by vehicles over the history of the rally. No exact figures exist for local fatalities or those injured but numerous incidents have been reported, including the death of a ten-year-old girl in Mali in 1988 and the deaths of a mother and daughter in Mauritania in the same year.[25] In 2003 a five-year-old Senagalese girl was killed[26] and in 2006 two boys aged ten and 12 were killed by rally vehicles.[27] In addition rally competitors have been accused of causing environmental damage to the countries that the rally passes through as well as killing livestock and endangering the habitats of native wildlife. In 1988 rally participants were blamed for starting a wildfire in Mali in which three people died. There is undoubtedly an environmental impact on the fragile desert ecosystem through which the vehicles race.[28]

Thus the negative impact of the race on the inhabitants of the countries through which it passes has been highlighted by critics of the rally. Some African news agencies have argued that the deaths of local inhabitants or pollution are of little interest to the race organisers. The Vatican, in its publication *L'Osservatore Romano*, described the race as a 'vulgar display of power and wealth in places where men continue to die from hunger and thirst'.[29] On occasion rally participants have also voiced their concerns over the poverty they encounter along the race's route and how disturbing they find this.[30] Race organisers have also been criticised for plotting a course through the disputed territory of Western Sahara without consulting the representatives of the Sahrawi people who reside there. The political scene in the part of Africa through which the rally takes place is extremely complex. Many of the countries in this region are relatively new, with borders established by European colonial powers such as France, Spain and Portugal in the nineteenth century.[31] Independence only came to many of these countries in the mid-to late twentieth century. One such example is the disputed territory of Western Sahara. This region was formerly a Spanish colony but since the Spanish withdrawal of 1975 the area has been occupied by Morocco. The local Sahrawi population, who are Moorish people descended from nomadic Bedouin tribesmen, claim it as their national territory. The Sahrawi people's political representatives are the militant Polisario Front, who demand independence for Western Sahara. In January 2001 the Polisario Front threatened to block the route of the Paris to Dakar Rally because the race organisers had requested permission to cross Western Sahara only from the Moroccan government and ignored the representatives of the Sahrawi people.[32] It took delicate negotiations involving the United Nations to bring this situation to a satisfactory conclusion. This highlights the difficulty in organising and running sporting events in this region of Africa due to the unstable political climate of many of the countries involved and illustrates that sport and politics in Africa are inseparable.[33] Many people in the region still see the Paris to Dakar Rally as an extension of old-style Western colonialism. The colonial powers may have withdrawn from Africa, but for some the competitors in the Paris to Dakar Rally continue to represent a 'symbol of colonial carelessness and arrogance'.[34] Countries such as Burkino Faso and the Ivory Coast have refused permission for the rally to pass through their territory for this reason.[35]

Further study of the region through which the rally takes place is required in order to fully evaluate its impact. The majority of the Paris to Dakar Rally takes place in the Sahara Desert, which is the largest hot desert in the world and a place where the presence of man is insignificant against the harsh terrain and climate.[36] It extends from the Atlas Mountains of Morocco in the north to the Sahel region of Mali in the south and across Mauritania, Niger and Chad, encompassing a vast wilderness of over 3 million square miles.[37] It is through this inhospitable region that the Paris to Dakar Rally unfolds. Areas such as the Sahel region in Mali are among the most sparsely populated in the world with the landscape under threat from a loss of biodiversity, degradation and desertification.[38] In fact it is estimated that the Sahara Desert is expanding south at a rate of almost 30 miles per year due to the effects of desertification. The people who inhabit this region are therefore extremely resilient and are constantly under threat from the elements, the harsh landscape and the unstable political climate. Two million people live in the Sahara, mostly in towns and villages and the cities on the fringes of the desert,[39] but over one-third of them remain nomadic, travelling with their flocks of sheep, goats and camels, living in tents and trying to etch out a living from the harsh desert landscape.[40] The largest ethnic nomadic group in the Sahara are the Tuareg. They are a nomadic pastoral people who inhabit the Sahara interior and are descended from Berber tribesmen. It is from the Tuareg that we get the iconic images of veiled camel riders crossing the desert or the Hollywood image of tribesmen attacking isolated 'foreign legion'-style forts in the desert.[41] The Tuareg are an indigenous people whose way of life has remained unchanged for centuries. They live mostly in Western Sahara, the Sahel and the Ténéré areas, which receive an average of 25mm of rainfall per year. The landscape is very important to these nomadic people, as it also holds religious and cultural significance for them. The Paris to Dakar Rally is an event that to some extent imposes itself on their landscape and so a balance must be drawn between the right of individuals to enjoy and participate in sport and the rights of indigenous people to live out their lives there. Indeed, in many instances it is the Tuareg that have rescued participants in the rally who have become lost in the desert.

Supporters of the Paris to Dakar rally argue that the race brings many economic benefits to the region in terms of the amount of money spent on food, drink, hotels and fuel. Many West African entrepreneurs rely on the rally for sales of their produce to participants[42], or from selling fuel and other goods to rally participants at an exorbitant rate.[43] However, the fact that arguably the Paris to Dakar Rally has stimulated tourism in West Africa and has brought money into the region is in itself not necessarily a positive development, as the influx of this wealth and tourism must be properly managed.[44] At present the area is ill-equipped to deal effectively with tourism expansion or this injection of cash from the rally as the infrastructure required to manage it properly is not in place.[45] An example of how the development of tourism and the influx of wealth into the region may not be welcomed by everyone is again evident by examining the plight of the Tuareg. The Tuareg people realise that money will end their way of life as it represents the end of self-sufficiency and a threat to their nomadic existence.[46] The Tuareg want to keep their culture alive and with it a way of life that has remained unchanged for generations. This highlights the need for investment in these areas to be undertaken responsibly and in a manner that is sustainable. In terms of the Paris to Dakar Rally, therefore, the cultural and social sensitivities of the local indigenous people must be appreciated so that the practices and values of the rally can complement those of the society with which it coexists.

The Development of Corporate Social Responsibility in the Dakar Rally

These criticisms of the race bring into sharp focus the concept of corporate social responsibility in motor sport, which indeed is a recent development in the study of sport generally. Originally the concept of corporate social responsibility applied only to ethical practices within large businesses, but in recent years this consideration has expanded into the management of sport as well. This is built upon the belief that sport should be viewed as an important aspect of modern life and bound by the same rules and values of any popular and widespread activity within civil society.[47] Corporate social responsibility is therefore the process of considering the interests of wider society by taking responsibility for the impact of activities in which one is engaged upon the everyday lives of people. The argument is that sport cannot be sustainable without 'preserving the integrity of the natural environment on which the sport itself depends'[48] and therefore sport cannot operate in isolation from the rest of society. Rather it must take the values and cultural norms of society and the impact of its actions on that society into account when planning and staging any large event.[49] To this end many commentators argue that sport has a moral obligation to be governed by the same principles and values present within other large corporations.[50] It has been argued that an overlap exists between the social responsibilities of sport and those of the corporate world as sport presents a bridge between social and economic aspects of society and offers an opportunity to improve the quality of life in society as a whole.[51] From this perspective the development of corporate social responsibility within sport requires organisations to consider the interests of investors, suppliers, consumers, employees, the community and the environment when engaging in their activities.[52] Thus in recent years the issue of corporate social responsibility has moved from being a business management practice to being a major issue in sport and so governing bodies within sport have been forced to sit up and take notice.[53] Sport now carries an expectation – and in some cases an obligation – to put something back into society by meeting the needs of all relevant stakeholders. Sports organisations need to clearly identify what they perceive their social responsibilities to be and to ensure the safety of participants and spectators as well by creating a link between sport, good governance and ethics.[54] Pivotal to this is an understanding of local social needs, a factor that is particularly relevant in the context of the Paris to Dakar Rally and, in a wider sense, the need for sport to be socially responsible.

A key area within corporate social responsibility is the requirement for sustainability and the need for sport to become a force for good in the development of long-term goals for host communities/regions.[55] Sustainable development in this context requires that the needs of the current generation are met without compromising the ability of future generations to meet their own needs.[56] This necessitates well-designed sports programmes that will contribute to economic and social development but at the same time remain environmentally aware. The negative impact of sport on the environment needs to be minimised,[57] and again this has relevance to the perceived environmental impact of the Paris to Dakar Rally on the landscape and environment of North and West Africa. The fact that sport is so uniquely placed to influence society means that these concepts of corporate social responsibility can be implemented in such a manner as to have much wider resonance beyond its immediate cultural boundaries.[58] It is therefore extremely important for sport to be pursued in a responsible and environmentally sustainable manner given the fact that the decline in environmental conditions reduces the health and living standards of communities.[59] The recent expansion of corporate social responsibility into sport combined with the well-documented criticisms of the Paris to Dakar Rally makes the race a prime candidate to explore the development of corporate social responsibility in motor sport. Once the criticisms of the race are addressed from a social perspective, utilising the concept of responsible and sustainable development, evidence of a clear practice of corporate social responsibility within motor sport is revealed.

In response to the criticisms directed against the Paris to Dakar Rally, the ASO began to take these issues much more seriously and develop policies that may be characterised as corporate social responsibility in action within motor sport. As a result of the poor publicity that the race received following a number of negative incidents in 1988, the organisers donated 11 motor pumps and 40 hand pumps to assist with irrigation in the communities located along the route of the rally.[60] This was the beginning of a process undertaken by the organisers of the rally to consider the interests of wider society by taking responsibility for the impact of its activities on the everyday lives of the people of the host regions. This work was expanded upon in the following years with more water pumps installed, medical equipment, school supplies and medical vaccines made available throughout Niger, Mauritania, Mali and Senegal.[61] ASO was also responsible for building schools in Zouerat, Mauritania and Koudathiou, Mali in 1997.[62]

In 2002 the ASO took a more strategic approach to corporate social responsibility and began to work in partnership with an organisation called SOS Sahel to establish a number of projects aimed at protecting the environment in West Africa under the brand name of 'Actions Dakar', *des projets pour l'Afrique*.[63] These projects cover a wide variety of activities, including the management of waste, the protection of natural resources, planting trees to limit the effects of desertification, educational projects and the installation of water pumps and irrigation systems. To date 136 projects have been funded with a total of 310,000 beneficiaries.[64] Moreover, in response to the criticism that the race caused excess air pollution, ASO commissioned an independent study in 2007 in collaboration with the Environment and Power Economy Agency to examine this issue. The resulting report confirmed that during the entire 2007 Dakar Rally the carbon emissions from the rally were approximately equivalent to a single Formula One race.[65] The Dakar Rally Road Safety Plan, which was published in 2007, targets the safety of the local population in the areas through which the rally passes. For example, drivers are instructed to observe local highway codes and speed limits through towns and villages as well as be extremely vigilant in populated areas. This policy is aimed at preventing the risk of accidents during the rally and enhances levels of safety for local populations.[66]

The 'Actions Dakar' project, it may be argued, is a good example of corporate social responsibility within motor sport. The nature of motor sport is such that it is impossible to make it entirely safe; however, the introduction of speed limits through villages by ASO goes some way towards making the rally less dangerous for local inhabitants and spectators. The organisers also pledge to source at least 70% of the food and drink required during the rally locally from countries that the rally passes through and employ as many indigenous people as possible, though some critics argue that this is mostly within low-paid jobs.[67] Other critics of the Actions Dakar project argue that the amount of investment in these countries is still minimal. The average size of funding to Actions Dakar projects is between 2,000 and 8,000 euro.[68] When these amounts are compared with entrance fees and the costs involved for competitors to enter the rally, it does appear that only a small percentage of investment is being put back into the countries affected by the event.

A small privateer entering the rally on a motorcycle will require a minimum of 40,000 euro to compete on a 'shoestring budget'.[69] When the cost of a new motorcycle at around 7,000 euro is factored in, together with the extra parts and mechanical works required to enter such a gruelling event – valued at approximately an additional 20,000 euro[70] – the cheapest an amateur rider can enter the Dakar rally for is estimated to be around 70,000 euro. In contrast the professional rally car teams with extensive financial backing and sponsorship can spend excessive amounts of money on the rally. For example Robby Gordon Motorsports required a budget of approximately 3,500,000 euro to enter two fully equipped state-of-the-art rally cars into the 2008 Dakar rally.[71] Some would argue therefore that the Actions Dakar project and associated humanitarian efforts are a 'smokescreen' designed to deflect criticism of the rally and not an attempt at genuine corporate social responsibility on the part of the rally organisers, given the comparatively small amounts of funding made available to the projects identified by Actions Dakar. The ASO argue, however, that the amount of funding is sufficient to make a significant difference in the lives of the people of the regions, with over 310,000 beneficiaries from the projects while a larger-scale financial investment would not necessarily reap such positive results. They contend that CSR is working well, either by accident or design, through the Actions Dakar project.

Recent Controversies and the Future for the Rally

The Dakar Rally drew publicity again in 2008 after race organisers cancelled the rally on the eve of the event when they stated they could not guarantee the competitors' safety following a terrorist threat. This was as a result of four French tourists being murdered by combatants linked to Al-Qaida in the Islamic republic of Mauritania.[72] In a statement the ASO said the threat of an attack was high and as eight of the rally's 15 stages were due to pass through remote areas of Mauritania they could not ensure the safety of the participants.[73] This again underscores the link between sport and politics in Africa. However ASO did stress that the race would return in future years as the Dakar Rally was a symbol that could not be destroyed.[74] As a result of these terrorist threats and the continued unstable political climate in Mauritania, Sudan and Chad, the rally organisers announced that the 2009 Dakar Rally would take place in South America through remote regions within Argentina and Chile.[75] This was the first time in 30 years that the race was not staged over its traditional route. However race director Etienne Levigne vowed following this temporary relocation that the event would return to its spiritual home in Africa the following year.[76]

The race in South America took place over similar terrain to that of Africa and received the same criticisms, specifically that it endangered the lives and culture of indigenous peoples. In this case those affected included the Mapuche, who are the indigenous inhabitants of Argentina and Chile.[77] The race was still referred to as the Dakar Rally despite taking place in South America and this has led to arguments that the race has become merely a brand name and has moved away from the event envisaged by Thierry Sabine in 1978. Nevertheless the rally remains dangerous, with French motorcyclist Pascal Terry being killed in an accident in Patagonia, Argentina, during the 2009 Dakar event.[78] As a result organisers will in future require all drivers to have competed in a round of the World Rally Championship and one Dakar Rally during the previous three years to gain entry to the event.[79] This could bring to an end the era of the amateur privateers who enter the race for the challenge and the adventure. The 2009 race was, however, viewed as a success with the Chilean government confirming that the 2010 Dakar rally would again be held in South America.[80] The traditional route of the rally through Africa is still viewed as being a security risk, with recent assessments from the United States government that the Islamic states of Sudan, Chad and in particular Mauritania could become the new 'Afghanistan' in providing a breeding-ground for militant terrorists.[81]

All of this may mean that it could be some time before the famous Paris to Dakar Rally takes place once more in its spiritual home of Africa. As a result of this other countries such as the United Arab Emirates are competing to host the rally in 2011.[82] While some critics view this as being the end of the Dakar Rally as we know it, others see it as a natural development as the race becomes more global. In the same way as the FIFA World Cup and the Olympic Games are held in various countries, so too, it is argued, should the Dakar Rally. This is because for some the rally represents first and foremost endurance racing through difficult terrain and as such does not necessarily have to take place in Africa. However the fact that it is unclear when, if ever, the race will return to the continent has thrown the future of the rally into doubt as it may have lost its mystique: for some, it was the iconic images of the Sahara that made the Dakar Rally unique. The future of the rally has also been thrown into doubt because of the recent global financial crisis. As a result of the economic downturn Mitsubishi pulled out of the rally in 2009 and the fear is that other manufacturers such as Volkswagen will do likewise.[83] All this leaves the long term future of the Dakar rally in some doubt.

As the Paris-Dakar rally has developed over the years it has shown great fluidity and adaptability. This is evident from the various routes that the rally has taken throughout its history. The ASO contends, therefore, that the temporary relocation of the rally to South America is merely another example of its adaptability and as the rally has a long standing tradition of evolution it will continue to grow. However, the fact that it no longer seems feasible to run the race through North and West Africa has called into question the long-term future of the event as it remains synonymous with the African continent. The fact that the ASO continues to use the Dakar name outside Africa has also been of some concern to politicians in Africa who feel that ASO is profiting from using the 'Dakar' image despite the race no longer taking place there.

In terms of corporate social responsibility, it remains to be seen if the ASO will continue to exercise a moral obligation and sustain its 'Actions Dakar' humanitarian work if the rally is not to be staged in Africa for the foreseeable future. It is likely, however, that this work will continue in the short term as the use of the name Dakar and the fact that so much damage has arguably already been done to the region would suggest that the humanitarian work undertaken by ASO will be sustained in the hope that the rally can return to Africa in the future. Indeed, ASO appears determined to stage the rally on the continent at the earliest possible opportunity; but if the political climate remains unchanged then the race could be held in various locations throughout the world over the next several years. The rally could therefore become an even bigger global event or conversely the allure of the race may diminish if it does not take place over its traditional route across the Sahara. The race organisers and supporters, however, feel that the event can only get bigger and more successful and will continue to attract new competitors and markets. At the same time they appear intent on continuing to assist and support the people of the rally's spiritual home through the delivery of much-needed humanitarian projects, which may point the way for others engaged in debates over the exact corporate social responsibilities held by sport governing bodies and their engagement with the environments in which they exist.

Notes

1. McCabe, *Against Gravity*, 286.
2. Hacking, *To Dakar and Back*, 1.
3. Michael Dobbs, 'Death of an Adventurer', *Washington Post*, 16 Jan. 1986.
4. Amaury Sports Organisation, 'Dakar, Retrospective', 2. Available at: http://www.dakar.com
5. Ibid., 8.
6. Hacking, *To Dakar and Back*, 5.
7. Amaury Sports Organisation, *Dakar, Retrospective*, 9.
8. Jones, *Dakar: The Challenge of the Desert*, 42.
9. Boorman, *Race to Dakar*, 240.
10. Amaury Sports Organisation, *Dakar, Retrospective*, 21.
11. Ibid., 46.
12. Ibid., 2.
13. McCabe, *Against Gravity*, 278.
14. Amaury Sports Organisation, *Dakar, Retrospective*, 51.
15. Ibid., 82.
16. McCabe, *Against Gravity*, 24.
17. *The Times* (London), 15 Jan. 1982.
18. Amaury Sports Organisation, *Dakar, Retrospective*, 52.
19. Ibid., 81.
20. Boorman, *Race to Dakar*, 122.
21. Amaury Sports Organisation, *Dakar, Retrospective*, 109.
22. Boorman, *Race to Dakar*, 217.
23. Ibid., 214.
24. Dobbs, 'Death of an Adventurer'.
25. James Brooke, 'Dangerous Paris Dakar Rally is Endangered', *New York Times*, 13 March 1988.
26. Brendan Gallagher, 'Dakar Rally's Dance with Death', *Daily Telegraph*, 9 Jan. 2009.
27. 'Second boy dies during Dakar', www.motoring.co.za, 14 Jan. 2006.
28. Andreason and Overton, *Creative Recycling*, 18.
29. James Brooke, 'Dangerous Paris Dakar Rally is Endangered', *New York Times*, 13 March 1988.

30. McCabe, *Against Gravity*, 227.
31. De Villiers and Hirtle, *Sahara: The Life of the Great Desert*, 12.
32. Zoubir and Karima Benabdallah-Gambier, 'Western Sahara Deadlock', 10.
33. Baker, 'Political Games', 290.
34. De Villiers and Hirtle, *Sahara: The Life of the Great Desert*, 289.
35. Brooke, 'Dangerous Paris Dakar Rally is Endangered'.
36. De Villiers and Hirtle, *Sahara: The Life of the Great Desert*, 3.
37. Ibid., 11.
38. Stroosnijder, 'Population Density', 3.
39. De Villiers and Hirtle, *Sahara: The Life of the Great Desert*, 159.
40. Ibid., 160.
41. Keenan, *Sahara Man*, 3.
42. Andreason and Overton, *Creative Recycling*, 18.
43. McCabe, *Against Gravity*, 245.
44. Trudel, 'IUCN education in Sahel and West Africa'.
45. Ibid.
46. De Villiers and Hirtle, *Sahara: The Life of the Great Desert*, 255.
47. Singh, 'Human Rights and Sport', 1.
48. Cappato and Pennazio, *Corporate Social Responsibility in Sport*, 4.
49. Ibid., 35.
50. Morgan, 'Patriotic Sports Ethics in Sport', 371.
51. Smith and Westerbeek, 'Sport as a Vehicle', 43.
52. Ibid., 44.
53. Davies, *Towards a Better World*.
54. Smith and Westerbeek, 'Sport as a Vehicle', 47.
55. Davies, *Towards a Better World*.
56. United Nations Inter-Agency Task Force on Sport for Development and Peace, *Sport for Development and Peace : Towards Achieving the Millennium Development Goals*, 10.
57. Ibid., 13.
58. Smith and Westerbeek, 'Sport as a Vehicle', 48.
59. United Nations Inter-Agency Task Force on Sport for Development and Peace, *Sport for Development and Peace : Towards Achieving the Millennium Development Goals*, 14.
60. Brooke, 'Dangerous Paris Dakar Rally is Endangered'.
61. Amaury Sports Organisation, *Actions Dakar: A Constant Solidarity*.
62. Ibid.
63. www.sossahel.org.
64. Amaury Sports Organisation, 'Actions Dakar'.
65. Amaury Sports Organisation, *The Dakar Carbon Footprint*.
66. Amaury Sports Organisation, *Dakar: Road Safety Policy*.
67. Boorman, *Race to Dakar*, 283.
68. 'Actions Dakar', Amaury Sports Organisation, press release, 27 Sept. 2007.
69. Hacking, *To Dakar and Back*, 29.
70. Boorman, *Race to Dakar*, 34.
71. *USA Today*, 7 Jan. 2008.
72. *The Times*, 24 Dec. 2007.
73. *The Guardian*, 5 Jan. 2008.
74. BBC, 4 Jan. 2008. Available at: http://news.bbc.co.uk/sport1/hi/motorsport/world_rally/7171426.stm
75. BBC, 26 March 2008. Available at: http://news.bbc.co.uk/sport1/hi/motorsport/world_rally/7315464.stm
76. Ibid.
77. *The Times*, 3 Jan. 2009
78. BBC, 7 Jan. 2009. Available at: http://news.bbc.co.uk/sport1/hi/motorsport/world_rally/7815495.stm

79. Associated Press, 3 March 2009.
80. Merco Press, South Atlantic News Agency, 9 March 2009.
81. Nicholas Schmidle, 'The Saharan Conundrum', *New York Times*, 15 Feb. 2009.
82. *The National*, 25 Feb. 2009.
83. Associated Press, 3 March 2009.

References

Amaury Sports Organisation. *The Dakar Carbon Footprint*. Paris: ASO, 2007.
Amaury Sports Organisation. *Dakar: Road Safety Policy*. Paris: ASO, 2007.
Amaury Sports Organisation. *Dakar, Retrospective: 1979–2007*. Paris: ASO, 2007.
Amaury Sports Organisation. 'Actions Dakar'. Newsletter, March, 2008.
Amaury Sports Organisation. *Actions Dakar: A Constant Solidarity*. Paris: ASO, 2008.
Andreasen, Jude, and Overton Cleve. *Creative Recycling: Handmade in Africa*. Philadelphia: Xlibris Corporation Publishing, 2004.
Baker, William. 'Political Games: The Meaning of International Sport for Independent Africa', in *Sport in Africa: Essays in Social History*, ed. William Baker. London: Africana Publishing, 1987.
Boorman, Charley. *Race to Dakar*. London: Sphere Publishing, 2006.
Cappato, Alice and Pennazio Vittorio. *Corporate Social Responsibility in Sport*. Turin: University of Turin, 2006.
Davies, Robert. *Towards a Better World – Sport, Citizenship and Development*. Lausanne: Worlds Sport Forum, 2002.
De Villiers, Marq and Hirtle Sheila. *Sahara: The Life of the Great Desert*. London: Harper Collins Publishing, 2004.
Hacking, Lawrence. *To Dakar and Back*. Toronto: ECW Press, 2008.
Jones, Jim. *Dakar: The Challenge of the Desert: Experience the World's Greatest Motorsport Event*. Llandybie: Dinefwr Press Ltd, 2003.
Keenan, Jeremy. *Sahara Man: Travelling with the Tuareg*. London: Murray Publishers, 2003.
McCabe, Edward. *Against Gravity: From Paris to Dakar in the World's Most Dangerous Race*. New York: Warner Publishing, 1990.
Morgan, William. 'Patriotic Sports and the Moral Making of Nations', in *Ethics in Sport*, eds. William J. Morgan, Klaus V Meier and Angels J Schneider. Leeds: Human Kinetics Publishin, 2000.
Singh, Paul. 'Human Rights and Sport'. *South African Journal for Research in Sport* 24, no. 2, (2002): 67–78.
Smith, Aaron C.T. and Hans M. Westerbeek. 'Sport as a Vehicle for Deploying Corporate Social Responsibility'. *The Journal of Corporate Citizenship* 25 (May 2007).
Stroosnijder, Leo. 'Population Density, Carrying Capacity and Agricultural Production Technology in the Sahel', in *The Sahel: Population, Integrated Rural Development Projects – Components in Development Projects*, ed. Birgit Brander Rasmussen. Aarhus: Aarhus University Press, 1994.
Trudel, Monique. 'IUCN education in the Sahel and West Africa', in *Planning Education to Care for the Earth*, eds. Joy Palmer, Wendy Goldstein and Anthony Curnow. Bellgarde-sur-Valserine: International Union for the Conservation of Nature, 1995.
United Nations Inter-Agency Task Force on Sport for Development and Peace. *Sport for Development and Peace: Towards Achieving the Millennium Development Goals*. New York: United Nations, 2003. http://www.un.org/wcn/content/site/sport/
Zoubir, Yahia H. and Karima Benabdallah-Gambier. 'Western Sahara Deadlock'. *Middle East Report* 227 (Summer 2003).

A History of the 'Triple Crown' of Motor Racing: The Indianapolis 500, the Le Mans 24 Hours and the Monaco Grand Prix

Philip O'Kane

University of Ulster at Magee, Londonderry, UK

This article provides a history and context to three of the most famous motor races in the world: the Indianapolis 500-mile race, the Monaco Formula One Grand Prix and the 24 Hours of Le Mans sports car race. The tradition and heritage of the races is examined in this piece alongside an analysis of the significance attached to each event and how, when viewed together, they have made a stellar contribution to the shared history of motor racing over many decades.

Introduction

Since the invention of the first motor vehicle in the late nineteenth century, man has had a desire to test the limits of both the human body and that of their automobiles under race conditions. The earliest races in the history of motor sport took place in France in the late 1880s and early 1890s as the French nation enthusiastically embraced the motor car, marking a fascination that has remained undiminished and unmatched by any other country throughout the world. The United States of America, always a champion of new technology and opportunity, also assisted in the development of both the motor car and in establishing motor racing as a global sport. The first recorded event in the USA was a street race in Chicago in 1895 and since then both France and the USA have stood apart from the rest of the field with regard to racing motor cars.

In the years following these early events various forms of motor racing emerged, including rallying, stock car racing, off-road racing, touring car racing and drag racing. The two most popular and prestigious forms of motor racing have, however, always been open-wheel racing and sports car racing. These two categories have commanded the public's imagination in a manner unmatched by any other genre of motor racing and are recognised as the most prestigious and glamorous categories in world motor sport. Open-wheel racing refers to a type of single-seater racing car in which the car's wheels remain uncovered while the car carries aerofoil front and rear wings in order to create down force, in turn permitting extremely high speeds to be achieved. The pinnacle of open-wheel racing is currently Formula One, and this has been the case since the Formula One world championship was inaugurated in 1950.

In the United States, however, the most popular open-wheel racing formula is Indycar racing, which has a huge global following and attracts top drivers from around the world. The other most famous form of motor racing is that featuring sports cars. Sports car races involve special prototype versions of established car manufacturers' road models, which are usually raced over long distances with two or more drivers working as a team. The glamour and prestige of both forms of motor racing have always attracted the leading drivers to compete against one another for the sport's top prizes.

It is no coincidence, therefore, given the history of the development of motor racing in both France and the USA that both countries in turn play host to the most renowned races within these two motor racing categories. There are many prestigious races within world motor sport, with each having their own unique tradition and attraction. However, some races, resulting from their heritage and legendary status, will always be viewed as having added significance in the minds of both drivers and fans alike. Within sports car racing the Le Mans 24 Hours Race is easily the most famous and recognisable meeting in the world, while in open-wheel racing the Monaco Grand Prix, which is the 'jewel in the crown' of the Formula One world championship, alongside the famous Indianapolis 500-mile race, held annually at the Indianapolis Motor Speedway in the USA, represent the most desirable open-wheel race victories in the world.

The significance of the Indianapolis 500, the Monaco Grand Prix and the Le Mans 24 Hours Race are unquestioned within the motor racing industry. Due to the long history and tradition of each race, winning all three events has, over time, come to symbolise and constitute the 'Triple Crown' or holy grail of motor racing. Spanning many decades, these races have achieved iconic status within motor racing and securing first place in any of the three events is considered to be the pinnacle of a driver's career. Arguably these races are viewed as being more important and prestigious than the three separate racing series that they incorporate, namely the IndyCar Series, the Formula One World Championship and the Le Mans Sportscar Series respectively.

As implied, winning any of these races attracts fame, prestige, wealth and respect among drivers and motor racing enthusiasts, whereas claiming all three race victories ensures legendary status. Achieving the latter is viewed as a remarkable accomplishment given the competition, difficulty and adaptability involved in each unique genre of racing. This is illustrated by the fact that only one driver has ever achieved this feat, that accolade being claimed by Englishman Graham Hill who won the Monaco Grand Prix five times (1963, 1964, 1965, 1968, 1969), the Indianapolis 500 in 1966 and the Le Mans 24 Hours Race in 1972. That this record has to date only been achieved on this one occasions illustrates how difficult winning all three events is; indeed only 11 other drivers in history have even won two out of the three races.

Despite the rich pedigree of each race and the fact that they are now collectively regarded as the 'Triple Crown of motor racing', this remains an unofficial designation; yet it retains a revered and mythical status among motor sport enthusiasts. Unlike other famous 'Triple Crown' events – in rugby or horse racing, for example – there is no trophy for winning the triple crown of motor racing; rather it is considered to be a moral victory, a badge of honour and an achievement that gives any driver who successfully achieves this legendary and near-mythical status in the sport of motor racing. In order to fully evaluate the difficulty involved in winning each race and the collective significance of the 'Triple Crown of motor sport' it in first necessary to look at the rich heritage and tradition offered by each race individually.

The Indianapolis 500 Mile Race

First run in 1911, the Indianapolis 500 Mile race, or 'Indy 500', is marketed as 'the greatest spectacle in racing'. The immortal words 'Gentlemen, start your engines!', first coined at the Indianapolis Motor Speedway, have alongside the race itself acquired legendary status over the years. The iconic race is staged annually on Memorial Day weekend in late May at the Indianapolis Motor Speedway, Indiana, USA, and is one of the largest sporting events in the world, with an attendance of over 400,000 people on race day. The speedway itself consists of a two-and-a-half-mile banked oval with four 60-foot-wide bends, which are approached at top speed by the participants. The lap record at the speedway was set in 1996 by Dutchman Arie Luyendyk who achieved an average lap speed of 237 miles per hour. The first race was held in 1911 and was won by Ray Harroun with an average speed of 74 miles per hour for the 500 miles. Such is the status of the Indianapolis Motor Speedway that in 1975 the US National Park Service listed it in the National Register of Historic Places.

The history of the speedway began in 1909 when Carl Fisher paid $300 an acre for the 80 acres of land that was to become the Indianapolis Motor Speedway.[1] The finished track was paved with over three million bricks and earned itself the nickname 'the brickyard'. The track was tarmacked in later years but still retains a yard of bricks along the start/finish line, which the race winner traditionally kisses in an established post-race ritual. The first race was held on Memorial Day 1911 and involved 40 cars, an amazing spectacle at that time. Safety was not an issue in those days with mechanics riding on board with the drivers. This lack of safety in the early years of the race is illustrated by the fact that during the 1915 race four fatalities took place over the course of the event. Despite the danger, however, or possibly because of it, the race grew in popularity and credibility. As the years passed by the cars and engines became more sophisticated, not least during the 1920s and into the depression era of the 1930s. Competition to win the race grew among racing drivers and in 1936 Lou Meyer became the first three-times winner of the event and was awarded the new Borg-Warner trophy, which has been presented annually to each Indy 500 champion since this inaugural ceremony. Meyer was also the first man to drink the now traditional pint of milk in the victory lane after the race.[2] During the Second World War the race did not take place and the speedway fell into disrepair. In 1945 the track was purchased by Tony Hulman and over the years the Hulman-George family did much to establish the Indy 500 as the global sporting event that it has now become. The race has been staged every year since 1946 and has become one of the most famous sporting events in the world as well as one of the most sought-after race victories among racing drivers.

The traditions that have grown up around the race have contributed greatly to its popularity and enduring appeal. Many fans see the customs and rituals that the race generates as representative of a particular form of American spirit. Organisers pride themselves on the fact that anyone can turn up at Indy in the month of May and attempt to qualify for the race, as unlike other racing series no one is excluded and there is an open call for entries. In recent years, however, due to spiralling costs fewer amateur drivers have arrived at the event attempting to qualify for the 33 starting places on the grid.

The race holds an important place in American culture and has become an annual pilgrimage for many American families. Many of the drivers who have raced at Indianapolis first attended the event as children with their families. Due to the fact that the race is run over Memorial Day weekend there are numerous references to the armed forces prior to the event, such as the playing of 'Taps' and the singing of patriotic songs to stir the crowd before the race such as 'America the Beautiful', 'God Bless America' and 'The Star-Spangled Banner'. Another pre-race musical tradition is the singing of 'Back Home Again in Indiana' after which the drivers receive a final blessing before they hear the immortal words 'Gentlemen start your engines!', the pace laps begins and the race commences. These pre-race ceremonies and traditions take some time and help build up the atmosphere among the 400,000-plus crowd. This all plays a part in establishing the race as the cultural reservoir that it has now become within the American psyche.[3]

There have been many famous races at Indy since Ray Harroun first took the chequered flag back in 1911. In the early years the race was quick to build up a reputation for speed and excitement, with Tommy Milton becoming the first two-times winner in 1923. The 1934 race was a classic duel between Bill Cummings and Mauri Rose, with Cummings emerging victorious in the closest finish up to that point; Rose went on to win the event three times. Indiana native Wilbur Shaw dominated the race in the pre-war years, claiming the title in 1937, 1939 and 1940. Shaw continued his association with the race after he retired by becoming president of the Indianapolis Motor Speedway. In 1936 Lou Meyer won the event for the third time before he went on to run his own team at Indy and die at the age of 91. To live this long was a rare feat for drivers from that era as sadly, due to the dangers and lack of safety, many competitors' lives were cut short following racing accidents. In the post-war years Moore Racing teammates Bill Holland and Mauri Rose dominated the race, with Bill Vukovich arriving on the scene in the early 1950s. Vukovich won the race in 1953 and 1954 and was pursuing a new record of three consecutive race victories in 1955 when he was tragically killed while leading the race.

The 1960s at Indy were famous for the so-called 'British invasion' as a number of famous Formula One names such as Jim Clark, Graham Hill and Jackie Stewart entered the race. In 1965 Scottish racer Jim Clark dominated the event, leading 190 of the 200 laps. A two-times Formula One World Champion, Clark lost his life at the Hockenheim circuit in Germany during the 1968 season. Undoubtedly, had he lived Clark would have gone on to have set many more motor racing records. The 1966 race was billed as the 'Battle of Britain' as Graham Hill overtook Jackie Stewart on his way to victory. Hill is still the only driver to have won the Indy 500, Monaco Grand Prix and Le Mans 24 Hours. Hill died in a light aircraft crash in 1975; appropriately his son Damon went on to become Formula One world champion in 1996.

The 1974 race was memorable for two reasons: it was the first time the event was held on a Sunday and eventual winner Johnny Rutherford drove an exceptional race after starting 25th on the grid. Legendary Texan A.J. Foyt won his fourth Indy 500 in 1977, having previously proven victorious in 1961, 1964 and 1967. Foyt also won the race as a team owner in 1999 when his driver Kenny Brack triumphed. The 1977 race was also famous for Tom Sneva claiming the first 200 miles per hour lap and

Janet Guthrie becoming the first woman to participate in the event.[4] There have also been numerous controversies in the race over the years, one of the most famous being in 1981 when Bobby Unser took the chequered flag with Mario Andretti in second place. However, controversy over a penalty that Unser incurred led to Andretti being declared the winner, but after an appeal from Unser he was later reinstated as the race winner. This controversy was repeated in 2002 with Brazilian driver Helio Castro-Neves declared race winner despite an appeal from Canadian Paul Tracy that he had made a legitimate last lap pass on the Brazilian.

The 1989 race is widely regarded as a classic, famous for the duel between Emerson Fittipaldi and Al Unser Junior. The two drivers had battled side by side for most of the race and with four laps to go Unser took the lead. Then with two laps remaining Fittipaldi pulled alongside Unser, but neither man would give an inch and they ran side by side for most of the lap before the two cars touched as Unser crashed out of the race and Fittipaldi went on to win. One of the most famous images from the race is Unser giving Fittipaldi the thumbs up sign, to acknowledge that it was merely a racing incident with neither man to blame, from beside his wrecked car as Fittipaldi drove round behind the safety car to claim victory on the last lap.[5] In 1995 Jacques Villeneuve, son of legendary Ferrari driver Gilles Villeneuve, came from two laps down to win the race, thereby completing a total distance of 505 miles.[6] Villeneuve went on to become Formula One world champion and has finished second at the Le Mans 24 hours race, meaning he has come closer than most to achieving the elusive Triple Crown.

There are many drivers who have immortalised their names at Indianapolis such as multiple race winners A.J. Foyt (four times winner), Rick Mears (four times winner) and three-times winners Mauri Rose, Wilbur Shaw, Lou Meyer, Johnny Rutherford and Helio Castro-Neves; however, two family names have dominated the history of the Indy 500 over the years. These are Andretti and Unser. Between them these two families have secured 135 starts in the race and ten victories. The Unser family have known both triumph and tragedy at the Indianapolis Motor Speedway. The first of the three brothers to race at the speedway was Jerry Unser in 1958 who was tragically killed in a crash during practice for the 1959 race. Jerry's brothers Al and Bobby went on to compete in 46 races at Indianapolis between them, with Al Unser winning the event four times (1970, 1971, 1978 and 1987) and Bobby Unser winning it three times (1968, 1975 and 1981). Al's son, Al Unser Junior, also completed 19 races, winning it in both 1992 and 1994. Jerry Unser's son Johnny was only seven months old when his father was killed at the Indianapolis Motor Speedway in May 1959; however this did not deter him from wishing to take part in the event and he went on to make five starts in 'the greatest spectacle in racing'.

The Andretti family name is equally synonymous with the Indy 500; however, unlike the Unsers the family has only one title to show for 62 race starts, Mario Andretti's 1969 triumph being their only victory there. Mario Andretti raced 29 times in the Indy 500 and his son Michael 16 times. Michael Andretti holds the unenviable record of being the driver to have led most laps at Indianapolis without actually winning the race. His brother Jeff and cousin John also met with little luck at the speedway. In fact the Andrettis have had so much bad luck at the Indy 500 that this has given rise to the phrase 'the Andretti curse' to explain numerous failures and misfortune over the years. The Andrettis have led deep into the race on many occasions only for victory to be snatched from their grasp. The latest example of this came in 2006 when, with four laps to go, Michael Andretti led the race, his son Marco Andretti was in second and Sam Hornish in third place. In a pulsating last four laps Marco took the lead from his father only for Sam Hornish to pass first Michael and then Marco on the last corner to win the race in the closest ever recorded finish at Indy.

As with all forms of motor racing, competing in the Indianapolis 500 is dangerous. Over the years a total of 41 drivers, 15 mechanics, four track officials and seven spectators have lost their lives at the Indianapolis Motor Speedway. Many of these fatal accidents involved young inexperienced drivers or amateur competitors. However, many experienced professional drivers have also lost their lives at the speedway, demonstrating how difficult and dangerous competing there can be. The 1938 race winner, Floyd Roberts, was killed during the 1939 race and in 1955 two-time race winner Bill Vukovich died while leading the event during his attempt to win three races in a row. The 1933 race was one of the most tragic, with five drivers and mechanics being killed. In 1996 the most experienced driver in the field, two-time pole position winner Scott Brayton, who had completed the race 14 times, lost his life in practice. That said, there have been numerous safety initiatives over the years with improved safer crash barriers, safety modifications to the driver's cockpits, fencing to protect spectators, first-class medical treatment on site and strict rookie orientation tests for new drivers.[7] However due to the nature of the race – with 33 cars racing at over 200 miles per hour on a banked walled oval – it can never be made completely safe.

Over the years the Indy 500 has been sanctioned by a variety of governing bodies. From 1911 until 1955 the race was organised and sanctioned by the American Automobile Association. In 1956 the United States Auto Club was founded and it sanctioned the race until 1978, when CART (Championship Auto Racing Teams) was formed and took over the running of the race. There was an uneasy alliance between CART and the speedway owners that lasted until the early 1990s when Indianapolis Motor Speedway president Tony George founded the Indy Racing League (IRL), which has sanctioned the race since 1996. This led to a split, with the CART teams refusing to enter the race from this point onwards and they in turn formed their own series. This divide in American open-wheel racing lasted until 2008, when the team series merged into the IndyCar Series; the fact that the CART series did not have the blue-riband Indy 500 event meant it found it increasingly difficult to attract manufacturers, drivers and sponsors and eventually closed its series and merged with the IRL. The CART series could not survive without the race, and this again illustrates the influence that the Indianapolis 500 exerts over fans, drivers, manufacturers and sponsors alike.

The import that the race commands is also illustrated by the fact that it attracts drivers from other racing series all over the world who come to Indianapolis to compete in the famous event. An early example of this is the famous Italian Grand Prix driver Alberto Ascari, who entered the race in 1952. The 1960s saw numerous Grand Prix drivers compete such as Jim Clark, Graham Hill and Jackie Stewart compete. These famous Grand Prix drivers have not always been successful, however, proving how difficult the race is to win. In 1992 three-times Formula One world champion Nelson Piquet broke both legs in a crash while attempting to qualify for the race, and in 1993 the reigning Formula One world champion Nigel Mansell led the race with 16 laps to go only to eventually finish in third place.[8] The race also attracts drivers from the world of stock car racing. There is a scheduling conflict, however, as the Coca-Cola 600, a stock car race that is run at night under lights at Lowes Speedway in North Carolina, takes place on the same day as the Indy 500. This has led some stock car drivers to attempt 'double duty', which is competing in the Indy 500 before taking a helicopter to North Carolina to compete in the Coca-Cola 600 later than day. Three drivers have attempted both races on the same day: John Andretti, Tony Stewart and Robby Gordon. Only Tony Stewart in 2001 completed both race distances, a total of 1,100 miles. Several amateur competitors also enter the race each year, and many of these drivers in particular have captured the public's imagination, including Jimmy Snyder, 'the Flying Milkman', in the 1930s; Danny Ongais, 'the Flying Hawaiian', in the 1970s and 1980s; and Dr Jack Miller, 'the Racing Dentist', in the 1990s. These drivers represent the romantic nature of Indianapolis as anyone, provided they have financial backing to purchase a car and have passed rookie orientation tests, can turn up at Indy in May and attempt to qualify for the race proper. The fans appreciate the struggle that many of these drivers encounter to make the field. In many cases merely qualifying for the race is a feat in itself worthy of the respect of followers. An example of a famous qualifying attempt is that undertaken by Robbie Buhl in 1999. With only a few minutes left in qualifying and frustrated with his driver's failure to qualify, team owner A.J. Foyt approached Robbie Buhl in the pit lane to ask him to qualify his car. Despite having not driven the car all month, Buhl jumped into the vehicle and with rain beginning to fall on a slippery track drove four laps at top speed to qualify on the last row with only seconds to spare. These courageous last-minute qualifying attempts have similarly captured the imagination of the fans at Indianapolis.

The Indianapolis 500 mile race is without doubt one of the greatest motor races in the world. It retains legendary status due to the rich history and heritage of the race and is the one that every racing driver wants to win. It is the challenge of the speed and danger combined with the pageantry and tradition that attracts both drivers and fans. It is one of the most enduring motor races in the sport's history and one that has entered popular culture as an iconic sporting event and thereby worthy of it's inclusion in the 'Triple Crown of motor sport'.

The Monaco Grand Prix

The Monaco Grand Prix has long been viewed as the 'jewel in the crown' of the Formula One world championship and one of the most prestigious motor races in the world. Formula One is seen by many as the pinnacle of motor sport and a series that all drivers aspire to compete in. The Monaco Grand Prix is the most important race in the Formula One calendar due to its history and prestige and also its glamorous location. The race takes place through the streets of the principality of Monaco, along the French Riviera, which has been ruled by the Grimaldi royal family since 1814. Monaco is famous for its conspicuous consumption, its wealth as well as its gambling centre of Monte Carlo. The fact that the principality is a tax haven makes it the playground of the rich and famous and for many the perfect venue for the high-octane sport of Formula One motor racing. The Formula One world championship in its current form was first staged in 1950 but many of the Grand Prix races on the calendar pre-date this, going back to the European Grand Prix motoring championship of the 1920s and the 1930s. The Monaco Grand Prix is one of the oldest races on the calendar, with the first running of the race taking place in 1929.

The Monaco Grand Prix is a notoriously difficult race to win, taking place as it does on a narrow street circuit through Monaco and thereby leaving no margin for error. The track does not possess the wide run-off areas and gravel traps common to other Grand Prix circuits. Despite the fact that the top speeds at Monaco are less than those at other Grand Prix tracks that have long straights, such as Monza in Italy or Spa in Belgium, it is an extremely dangerous and demanding circuit due to the tight corners and streets, frequent elevation changes and the famous tunnel that all combine to make Monaco a unique and challenging race track. Some of the corners at the Monaco circuit are famous within motor sport – corners such as Sainte Devote, Rascasse and Casino Square have reached mythical status among drivers and Grand Prix racing fans. The layout of the circuit has remained largely the same since the first race was held in 1929, but with an increased lap speed in excess of 70% over the years demonstrating the considerable technological advances that Formula One has made over this period.

That first race in 1929 was the brainchild of Monaco native and general commissioner of the Automobile Club de Monaco (ACDM) Anthony Noghes, who in 1925 envisaged a motor car race around the narrow streets of Monaco. There already was a tradition of motor sport in Monaco with the Monte Carlo Rally being held from as early as 1911, but the race envisaged by Noghes was a street race through the tight roads and steep inclines of Monaco. He mapped out a circuit which has become the most famous Grand Prix track of all time.[9] Thanks to Noghes's persistence and with help from both the Automobile Club de Monaco and the Association Internationale des Automobile Clubs Reconnus (AIACR), the inaugural Monaco Grand Prix was held in 1929 with a total prize money of 179,000 francs on offer, including 100,000 francs for the winner. An invitation-only event, the race was won by British driver William Grover-Williams in a Bugatti. The glamour and prestige of Monaco together with the prize money on offer meant that the Monaco Grand Prix soon grew in prominence. The race quickly built up a reputation as being extremely challenging with the tight and twisted nature of the circuit meaning that only the drivers with the best car control could aspire to win there.

Throughout the 1930s, as the Monaco Grand Prix grew in stature, the race was dominated by the Bugatti race car company, who won the first three races, and the other big car manufacturers of the time, Alfa-Romeo and Mercedes-Benz. In 1931 Monaco native Louis Chiron, driving a Bugatti, held off Luigi Fagioli in a Maserati to become the first, and to date the only, Monaco-born winner of the race. The 1932 event was famous for being the only win at Monaco by racing legend Tazio Nuvolari, who took Alfa-Romeo's first title at the famous circuit. Nuvolari was popular with the fans because of his fearless driving style; easily recognisable in his red leather helmet, Nuvolari was pulled 17 times from the wreckage of race cars and broke almost every bone in his body but always came back to race in his own indomitable style. This led many fans to joke that Nuvolari had in fact made a pact with the devil.[10] He almost won the 1933 Monaco Grand Prix as well after a race-long duel with Achille Varzi led to Nuvolari's car breaking down on the last lap.

Mercedes-Benz dominated the race in the late 1930s, winning it three years in succession before the onset of the Second World War witnessed the end of the Monaco Grand Prix until 1948. In these post-war years the race was only held sporadically, with the 1948 race followed by meetings in 1950 and 1952. The 1950 race is famous as it was the first win at Monaco for legendary five-times Formula One world champion Juan Manuel Fangio from Argentina, who would go on to win the Monaco Grand Prix again in 1957. In 1955 the race finally became a permanent fixture on the Formula One World Championship calendar and it has been held annually ever since. It was the dawn of the Formula One World Championship that was to elevate the race to legendary status as it became the 'jewel in the crown' of F1. The advent of the Formula One World Championship also made the Monaco Grand Prix the most difficult of the Triple Crown events to win, as there were no one-off entries allowed in Formula One – meaning that any driver who wanted to win at Monaco had to find a seat in a Formula One team for the entire season. For this reason sports car and Indycar drivers are now less likely to accomplish the Triple Crown.

The early years of the Formula One World Championship were dominated by the ongoing rivalry between the two greatest drivers of that era, Juan Manual Fangio and Stirling Moss from England. Between 1950 and 1961 Fangio won the Monaco Grand Prix twice (1950 and 1957) while Moss won it three times (1956, 1960 and 1961). The rivalry between these two legendary drivers was played out on the grand stage of the Monaco Grand Prix and captured the public's imagination. In so doing it helped to establish both the fledgling Formula One World Championship and the Monaco Grand Prix as truly global events: while Fangio won the championship a record five times Moss was runner-up on four occasions, always narrowly missing out on the title. This was due to a combination of bad luck and his stance of only driving British-made cars. This inevitably meant that he was often driving uncompetitive cars compared to those of the top teams of Ferrari, Maserati, Alfa-Romeo and Mercedes-Benz. Indeed the fact that he won the Monaco Grand Prix three times is testament to his remarkable skill as a driver. In wet conditions, such as at the 1960 Monaco race, he was unequalled with his bravery and car control in difficult conditions. Legendary. Fangio was also a highly skilled driver renowned for his accuracy and precision. Moss once said of Fangio that he took the exact same line on each lap of a race without fail.[11] It was also a case of youth against experience as Fangio was already in his 40s when he first raced Moss in the early 1950s. The 1956 race was a classic battle between the two drivers, with Moss holding Fangio off to win after an exciting duel in which Fangio set the fastest lap of the race on the last lap in his attempts to catch and overtake Moss. Fangio won the race for the second time in 1957 when Moss crashed out early on.[12] This was to be Fangio's last race at Monaco as he retired the following year. Ironically, Moss also won on his final appearance at Monaco in 1961 when he famously held off the charge of three Ferraris in his Lotus to take the chequered flag; sadly Moss was forced to retire from competitive racing in 1962 as a result of injuries sustained at a crash at Goodwood that brought his career to a premature end.

Over the years the Monaco Grand Prix has produced some classic races and indeed some legendary drivers, none more so than five-times race winner Graham Hill, who dominated the meeting in the 1960s, earning a reputation as the 'King of Monaco'. Hill won the race in 1963, 1964, 1965, 1968 and 1969; these five wins, combined with his race victories at Indianapolis in 1966 and Le Mans in 1972, have seen him go down in history as the only driver to complete the famous Triple Crown of motor sport.[13] Hill also won the Formula One World Championship in 1962 and 1968. In 1969, however, Hill broke both legs in a high-speed crash at Watkins Glen circuit in the USA and was out of racing for many years. He battled back to win Le Mans and to re-enter the Formula One championship; however, he never quite recovered to the standard he displayed before the accident and he announced his retirement after failing to qualify for the 1975 Monaco Grand Prix. Sadly Hill was killed in a light aircraft crash six months later. As mentioned, his son Damon was to follow in his father's footsteps by winning the Formula One World Championship in 1996, but he never emulated his father's achievement of winning the Monaco Grand Prix.

Other drivers of Graham Hill's era who also earned fame at Monaco included Jackie Stewart, who won the race three times (1966, 1971 and 1973) and Austrian Niki Lauda who triumphed there in 1975 and 1976. Lauda, a three-times Formula One World Champion is famous for his comeback from a near fatal accident at the Nürburgring in Germany in 1976 which left him permanently scarred as a result of his car becoming engulfed in flames following the accident. His win for Ferrari in 1975 was the famous Italian manufacturer's first win at Monaco for 20 years. There have been many classic races at Monaco including the 1970 race when Jochen Rindt won from the fourth row of the grid after a fierce battle with Jack Brabham and Jackie Stewart as well as the 1972 race when Jean-Pierre Beltoise won with a brilliant drive in extremely wet conditions. The 1981 race was won by Gilles Villeneuve in an ill-handling Ferrari that only a driver with his artistic car control could have achieved success with. Villeneuve was popular with the Ferrari fans due to his fearless driving style and it was a great loss to the sport when he was killed at the 1982 Belgian Grand Prix; since then the Ferrari Number 27 car has always been associated with his personage. Gilles's son Jacques Villeneuve also became a famous racing driver, winning the Indianapolis 500 and the Indycar championship in 1995 and the Formula One World Championship in 1997. The younger Villeneuve, however, has never won the Monaco Grand Prix despite having competed in it ten times to date.

From 1984 until 1993 the Monaco Grand Prix was won by only two drivers, Frenchman Alain Prost and Brazilian Ayrton Senna. The rivalry between these two drivers was legendary. Prost, who won the race four times (1984, 1985, 1986 and 1988), has said that the Monaco Grand Prix was his favourite event due to the mythical status of the race and the concentration, finesse and tactics required to win it. His great rival Ayrton Senna won the race six times (1987, 1989, 1990, 1991, 1992 and 1993), a record that still stands, and had it not been for his death in the 1994 San Marino Grand Prix he would probably have gone on to win the race on several more occasions. A three-times Formula One world champion, Senna is regarded by many as being the greatest Formula One driver of all time: his car control was unequalled and in wet conditions his skill has never been matched. His five successive wins at Monaco will probably never be equalled. Ironically, like Juan Manuel Fangio and Stirling Moss before him, Senna was to win the final time he competed at Monaco in 1993. However, his 1992 race victory was probably his finest and most satisfying of all. The Williams-Renault of Nigel Mansell was dominant that year, with the McLaren-Honda being driven by Senna no match for it. Senna's mastery of the Monaco track, however, and his car control enabled him to beat Mansell in a memorable race. The last six laps of the race have gone down in the motor racing hall of fame as Mansell, in a much quicker car, caught Senna by two seconds a lap after a late pit stop for new tyres; but despite his best efforts he could find no way past Senna. The talented Brazilian used all his considerable talent to keep Mansell at bay and win the race.[14]

Senna's brilliance at Monaco has been put down to his incredible car control and his ability to carry speed through the tight corners of the circuit as well as his ability to weave his way through back markers and traffic quickly and efficiently. Senna's mantle as 'the greatest driver on the planet' was claimed by Michael Schumacher, who won the Monaco Grand Prix five times to equal Graham Hill's record (1994, 1995, 1997, 1999 and 2001) as well as the Formula One World Championship a record seven times. Motor racing enthusiasts find it a great pity that Senna and Schumacher never raced each other in their prime as Schumacher was still in the early stages of his career in Formula One when Senna was killed. Schumacher's five world titles and three Monaco wins with Ferrari have forever made him a legend with the Ferrari *tifosi* fans both in Italy and around the world. He also holds the lap record at Monaco as well as the record for the most Grand Prix race wins of all time, 91, a number of records that are sure to last for many years to come. Schumacher's win at Monaco in 1997 was the first win for Ferrari at the circuit since the great Gilles Villeneuve won there in 1981. Other notable races in recent years at Monaco include 1996, which was won by Frenchman Olivier Panis from 14th on the grid in a race where only four cars finished, and the 2003 race, which was won by Colombian Juan Pablo Montoya to put alongside his Indianapolis 500 victory in 2000 and make him the only active driver who could equal Graham Hill's feat of capturing the Triple Crown of motor sport.

The nature of the Monaco circuit, at which the speeds are lower than at other Grand Prix tracks, has resulted in fewer fatal crashes over the years, but the tight nature of the circuit and the challenge of the elevation changes and the contrast between light and dark on the exit from the famous tunnel have led to many spectacular crashes over the years. The two most notable collisions in the history of the race came in 1955 and 1965 when on both occasions cars flew off the circuit into the harbour. In 1955 two-times Formula One world champion and Italian racing legend Alberto Ascari missed a chicane and crashed his Ferrari into the water of Monaco harbour, miraculously escaping unharmed. Tragically, however, Ascari was killed only four days later on 26 May 1955 in a testing crash at the Monza circuit near Milan, Italy. The second time that a car found its way into the harbour at Monaco was during the 1965 race when Australia driver Paul Hawkins accomplished the feat after spinning out of control. Hawkins was unharmed in the crash, which has been immortalised in film as footage of the crash was used in the 1966 film entitled *Grand Prix*.[15]

To date there have only ever been two fatal crashes at the Monaco circuit. In 1952 Italian driver Luigi Fagioli was killed in a crash while practising for a support race during the Grand Prix weekend; a veteran of the Monaco Grand Prix Fagioli had won the 1935 race driving a Mercedes-Benz and was 54 years of age when he lost his life. The second fatal crash at Monaco also involved an Italian driver when Lorenzo Bandini died at the wheel of his Ferrari during the 1967 race. Bandini was running second in the race when he lost control of his car and overturned following contact with the guard rail; the Ferrari's fuel tank erupted and ignited a number of straw bales at the side of the track, resulting in an inferno that tragically claimed Bandini's life.[16] In 1992 the Lorenzo Bandini trophy was established in Brisighella, Italy to be presented annually to an outstanding figure from the world of motor racing and someone who best displayed Bandini's spirit and passion for motor racing.

Following Bandini's crash, thanks largely to safety measures introduced into Formula One during the 1970s, there were to be no more fatal crashes at Monaco, though there were some spectacular ones. These included the first corner crash in

1980 when Derek Daly's Tyrell was catapulted into the air before crashing down on both his teammate Jean-Pierre Jarier and the McLaren of Alain Prost; or the fiery collision between Nelson Piquet and Ricardo Patrese at Sainte Devote in 1985. In 1994 however, the Formula One fraternity came to Monaco in a state of shock following the death of three-times Formula One World Champion Ayrton Senna at the previous Grand Prix at San Marino. During practice for the race itself Austrian driver Karl Wendlinger lost control coming out of the famous tunnel close to the harbour at Monaco and hit the wall sideways with considerable force. Wendlinger was knocked unconscious in the crash, suffering serious head injuries; he eventually recovered after being in a coma in hospital for weeks.[17]

The Monaco Grand Prix is representative of everything that attracts drivers and spectators to motor racing – speed, glamour, excitement and prestige. The location for the race in the principality of Monaco on the French Riviera with its long association with the rich and famous has made it an ideal setting for the glitz and glamour of Formula One. The winner of the race is presented with their trophy each year by the ruling monarch of the Grimaldi family, while the race has been run during the reign of three monarchs, Louis II, Rainier III and Albert II. The race grew both as a result of its location but also because of its association with Formula One, the most popular form of motor racing in the world. Monaco is the one Grand Prix that every driver wants to win above all the rest of the races on the Formula One calendar and over the years some of the greatest drivers in history have dominated the event, including such as Nuvolari, Fangio, Moss, Hill, Stewart, Prost, Senna and Schumacher, who have all found fame on the streets of Monaco.

The 24 Hours of Le Mans

The 24 Hours of Le Mans is a French sports car endurance race which was first run in 1923. It is the oldest and arguably most prestigious sports car race in the world and has attracted drivers and car manufacturers from all over the world during its long history. The race has made the name Le Mans synonymous with motor racing and in particular with sports car racing. The race itself lasts for a 24-hour period, testing not only the speed of the car and the ability of the driver but more importantly the durability and reliability of the vehicle. Designed to test the robustness of the car, the 24 Hours of Le Mans is an endurance race where speed is not the most important factor and, as a result of this, the car manufacturers take the plaudits at Le Mans as much, if not more so, than the drivers. This quest for victory at Le Mans has led to many technical innovations over the years from the car manufacturers as they attempt to successfully combine speed and reliability in pursuit of victory.

The track at Le Mans is also very different from many other circuits in that it incorporates both permanent racetrack as well as public roads and has traditionally had some of the longest straights of any racetrack in the world. Since the inaugural event in 1923 the circuit has undergone many changes, mainly as a result of safety concerns. For many years the track included the famous Mulsanne straight which was 3.7 miles (6 km) in length. The sheer expanse of this straight made it extremely dangerous and saw top speeds soar over the years, with the Peugeot team breaking the 250 miles per hour barrier in 1988.[18] As a result of these increases in speed along the straight, the track was modified, with more chicanes and bends introduced to reduce speeds. The fact that the track also includes both permanent racetrack and public roads presents an additional difficulty for drivers as the public roads tend to have a much more uneven surface than the racetrack, leading to handling problems as well as reduced grip, which increases the reflexes and car handling skills required from the drivers.

The race normally consists of approximately 50 cars, though in some years the entry list has been significantly less, with only 17 cars entering in 1930, for example. As well as there being one overall winner there are also a number of other classifications in the field divided by engine size and so on: this keeps the racing competitive throughout the field. In the early days of Le Mans most entries consisted of two competitors, though in some instances drivers attempted the race distance single-handedly, a feat that was banned following a crash in 1955. Nowadays most car entries list three drivers, with no individual allowed to drive for more than 14 hours and only four consecutive hours racing permitted in any one stint.

The first 24 Hours of Le Mans was held on the 26 and 27 May 1923 and began with the waving of a French tricolour, a tradition that still exists today. There had been earlier races at Le Mans, most notably the French Grand Prix as far back as 1911, but this new sports car endurance race represented something different. It was the brainchild of George Durand, general secretary of Automobile Club de l'Ouest; Charles Faroux, the editor of French motoring magazine *La Vie Automobile*; and industrialist Emile Coquile. The first race drew 33 competitors, almost exclusively French apart from two Belgian entries. The race was run in poor weather and won by Andre Lagache and Rene Leonard driving a French-manufactured Chenard & Walcker car.[19] From 1924 onwards the race was changed to its now traditional mid-June date in order to allow for better weather conditions and more hours of daylight. As the race became established in the early years it drew a more international field, with Italian, British and American entries competing from as early as 1925. This growing international dimension to the race is highlighted by the fact that following the 1926 win by the French-manufactured Lorraine-Dietrich team a French car would not win the race again until 1937. The Le Mans races of the late 1920s were dominated by British manufacturer Bentley, who won four consecutive races between 1927 and 1930. This Bentley dominance led to the growth of fierce competition between manufacturers, with both Bugatti and Alfa-Romeo at the forefront of technical innovation in order to make their cars faster and more reliable for Le Mans. The 1931 race was famous for the duel between Alfa-Romeo and Bugatti, with the Italian Alfa-Romeo team triumphing over its French rival. The 1933 race is another that has gone down in the motor racing hall of fame as a 'classic', with 1932 Monaco Grand Prix winner and motorcycling legend Tazio Nuvolari competing for the first and only time at Le Mans. Driving an Alfa-Romeo, Nuvolari and team-mate Raymond Sommer won an exhilarating race in which the lead changed hands no fewer than three times on the final lap. By the late 1930s Bentley, with five wins, and Alfa-Romeo, with four, had stamped their mark of authority on Le Mans. However, the spectre of war loomed over Europe and there were no races held at the famous circuit between 1939 and 1949. The Le Mans circuit was used as a base by the RAF early in the war,m but when France fell to Germany the Luftwaffe used the circuit as an airfield and it was heavily bombed, ironically by the RAF.[20]

Due to the nature of the 24 Hours of Le Mans a great deal of emphasis is placed on the car as well as the driver. This is partly because car manufacturers have slightly more design freedom at Le Mans than in other racing series such as Formula One or Indy Car Racing, where cars must all conform to similar chassis, design and engine regulations. While regulations exist at Le Mans, notably in regard to engines, the car manufacturers have more freedom in car design. Manufacturers therefore see the race as an opportunity to prove that their sports cars are both fast and reliable and therefore a much better product than those offered by their competitors in the race and also in the wider marketplace. Thus in the minds of sports car manufacturers the race at Le Mans presents the best possible stage to advertise and prove the speed and reliability of their cars. As a result of this, the history of Le Mans over the years is very much the history of fierce competition between famous car manufacturers.

The first race at Le Mans following the Second World War signalled the arrival on the scene of arguably the most famous sports car manufacturer of them all, the legendary Ferrari team. Ferrari won the 1949 race in a car driven by Luigi Chinetti and Peter Mitchell-Thomson. Enzo Ferrari had founded Scuderia-Ferrari in 1928 in Maranello, Italy, and the team quickly became noted for its racing cars. The Ferrari cars are today famous all over the world, with the 'prancing horse' emblem instantly recognisable. Enzo Ferrari claimed he used the prancing horse or *cavallino rampante* in honour of Italian First World War flying ace Count Francesco Baracca, who was killed in action and who also used the *cavallino rampante* as his emblem.[21] The 1949 win for Ferrari at Le Mans was the start of a long tradition at the race that has yielded nine victories to date. The 1950s became known as the 'golden age of Le Mans', with Ferrari and also famous manufacturers such as Jaguar and Mercedes-Benz bringing glitz and glamour to the race as competition between these marques was fierce. Ferrari and Jaguar dominated the race until the mid-1960s, with Ferrari winning an unprecedented six races in a row, including victories for Formula One world champions Phil Hill and Jochen Rindt as well as famous Italian driver Lorenzo Bandini.[22]

Ferrari's dominance was challenged in the mid-1960s by the powerful American car giant Ford, which had set its sights on winning the race in order to show the might of American race car technology. This was a target that it achieved in 1966, and it went on to win the race for the following three years as well. Its 1967 race win over Ferrari was notable for the fact that Indy 500 winner A.J. Foyt added a Le Mans win to his CV and his co-driver Dan Gurney, a two time Indy runner up, famously sprayed a bottle of champagne on the podium after the race – the first time that this was done and a tradition that is still enacted at motor races around the world today. The most successful manufacturer ever at Le Mans, however, is German marquee Porsche with 13 wins to date. Porsche emerged in the late 1960s and won its first Le Mans in 1970 with Hans Hermann and Richard Attwood. Porsche cars quickly became popular among drivers and teams at Le Mans with 37 of the 49 starters in the 1971 race driving Porsches. This was the start of a long tradition for Porsche at Le Mans, a tradition that still survives today, as alongside Ferrari, Porsche is the most recognisable household name in the world of sports car production. Many of the successful drivers in the history of Le Mans have won the race driving a Porsche; these include Jacky Ickx, Derek Bell, Michele Alboreto and Tom Kristensen, for example. Other manufacturers to have made an impact at Le Mans include Audi, which has been dominant in the twenty-first century, winning eight races, and French marquee Peugeot. Interestingly only one Japanese manufacturer has ever won the race, that sole victory coming in 1991 for Mazda.

The powerful Japanese manufacturers of Honda and Toyota have yet to make a concerted effort to win at Le Mans despite being extremely successful in other forms of motor racing.

The dangers of racing at Le Mans have been acutely highlighted over the years and none more than at the tragic 1955 race. During this race the Mercedes-Benz of Pierre Levegh collided with the Jaguar of Mike Hawthorn, which resulted in Levegh's car becoming airborne and crashing into the grandstands killing both Levegh and over 80 spectators.[23] The high rate of fatalities was as a result of the fuel tank on the Mercedes exploding. It is the worst motor racing accident in history in terms of fatalities and one that had far-reaching consequences for the Le Mans race. In the immediate aftermath of the crash all motor racing was banned in France, Germany and Switzerland until essential safety work was carried out at racetracks. Such was the negative reaction to motor racing in the aftermath of the crash that the ban on motor racing in Switzerland still stands to this day. The race also had a crushing effect on Mercedes, with the German manufacturer withdrawing from all forms of motor sport for the next 30 years as a result of negative publicity following the crash.

There had been fatal crashes at Le Mans before 1955, most notably the death of Marius Mestivier in the 1925 race; the collision that killed both Pat Fairchild and Rene Kippeurth during the 1937 race; and the fatal crashes of Jean Lariviere in 1951 and Tom Cole in 1953. However, the loss of so many lives in 1955 and the fact that the vast majority were spectators made safety more of an issue. As a result, safety for spectators became paramount and tracks and grandstands were improved significantly over the next number of years. Racing was still dangerous for drivers, however, as illustrated by the fatal crashes of successful sports car racer Lloyd Casner at Le Mans in 1965 as well as the deaths of experienced Formula One drivers Walt Hausgen (1966), Lucien Bianchi (1969) and Jo Bonnier (1972) in crashes at the Le Mans 24 Hours. Safety was improved for drivers after the 1971 first lap crash that claimed the life of amateur driver John Woolfe. This year marked the last use of the so-called 'Le Mans race start', where the drivers would run to their cars, jump in and drive off as quickly as possible. In an effort to save time many drivers did not secure their safety belts until the second or third lap. This practice led directly to the death of John Woolfe on the first lap of the 1971 race and the decision of the race organisers to end this type of race start. There have been fewer fatal crashes in recent years, but competing at Le Mans is still extremely dangerous, as illustrated by the tragic death of Austrian Formula One driver Jo Gartner during the 1986 race and the death of much-heralded young French driver Sebastien Enjolras, who was killed in a qualifying crash in 1997 at the age of only 21.[24]

Despite the ever-present dangers of the Le Mans 24 Hours the race has always attracted the best drivers from around the world. As well as sports car specialists, drivers from other series are drawn to the race because of its challenge and prestige. One of the earliest 'celebrity drivers' to enter Le Mans was Italian motor racer Tazio Nuvolari, who took part in the 1933 race. Nuvolari was a household name at the time, having won the 1932 Monaco Grand Prix and being the reigning European champion in Grand Prix motor racing. He had also proved himself in endurance racing by winning the famous Mille Miglia, a one-thousand-mile open road endurance race that took place in Italy from 1927 until 1957. In his only ever appearance at Le Mans, Nuvolari won the 1933 race in an Alfa Romeo to secure his reputation as the greatest driver of his generation. Other Grand Prix drivers would follow in Nuvolari's footsteps including 1961 Formula One world champion, Phil Hill, who won Le Mans in 1958, 1961 and 1962. As the only US-born Formula One world champion to date, it is ironic that Hill never competed in the Indianapolis 500. The 1955 Monaco Grand Prix winner Maurice Trintignant won the Le Mans 24 hours in 1954 and 1958 but never competed at Indianapolis. The 1970 Formula One world champion Jochen Rindt won the Le Mans 24 Hours in 1965 and raced in the 1968 and 1969 Indianapolis 500s without success before winning the Monaco Grand Prix in 1970. Tragically, however, Rindt was killed in practice for the 1970 Italian Grand Prix, making him the only posthumous Formula One world champion in history. Other notable Grand Prix drivers to triumph at Le Mans include New Zealander Bruce McLaren, who won Le Mans in 1966, having previously won the Monaco Grand Prix in 1962. Sadly McLaren never got the chance to compete for the Triple Crown of motor sport at Indianapolis as he was killed in a crash at Goodwood in England in 1970.

It was 1972 before a driver managed to win all three events in the Triple Crown, British driver Graham Hill becoming the first, and so far only, man to achieve this accolade. Having previously won the Monaco Grand Prix a record five times (1963, 1964, 1965, 1968 and 1969) and having won the Indianapolis 500 in 1966 Hill triumphed in the 1972 Le Mans 24 Hours Race driving a French-manufactured Mantra along with teammate Henri Pescarolo – a unique record that has so far lasted for 38 years. Belgian Formula One driver Jacky Ickx was to achieve significant success at Le Mans, winning the race six times, a record that stood for 26 years. Despite a long Formula One career, which included 120 race starts and eight wins, Ickx was never fortunate enough to win at Monaco, a fact that again highlights just how impressive Graham Hill's feat of winning all three Triple Crown races actually is. The skill required to win in one racing category does not always translate itself into wins in the other racing series, which makes the adaptability to win at all three circuits unique. This is also highlighted by the fact that the most successful driver ever at Le Mans with eight wins is sports car specialist Tom Kristensen from Denmark, who has never competed in Formula One or at Indianapolis. Kristensen has won the race eight times to date, between 1997 and 2008, which illustrates again that some drivers can be dominant in one particular series but this does not necessarily mean that they have the skills required to win at all three Triple Crown events. One ex-Formula One driver who is still chasing a Le Mans win is 1995 Indianapolis 500 winner and 1997 Formula One world champion Jacques Villeneuve, who came second in the 2008 Le Mans 24 Hours. Such is the lure of the race that he has vowed to keep returning to Le Mans until he wins the race in order to complete his own unique triple crown.

The race has established itself to such an extent over the years that the very name Le Mans conjures up images of intense endurance motor racing. The race has pervaded all forms of popular culture, from film and television to books and computer games. The rich heritage that it has established as the most famous sports car race in the world has ensured its continued survival over the years and has made it the third great race in the 'Triple Crown'. The fact that it is an endurance sports car race makes it more alluring than its two illustrious open-wheel equivalents at Indianapolis and Monaco and arguably it gives the 'Triple Crown' an added dimension by making reliability and endurance as important as outright speed.

Conclusion

There can be little doubt therefore over the merits of these three races to justifiably lay claim to the combined title of the greatest motor races on earth. They are the most important and prestigious events in the most popular motor racing categories and series in the world, therefore guaranteeing their accepted status. Known as the 'Triple Crown of motor racing', they can be collectively analysed as one because of their long-standing tradition and shared history in the development of motor racing.

There is a tendency within sport to combine a number of sporting victories together in order to elevate an achievement to legendary status – double- or treble-winning football teams for example, or Grand Slam victories in tennis. The combined victories propel each individual victory into something more significant in sporting terms. Sports such as horse racing and rugby have long-established Triple Crown events. In thoroughbred horse racing, for example, in the United Kingdom since 1853 the 2000 Guineas Stakes, the Epsom Derby and the St Leger Stakes have made up the 'Triple Crown of horse racing' while in the United States, the Kentucky Derby, the Preakness Stakes and the Belmont Stakes have been recognised as constituting a triple crown since 1923.

The same is true in rugby union with England, Ireland, Scotland and Wales having contested a Triple Crown since 1894. To achieve the 'rugby union Triple Crown' one side must beat the other three in the Six Nations Championship which is held annually and also now involves France and Italy. Ironically, there was no trophy for winning the rugby union Triple Crown until 2006 and it was known for many years as the 'invisible trophy'. Despite this, however, it was one of the most sought-after achievements in world rugby. The figurative use of the term 'Triple Crown' as a badge of honour did not lessen the significance of winning the rugby union Triple Crown; if anything, it made the achievement more important due to the tradition upon which it was based. This can also be applied to the Triple Crown of motor racing: there is no trophy to be awarded for winning all three races, yet drivers desperately want to win the three events because of the prestige attached to this achievement.

Despite the differences in each race there are a number of common themes that bind the three events together. While driving styles and race tactics differ between each, outright speed and phenomenal car control are required to win any of the races. Winning all three displays a talent for speed and car control combined with an adaptability to modify racecraft and driving style, which can only be achieved by a world-class racing driver at the top of his game. The three races can be examined as one due to the fact that they are the most prestigious and important races in open-wheel and sports car racing, the two motor racing categories with the widest popular appeal. Representing some of the oldest motor racing events on the planet, these three races can justifiably be used to analyse the history of motor racing due to the overlap of racing drivers and car manufacturers in the three events throughout their history. The fact that each Triple Crown event has attracted the best drivers and car manufacturers in the world means that there can be no proper analysis of the achievements of these drivers and marques without examining their performances in totality in both open-wheel racing and sports car racing. As the most important races in these two motor racing categories are incorporated into the Triple Crown of motor racing, it therefore represents a perfect stage for the examination of any history of world motor racing.

These three famous races each bring their own unique features and characteristics to the fore. The Indianapolis 500 is a cultural icon in the United States and for many it is representative of the American spirit and American identity, while the Monaco Grand Prix also plays a key role in the sporting and cultural identity of the small principality of Monaco. The circuits at which the three races take place all differ markedly – from the high speeds of the banked oval at Indianapolis to the narrow tight streets of Monaco and the combination of racing track and public roads at Le Mans. It is the different nature of the circuits that makes each race so challenging and which makes the feat of winning all three so commendable. These Triple Crown events are representative of all the elements which together make motor racing so popular: high speeds, exciting circuits, glamorous locations, advanced technology and bravery and car control from the drivers. Despite the various differences between each race they are linked through their established heritage and tradition. It is these elements, together with the adaptability required from drivers who attempt to win all three races, that make the Triple Crown of motor sport such a prestigious and uniquely challenging undertaking.

Notes

1. Kramer, *Indianapolis Motor Speedway*, 13.
2. Reed, *The Race and Ritual of the Indianapolis 500*, 58.
3. Ibid., 233.
4. Kramer, *Indianapolis Motor Speedway*, 197.
5. Reed, *The Race and Ritual of the Indianapolis 500*, 174.
6. Collings, *The New Villeneuve*, 165
7. Reed, *The Race and Ritual of the Indianapolis 500*, 104
8. Allen and Mansell, *Nigel Mansell*, 349.
9. Lehbrink and Schlegelmilch, *Grand Prix de Monaco*, 11.
10. Ibid., 35.
11. Ibid., 75.
12. Donaldson, *Fangio*, 264.
13. Lehbrink and Schlegelmilch, *Grand Prix de Monaco*, 159.
14. Hilton, *Ayrton Senna*, 110.
15. *Grand Prix*, directed by John Frankenheimer. Metro-Goldwyn-Mayer, 1966.
16. Williams, *Enzo Ferrari*, 245.
17. Watkins, *Life at the Limit*, 175.
18. Blumlein, *Le Mans*, 51.
19. Ibid., 2.
20. Ibid., 21.
21. Williams, *Enzo Ferrari*, 25.
22. Clarke, *Le Mans*, 149.
23. Donaldson, *Fangio*, 231.
24. Blumlein, *Le Mans*, 61.

References

Allen, J. and N. Mansell. *Nigel Mansell*. London: CollinsWillow, 1995.
Blumlein, David. *Le Mans: A History*. London: Bookman Publications, 2003.
Bretzel, Giacomo. *Grand Prix de Monaco Historique*. Paris: Somogy, 2001.
Clarke, R.M. *Le Mans: The Ferrari Years 1958–1965*. Cobham: Brooklands Books, 2004.
Collings, Timothy. *The New Villeneuve*. London: Bloomsbury Publishing, 1997.
Donaldson, Gerald. *Fangio: The Life Behind the Legend*. London: Virgin Books, 2009.
Hilton, Christopher. *Ayrton Senna*. Nordiska: Haynes Publishing, 1994.
Holder, Bill. *The History of the Indianapolis 500*. Philadelphia, PA: Bison Group, 1992.
Kramer, Ralph. *Indianapolis Motor Speedway: 100 Years of Racing*. Lola, WI: Krause Publications, 2009.
Laban, Brian. *Le Mans 24 Hours: The Complete Story of the World's Most Famous Motor Race*. London: Virgin Books, 2001.

Lehbrink, Hartmut and Rainer. Schlegelmilch. *Grand Prix de Monaco*. Oldenburg: Konemann, 1998.

Reed, Terry. *The Race and Ritual of the Indianapolis 500*. Washington, DC: Potomac Books, 2005.

Tipler, John. *Graham Hill: Master of Motorsport*. Derby: Breedon Books, 2002.

Wagstaff, Ian. *The British at Le Mans: 85 Years of Endeavour*. London: Motor Racing Publications, 2006.

Watkins, Sid. *Life at the Limit: Triumph and Tragedy in Formula One*. London: Macmillan, 1997.

Williams, Richard. *Enzo Ferrari: A Life*. London: Yellow Jersey Press, 2002.

NASCAR Stock Car Racing: Establishment and Southern Retrenchment

Ben Shackleford

Independent scholar

Stock Car racing within the United States emerged as a national phenomenon fostered by two main competing organizations, the National Association for Stock Car Automobile Racing (NASCAR) and the Competition Board of the American Automobile Association (AAA). As initial success waned, the stock car format found revitalization where the violence and danger of the sport resonated with growing idealization of the traditional Southern culture.

On 14 December 1947 a group of drivers, mechanics and racing promoters gathered in the Ebony Lounge of the Streamline Hotel in Daytona Beach, Florida, to discuss the future of production-based automobile racing in the United States. Through advertisements placed in various motor sport publications, they were invited by racing promoter Bill France to agree a system of rules for a new production-based championship series.[1] Because most of the attendees knew each other through racing competition or joint promotional ventures, it was as much a social event as a business meeting. Among the community of racers these activities often overlapped, so the idea of gathering to discuss racing in a resort town combined business and pleasure in the same way as racing.[2] Throughout the four-day meeting, a free-flowing keg of beer kept everyone in friendly spirits and open to new ideas.[3] The result of this meeting was the formation of a businesslike sanctioning agency for professional production-based racing in the United States, the National Association of Stock Car Automobile Racing or NASCAR. How this organisation came into being and how it managed technological change, differentiated the business of sanctioning stock car races from existing racing authorities and facilitated the creation of competitive spectacle is the core of the NASCAR story.

At the time of the meeting and indeed since the dawn of motor sport in the United States, there was another, larger sanctioning body to contend with. In 1947, the Contest Board of the American Automobile Association (AAA) was, like most institutions, returning to normality after the Second World War. In the wake of hostilities, the racing business was booming. Though the AAA was aware of the tremendous demand for automobile racing, it was unwilling to sanction events using production-based equipment. Indeed, a bulletin issued by the AAA Contest Board on 7 January 1948 acknowledged the dearth of race cars to meet the needs of competitors and thus the expectations of fans. Yet even though this communiqué relates that 'Based on information given the Board by those actively participating in automobile racing from all sections of the country, it was quite evident that there was a shortage of racing equipment during the past season', there was no move to accept production-based chassis for speedway competition.[4] Indeed the AAA seemed little interested in letting the so-called 'jalopies' occupy even the margins of motor sport.

The same bulletin also stated that "There is no change in the policy of the Board with respect to the sanction and supervision of stock car racing events'. The AAA emphasised that it would

> only issue our sanction for stock car racing events which were limited to cars of strictly stock status. We will not issue sanctions for the 'so-called' stock car races which permit all types of modifications of the engine and chassis. It is our feeling that these races contribute in no way whatsoever to the benefit of the motoring public.[5]

Though they would permit the use of modified production engines in competition, these engines had to be installed in what they considered 'real racecars', built on special chassis. By insisting on sanctioning only races using purpose-built cars, the AAA Contest Board rejected a vast group of dedicated and capable racers working the smaller tracks across the nation. For entrepreneur Bill France, its refusal to deal with any racing that smacked of mass-production was a stroke of tremendous good fortune. Organising these racers into a national series was left to the men gathered in the Streamline Motel and others like them.

With his opening remarks on the first day of the meeting in 1947, France outlined his perspective on how production-based automobile racing could become a respectable and profitable sport for drivers, mechanics, car owners and racing promoters alike. He referred to a 'golden age' of stock car racing when factories would sponsor racing teams to travel around the nation promoting their brand.[6] He spent a considerable amount of time describing the state of chaos that stock car racing had descended into before the Second World War. During this time, the racing business was, at best, a gamble. According to France, who was a race promoter before 1941, drivers seldom knew if prizes would be paid, promoters rarely knew if drivers would show for a race, and there were no consistent procedural rules or technical specifications.[7] On all but the highest levels it was a sport created and carried out largely on an ad hoc basis.[8]

After offering a brief biography on his qualifications as a racer and experience as a promoter, France turned to the heart of his opening comments: his plans for managing the creation of a national production-based racing series. He began by describing the advantages offered by creating a national championship series. He argued that racers would be free to travel around and compete at different venues if they could rely on a uniform set of rules to prevent disparity between race vehicles. The criteria governing vehicle specifications had evolved differently in different regions. Lack of uniformity between race cars from different regions kept racing local and comparatively 'small-time'. What racers and promoters didn't want was technological disparity to ruin competition, but numerous local sets of rules did stifle competition. While these differences between rules might have been inconsequential, the perception of technological inequity was enough to keep racers from travelling to a race where they stood less chance of winning or needed to invest in extra equipment to meet different specifications. To illustrate this point, France asserted that a fast driver in an average car would always lose to an average driver in a 'hot' car.[9] The idea was to produce a formula describing the race vehicles that permitted the maximum number of competitors to enter machines of near equal specification.

Based more on keeping racing machines economical than on the reality of what came off production lines, this stance had tremendous long-term ramifications. Once established, this fundamental principle would permit NASCAR, over the course of the next 30 years, to develop an inexpensive 'stock' race vehicle appropriate to the task of resembling a true production car while racing at very high speeds. By borrowing components freely from the production line and the after-market while stemming costly investment in technical novelty, Bill France was opening a crucial area for interpretation of the rules. Ultimately this practice removed absolute control over the technology of competition from the auto makers and secured management of the racing technology for NASCAR.

Beyond providing NASCAR with leverage to control the NASCAR stock car championship, this stance also had ramifications for the public face of motor sport. France's theory of regulation suggested that serving the public need as a race organiser was more about providing entertainment than providing a test or exhibition of genuine production cars. This attitude set NASCAR apart from the AAA, whose rulebook indicated that 'the Contest Board ... found opportunity to render a service greater than its founder envisioned. Under its supervision automobiles and their engineering were tried in races, tours, hill climbs and other tests, and this great laboratory process helped produce the great cars we have today.'[10] Though NASCAR would use the rhetoric of 'the track as a laboratory', its rules made clear that any testing function of competition was subordinate to cultivating entertaining racing.

After the first day of the meeting to form NASCAR, it was clear that the only factors preventing stock car racing from becoming a success were regularisation, integration and respectability. The points outlined by Bill France all focused on creating a legitimate, professional sporting series out of production-based racing. Regularisation would come with rules, schedules and procedures to bring about the consistent production of close competition between equivalent racing cars. Accepting and organising existing grass-roots racing enterprises would integrate the participants of production-based racing into an informal system that fed talent to the top tiers while reaping profits throughout the lower levels. In addition to bringing in capital and cultivating new talent, this structure helped focus attention on NASCAR as the single entity responsible for organising production-based racing in the United States. These first two issues dealt more with people already committed to racing production-based vehicles and as such success could be realised largely through organisation. Cultivating respect for production-based racing dealt with shifting the attitudes of fans and the general public and was a more complex matter.

Respectability, an issue that went to the core of production-based racing and more established forms of purpose-built racing, would take more time to build. The massive task of organising and administrating races at the grass-roots level nationwide would help gather respect. In addition, standardised rules and a regular schedule of events could enhance the credibility of NASCAR. Yet these instrumental issues would not negate the considerable power exercised by the AAA, the organisation competing with the NASCAR for control over racing in the United States. For France one crucial aspect of respectability – not shared by all meeting attendees – was the exterior appearance of the cars. Though unforeseen, this issue would ultimately find resolution with the creation of the Grand National stock car championship as the top tier of production-based racing. Respectability among the fans meant having the sort of clean, well-maintained machinery the 'average person' could identify with. Competition with such cars would fill the stands of race events with those eager to see close competition between racing drivers in machines similar to those on the showroom floor. In choosing the strictly stock format, NASCAR chose the arena for struggle with AAA over legitimate racing in America.

Nationwide ubiquity on the scale described by France and in NASCAR's rules had never been attempted in motor sport. During the second year of operation, NASCAR, on all three levels of competition, sanctioned more races than the AAA Contest Board across all the levels that the latter sanctioned.[11] Creating this sort of scale of regulation over such a short period of time was only possible because smaller racing leagues existed to be unified and because automobile mass production allowed material uniformity across the nation.

Apparently the bulk of meeting attendees at the Streamline Motel agreed with Bill France's assertion that mechanical ubiquity and technological parity translated into good competition on tracks full of economical race cars. The work of the technical committee amounted to 35 statements governing the construction of a stock car for NASCAR competition.[12] Rules permitted the use of any cylinder head, as suggested by Bill France, and even the use of hot-rod components such as superchargers and magneto ignition.[13] Even though it would be a year until the 'strictly stock' racing began, the pattern for regulating competition was set. NASCAR levelled the playing field by mandating similar equipment based on cost, not origin. This attention to uniformity and economy helped fill the field with race cars without arousing resistance from race promoters.

Though the mythology surrounding NASCAR's creation often suggests that introducing 'strictly stock' racing was a unified, long-term plan conceived and executed by Bill France, there was no mention of racing 'strictly stock' cars during the organisational meeting. While it is possible that France planned to introduce the strictly stock format from the beginning, he did not share these plans with the racers gathered in Daytona.[14] What seems more likely is that France introduced the strictly stock format in 1949 as much as a means of fielding a group of respectable-looking newer cars and of distinguishing NASCAR from existing forms of 'modified' and 'sportsman' classes. The eventual shift to strictly stock, through starting with specifications created by manufacturers, would also prove an easy way of creating a baseline from which rules governing the parameters of race cars evolved.

For those meeting at the Streamline, the parameters of car construction had more to do with existing conventions built by 'modified' and 'sportsmen' competition on tracks across the country. After agreeing on the details of competition, rules governing car construction and guidelines for a competitive schedule on Monday, Tuesday and Wednesday were reserved for creation of a points scheme whereby the champions on each tier would be established. A championship based on total points awarded for finishing positions over the course of a racing season was not novel. AAA racers in the Championship, Sprint and Midget series had been run in pursuit of a national championship for decades. However, the NASCAR points system proposed by driver Red Byron, and adopted late on the Wednesday afternoon awarded points and money more deeply into the field of finishers than other established series.[15] The points system was linked directly to the system of payout for each race and rewarded consistency in competition almost as much as victory. Unlike the AAA, where points were offered to the top 12 finishers in large events, NASCAR awarded points to the first 22 finishers.[16] The relatively 'flat' distribution of points leading to the NASCAR championship favoured consistent participation and had the effect of encouraging drivers to compete in the maximum number of events. Because pay was to be distributed relative to points, NASCAR racers also enjoyed distribution of pay deep into the ranks of competitors. Spreading the proceeds among the racers, even if it meant giving less money to the top finishers, made racing a possible career for entrepreneurial driver/owners. In contrast to the patron/professional operator format of AAA racing (an arrangement reminiscent of thoroughbred horse racing), NASCAR's relatively flat distribution of points and money throughout the ranks helped keep more competitors of limited means financially viable. Although it would take a lot of success to get rich in NASCAR, racers could continue competing because they usually took home some prize money. A widespread distribution of rewards also helped build a cadre of professional racers willing and able to drive a full season.[17]

With the creation of NASCAR, the relationship between motor sport and business was recast. In contrast to the AAA, NASCAR racing was more about providing entertainment than facilitating racing in the public interest. For NASCAR it was important to have close racing and stands full of fans each week. The AAA Contest Board, apparently influenced by the public service and automotive advocacy role played by the AAA, was more interested in simply facilitating the sport of automobile racing. Even the AAA rule book justified racing as an experiment conducted on the behalf of public interest suggesting that

> The need for testing will remain as long as there are cars and a public which buys them. The element of sport which has surrounded the automobile from its earliest days will live. People will always like to witness tests of speed and there will always be adventurous men who enjoy the thrill of participation in them. Adventure, engineering, sportsmanship, fame, fortune careers and scientific testing are combined in automotive competitions as in no other activity in the world.[18]

In contrast, NASCAR promoted races with unapologetic concern for the entertainment aspects of the sport. Though NASCAR did describe its racing as a laboratory for the automakers in Detroit, this was typically proposed as a benefit secondary to entertaining the masses. Entertainment using production-based vehicles that looked like cars straight from the stock of auto makers was their primary mission.

When the Ebony Lounge at the Streamline Motel emptied on the Wednesday evening, the foundation for a stock car racing empire was in place. The rule book resulting from four days of meetings united technological specifications and event scheduling under the auspices of a national championship. Bill France had effectively brought competing promoters into the fold by promising consistent racing action between closely matched cars. By designing an approach that promised to make stock car racing a regularised, integrated, and respectable enterprise, NASCAR was in a position to capitalise on America's growing fascination with fast cars.

The names of the notable drivers, car owners, and promoters that met to form NASCAR were printed on the cover of the 1948 *Rule Book*.[19] Despite this show of solidarity between racers from differing regions with different occupations, in time control over NASCAR and its mandates would become concentrated in Daytona in the hands of NASCAR president Bill France. Just how voluntarily the charter members allowed power to become so concentrated is unknown. It does, however, seem likely that much of the drudgery of starting up a racing series, endless travel, settlement of countless disputes and operating on a shoestring budget was willingly transferred to France.[20] That is to say that he gathered power because he was always on hand to assume responsibility.

In addition to putting in long hours organising, officiating, 'schmoozing' and travelling, concentrating this power was due in no small part to continued, subtle revision of the rule book presided over by Bill France. Over time, the responsibility for decisions about racing procedure and racing equipment was ceded to France and NASCAR. With each subsequent rule book, the list of rules governing procedure and technology lengthened; the list of people responsible for the rules grew shorter.

Most importantly, NASCAR's rule book, though conceived as a yearly set of regulations, became a flexible tool for the exercise of discretionary power. The areas of jurisdiction wherein NASCAR officials (Bill France was the top NASCAR official) could exercise discretionary judgement and change rules at a moment's notice became useful grey areas that permitted on-the-spot manipulation of events in 'the spirit of competition'.[21] In time, the discretion with which decisions could be made broadened until Bill France could alter whole sections of the rule book any time he felt it necessary. While such potential for caprice infuriated many competitors even as it reinforced France's paternalistic management style, it also gave NASCAR the sort of flexibility it would need to rein in headstrong competitors and consistently produce close competition.

Yet extending control over the racers working under NASCAR sanction was not sufficient to guarantee control over stock car racing in the United States. Beyond concerns about meeting the demands of potential fans, Bill France had to be concerned about the larger context of the motor racing world into which NASCAR was born. Even though NASCAR was the first organisation to capitalise on the production-based format on anything like a national scale, it was still the newcomer. The AAA Contest Board claimed the sole right under authority of the *Federation Internationale de l'Automobile* (FIA) 'to authorise and supervise automotive competitions and tests of any kind'[22] and was not amused by the upstart racing group in their 'stock' cars. Just seven months after the first NASCAR strictly stock race in June 1949, the AAA declared war on NASCAR. A press release describing the February meeting of the Contest Board states that 'Effective immediately the contest board will sanction and supervise legitimate stock car racing events on tracks one mile or more in length where a creditable race can be held under approved racing conditions and only by accredited AAA promoters.'[23]. This decree, using language suggesting that NASCAR racing was not legitimate or creditable, drew the AAA into direct competition with NASCAR.

Though the AAA had long maintained specifications for 'strictly stock' cars, these standards were largely reserved for vehicles competing in performance trials. In keeping with the AAA perspective of public service, these trials and speed runs were conducted with laboratory precision, not the competitive gusto of a stock car racing event.[24] The AAA had demonstrated an unwillingness to consider sanctioning sportsmen and modified 'jalopy' racing (according to one account, even Bill France had approached the AAA about organising a national championship for production-based racing just before he organised NASCAR[25]) infringing on AAA's talent was a different matter. The Contest Board wanted to sanction the top level of competition for any type of auto racing in the United States. With the strictly stock formula introduced in the summer of 1949, NASCAR established a new top tier of production-based racing and the AAA wanted control.

Further comments in the same bulletin suggest that NASCAR may have attracted (or possibly poached) some talented drivers from the ranks of AAA competitors. The memo continues: 'In the future, AAA registered drivers will not be allowed to participate in any unsanctioned races except where local concessions have been officially granted for small car events.' [26] Clearly there was to be no quarter given to this upstart sanctioning agency. The AAA wanted to control where its drivers raced and was prepared to punish drivers willing to compete in production-based events. Apparently in the eyes of the Contest Board it was fine for the upstart sanctioning body to preside over a national championship provided it did not impinge on AAA prestige. However, when NASCAR's purview began to threaten AAA Contest Board jurisdiction, they struck back.

Despite the scathing tone of the Contest Board announcement regarding the 1950 season, the struggle between NASCAR and the AAA began with more of a whimper than a bang. The first year of the AAA 'strictly stock' racing series amounted to only five races. Worst still, the second season was limited to only three contests. The struggle began to heat up when NASCAR responded in 1951 by accepting into its ranks 1949 Indy 500 champion Bill Holland, who was on AAA suspension for competing in a charity event outside Contest Board sanction.[27] Losing an ex-champion from the premier motor sport event in the nation (and probably the world) to the upstart rabble in their jalopies was a tremendous blow to AAA prestige.

To offset the loss of an Indianapolis champion into the ranks of stock car drivers, the AAA lured top NASCAR performer Marshall Teague to AAA stock competition in 1952.[28] Teague was one of the top drivers for the Hudson racing effort, a high-profile effort during the early years of NASCAR, winning five out of 15 starts in 1951. His departure for the AAA ranks, with a Hudson sponsorship, was a blow to NASCAR. There was, however, a glimmer of redemption. In contrast to the lukewarm performance registered by Holland after his defection to NASCAR, Teague's dominance of the AAA racing seemed to suggest that NASCAR racers were, on the whole, a speedier lot. This may well have been, in part, because of the more liberal allowances for vehicle modification enjoyed by NASCAR mechanics.

From the beginning, alterations in the interest of safety and speed were permitted. NASCAR allowed changes in carburettor jetting, water pump impellers could be altered and 'wheels, hubs, steering parts, radius rods and sway bars [could be] reinforced and strengthened in any manner'.[29] To build a successful series, it was the appearance rather than the substance of strictly stock that mattered. With each passing year, chassis and engine specifications changed to facilitate economical, competitive racing. Innovations were suppressed, weak systems reinforced and unfair advantages negated.[30] For Bill France (and therefore for NASCAR) the technical details of the car were subordinated to the business of providing entertaining racing. If calling a car strictly stock was a quick and easy way to build a racing series full of respectable-looking cars, then so be it.

It turns out that AAA fears about NASCAR encroaching on its territory were not unfounded. The production-based approach to sanctioning races initiated during the inaugural meeting of 1947 proved a substantial success. By imposing order on existing forms of production-based racing, NASCAR became the largest sanctioning body in the United States almost overnight.[31] As one report indicates, in '1951 NASCAR sanctioned 585 races on 91 tracks and awarded $779,589 in purses plus $40,000 in point money',[32] with much of this going to racers in the 'sportsmen' and 'modified' ranks. Apparently, administering several tiers of racing helped fuel phenomenal growth. The same article suggested that NASCAR was 'racing's Cinderella organisation' and that stock car racing under NASCAR 'has grown more than 400 per cent in three years of racing'.[33] As NASCAR grew but still struggled with the AAA, it developed an expanding schedule of races each year. This approach satisfied two objectives. NASCAR was paid by the race for its sanction. If Bill France wanted NASCAR to become a big player in the world of motor sport, he needed to take advantage of the growing demand for racing and expand, even if it mean conflict with the AAA.

Despite AAA criticism and competition, between 1949 and 1955 NASCAR realised dramatic growth. After staging only eight races in 1949, between the 1950 and 1955 the number of high-profile NASCAR Grand National events increased from 19 to 45.[34] In contrast, the AAA averaged little more than 11 races per year between 1950 and 1955.[35] By 1955, there were 45 races in the Grand National championship series, with over $225,000 in prize money awarded. The AAA could not boast such impressive figures, as it sanctioned only 13 stock car races in 1955 and awarded just over $107,700 in prize money. Though at $85.84 the AAA 'purse per mile'[36] average for 1955 was more than twice the average for NASCAR races, the latter offered more opportunities to win money.[37] NASCAR also offered an array of opportunities for gathering money in production-based racing among its lesser tiers of competition. On the AAA stocker circuit, animosity against production-based racers and a lack of experience in open-wheeled cars probably kept drivers from working when a stock event was not on the schedule.

Over the course of five years NASCAR's national sanctioning activities had grown to dwarf those of the AAA. In 1949, before entering direct competition with NASCAR by sanctioning stock car races, the AAA oversaw 446 events. In 1955, the AAA sanctioned a total of 123 events. In contrast, NASCAR had grown from sanctioning 67 races in the Modified, Sportsmen and Grand National classes in 1949,[38] to sanctioning 1,142 races in all tiers of production-based racing in 1955. In assuming complete control over the majority of racing action across the nation by 1955, NASCAR had demonstrated the popularity and the profitability of production-based racing.

Despite the inertia accompanying NASCAR's growth, events outside American racing would ultimately bring the conflict between NASCAR and the AAA to a close. Following the death of six drivers in AAA-sanctioned events, and the disastrous death of over 100 spectators at the 24-hour race at LeMans, France (addressed by both O'Kane and ÓCofaigh in this collection), much public criticism was levelled against automobile racing.[39] On the floor of the US Senate, Senator Richard Neuberger of Oregon stated that 'I doubt is there is as much blood shed in Spanish bull rings as is occurring on automobile race tracks in this country'.[40] In response to the growing amount of bad publicity associated with motor sport, in early August 1955 the president of the American Automobile Association, Andrew J.

Sordini, announced that 'Upon the completion of the schedule of events already undertaken for the year 1955, the AAA will disassociate itself from all types of automobile racing in the United States'.[41] With one quick statement the conflict between NASCAR and the AAA was ended. Though the AAA Contest Board's activities were reorganised under the auspices of the new United States Auto Club, NASCAR's role as premier sanctioning agency for production-based motor sports in the United States was never again challenged. USAC stock car racing continued the championship series begun by the AAA, but it never developed enough momentum to seriously challenge NASCAR.

At the close of 1955, NASCAR stood alone among sanctioning agencies. In just over eight years Bill France had established a national championship for stock car racing that operated without significant competition across the United States.[42] In seven seasons, the NASCAR Grand National series had grown to such prominence that factory sponsored racing teams were commonplace.[43] The year after the withdrawal of the AAA from racing, Grand National competition enjoyed a banner year. NASCAR sanctioned 56 Grand National races in 1956, and paid out substantially more prize money than in 1955.[44] As a result of dictatorial management and general public enthusiasm for fast production-based cars, NASCAR had become well-established in a very short time despite isolated outcries regarding safety issues.

Perhaps because of the close identification with the equipment possible in the case of stock car racing, the public discussion of violence in racing often included references to the barbaric carnage supposedly staged weekly for degenerate Southern fans. As the largest sanctioning body in the country, NASCAR was certainly a target for criticism. 'I believe the time has come for the United States to be a civilised nation and to stop the carnage on racetracks,' Senator Neuberger commented. 'The deaths on our highways are sad and tragic, but at least they are not purposely staged for profit and for the delight of thousands of screeching spectators.'[45] Where action was initiated to diminish violence on the track, even if intended to apply to all forms of sport, it impacted NASCAR the most.

In June 1957, the Automobile Manufacturers Association (AMA) enacted a ban on factory support for any automobile racing.[46] Carnage in the annual sports car endurance race at Le Mans, France in June of 1955 and numerous deaths on the AAA Championship circuit during the mid-1950s prompted the AMA ban.[47] As a result, the important support that had helped cultivate a national reputation for stock car racing during the 1950s was withdrawn. Yet there was little impact on AAA-style racing using purpose-built equipment or on sports car racing. Neither of these forms relied heavily on products or prestige from American auto makers. Unfortunately for NASCAR, the evacuation of support for a series dependent on production-based cars was significant. For five years attendance declined as racing teams lost major factory participation while other forms of racing suffered little change in momentum[48] (see Figure 1).

At various times during the decade, financial and technical support for racers from auto makers such as Hudson, Oldsmobile, Pontiac, Studebaker, Ford, Chrysler and Chevrolet had helped NASCAR achieve success and respectability. With the withdrawal of factory support in 1957, NASCAR focused less on expanding nationally and more on consolidating growth in regions most amenable to stock car racing. For NASCAR the decade between 1955 and 1969 was a period of Southern retrenchment that allowed stock car racing to recover from the loss of factory sponsorship and consolidate a loyal fan base within the south-eastern United States. This period heavily influenced the composition of NASCAR patrons and shaped eventual perceptions of stock car racing when it again appeared on the national scene.

Popular histories often cite the moonshining roots of some competitors as evidence that NASCAR was 'Southern' from the beginning.[49] Yet any such regional association was not initially embraced by NASCAR. During the first decade there was much official emphasis devoted to shaking any regional association with the South. Indeed, NASCAR spent much of its first five years trying to make stock car racing a genuinely international sport. Between 1949 and 1954, NASCAR staged races in 23 different states and Canada – see Figure 2. During this period, there were more races in the state of New York than in Alabama, Arkansas, Louisiana, Tennessee and Texas combined.[50] Not until the five seasons between 1955 and 1959 did NASCAR competition begin to concentrate its competitions in the South – see Figure 3.

NASCAR event scheduling policy was clearly intended to develop a racing series unifying production-based racing across North America. Even its letterhead hinted at this ambition, presenting the ambitious (if somewhat confusing) title of NASCAR International (NASCAR is short for the National Association of Stock Car Automobile Racing).[51] Despite such ambitious nomenclature, by the time NASCAR racing resumed earnest national growth in the 1970s, stock car racing had become known as a particularly Southern endeavour.

Much of this persistent association with region resulted from historical happenstance and the demographics of mass entertainment. When NASCAR was formed, potential fans in other regions were already concentrated in urban areas and following professional 'stick and ball' sports. During the 1920s, while Southern workers struggled within an agricultural and emerging textile production economy, working-class fans elsewhere became affluent enough to begin following sports as entertainment. Working-class fans of the East Coast and industrial Midwest

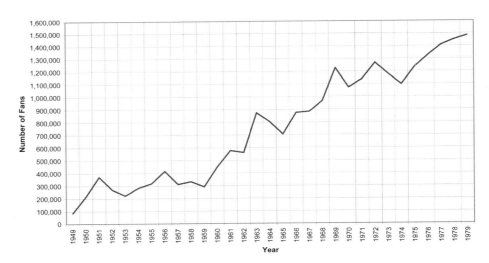

Figure 1.   Total reported annual attendance at NASCAR events, 1949–79.
Source: data extracted from Fielden, *Forty Years of Stock Car Racing.*

embraced sports such as professional baseball, football and basketball. Teams from the National Football League (1903–32), American Basketball League (1925–55), and the International Roller Derby League, among others, were building fan bases in larger urban centres across the northern United States.[52] Where auto racing other than the major AAA Championship series did occur, it was small-time and subject to the whims of racers, promoters and weather. Though numerous local dirt tracks hosted a full schedule of midget and jalopy racing events, they were far too

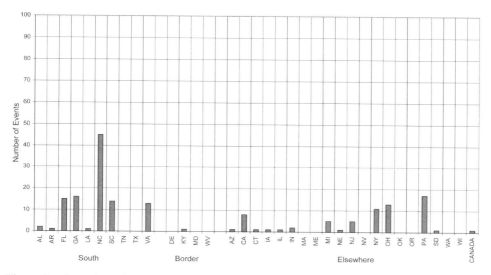

Figure 2.   Location of NASCAR events by state and region, 1949–54.
Source: data extracted from Fielden, *Forty Years of Stock Car Racing*.

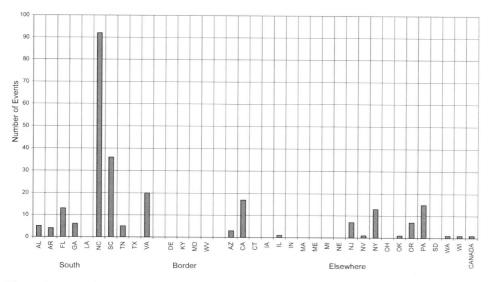

Figure 3.   Location of NASCAR events by region and state, 1955–59.
Source: data extracted from Fielden, *Forty Years of Stock Car Racing*.

disorganised, and frequently too far removed from urban centres, to enter direct competition with established professional sports.[53]

The timing of NASCAR's growth suggests that it was the expectations of Southern fans that made it grow into a regionally defined sport. As the Southern industrial working class emerged economically during the decades following the Second World War, NASCAR stock car racing offered entertainment. This 'demand pull' also influenced NASCAR because stock car racing served a region longing for emblems of identity in a time of social upheaval. If Boston, Pittsburgh, Baltimore and Chicago had pro baseball teams, and working class fans in Philadelphia and Cleveland could cheer for pro football teams, Southern fans could rally around the amazing feats of drivers in 'production' cars.

Meeting the demand for sports entertainment meant that money existed to create such demand. As the Southern states realised explosive economic growth following the Second World War, the means to take advantage of mass entertainment were available to the masses for the first time.[54] Across the nation automobile ownership was becoming virtually universal, roads were being built at a rapid pace and the car was in vogue as a symbol of status and taste.[55] In the South, the emergence of the automobile as a consumer durable of profound symbolic and immense practical value is reflected in the high ratio of car ownership. During the years 1950 to 1975, Southern states consistently reported more cars per driver than the national average.[56] The economic emergence of the South only sharpened the separate impact of these trends. Also between 1950 and 1975, automobile ownership per 1,000 citizens realised an average national increase of less than 20%, while during that same period automobile ownership in the South increased by more than 26%.[57]

One way that North Carolinians celebrated the American automobile was staging, attending and competing in stock car races. Between 1955 and 1964, more than one-third of all Grand National races were staged in North Carolina.[58] Even as late as 1979, the state still accounted for well over a quarter of all NASCAR Grand National races yet run[59] (see Figure 4). The connection between the growing road system and racing stock cars is telling. The growing infrastructure helped bring fans to tracks and the growing economy provided dollars for fans, racers and promoters to spend on racing events. New roads and a higher percentage of drivers helped build the association between action on the track and the common experience of the fans. More cars and roads across the South helped foster a dimension of vicarious association possible with stock car racing. Beyond these practical matters, stock car racing, as a powerfully symbolic manner of celebrating the use-value of the automobile, found devoted fans in North Carolina. This atmosphere celebrating automobility, as centred in North Carolina, found patrons expressing enthusiasm for use of the automobile by driving to a racetrack and watching production based cars similar to their own compete.

For the cultivation of devoted fans, the timing of the creation of a large stock car series could scarcely have been more fortuitous. As radio and television acquainted the South with the rest of the nation, working-class whites in Dixie sought new symbols to help maintain distinct regional flavour. The birth of NASCAR in 1948 coincided with the beginning of a national push for civil rights with other, more fundamental, threats to the established culture of the region. As lunch-counter sit-ins, ranting segregationists and televised confrontations between peaceful protesters and police in riot gear brought scorn upon the South, stock car racing found a solid

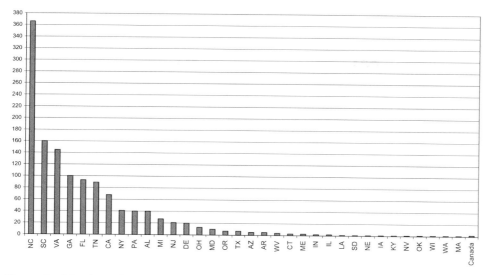

Figure 4.   Number of NASCAR events, 1949–79, by US state.
Source: data extracted from Fielden, *Forty Years of Stock Car Racing*.

fan base among the working-class whites of the southern Piedmont.[60] As Dewey Grantham comments on the civil rights movement, 'The Second Reconstruction was clearly the result of outside forces impinging on the South'.[61] For white Southern workers, a group often manipulated with segregationist rhetoric and historically most threatened by desegregation,[62] the thrill of racing created new symbols of white Southern character and distinction. By the early 1960s, the equipment and superspeedways of NASCAR stock car racing were sufficiently evolved to help sustain the mythology of Southern white supremacy. The sight of an ostensibly mundane 'stock' race car travelling at phenomenal speeds on the banks of a superspeedway suggested that stock car drivers could accomplish fantastic feats with ordinary equipment. Even if the competitors were not vehemently racist or perhaps not even white, their exploits were carried out primarily for working-class audiences in an increasingly Southern sport. For some, dramatic wrecks and hard-fought finishes likely offered redemption for Southern masculinity damaged by the lost cause, reconstruction and the unswerving march of the civil rights movement.

Other features of stock car racing were appealing to Southern working-class fans. A market study conducted for Ford at Darlington and Charlotte in 1963 found traditionally Southern themes present among NASCAR stock car racing fans. In addition to exploring the role of violence, the study suggested that patrons were frequently disaffected working-class men. A synopsis of this research reported that

> The findings indicate that stock car racing represents the American version of bull fighting whereby the fan achieves significant pleasure viewing the combined act of violence and competition. Violence if equated with accidents, bloodshed, and death, while competition is equated with drivers and or makes. Not surprisingly the dominant characteristics of the fans are youth, employment in subordinate jobs, and an extreme love and knowledge of automobiles, engines, etc. The great attraction of stock car

racing to this group is the opportunity to release feelings which have little chance to be expressed fully in the course of daily, and frequently dull, routines.[63]

This appraisal confirms Dewey Grantham's later assessment that

Televised scenes of demonstrators being attacked with fire hoses and police dogs, reports of the bombing of black churches, and the beating and murder of civil rights volunteers shocked millions of people in the United States and reinforced the outside perception of the South as the nation's most violent and savage section.[64]

Though not exclusive to stock car racing or even racing in the South, violence during competition was embraced by Southern working-class fans who accepted danger and violent behaviour between contestants as normal, perhaps even praiseworthy. As John Shelton Reed suggests in The Enduring South, 'the historical record and actual crime statistics suggest that Southerners do have a "tendency to appeal to force" to settle differences and it may be supposed that they view such resort as more often legitimate than do non-Southerners'.[65] Southern working-class fans were perhaps more willing to condone, even celebrate, the violent nature of stock car racing. One survey published by Reed indicates that among all Southerners, urban uneducated skilled labour, the same sort of folks working on the weaving floors of Piedmont textile mills and in the bleachers at stock car tracks, were more likely to condone violence than their counterparts outside the South.[66]

As the Ford-sponsored study suggested, while outsiders condemned such violence, Southerners revelled in it. Harsh appraisals of Southern violence, especially when broadcast nationally, could not have been lost on race fans.[67] Even as the superspeedways hosted their first events, in the political arena segregationist practices associated with the South were being beaten back by external forces. What better way to show indifference or defiance to opinions and initiatives from without than attend a violent stock car race?

Celebration of such a contrast extended notions of transgression and rebellion in evidence at racetracks into the national arena. Though NASCAR stock car racing sprang from activities contrary to the sensibilities of Southern authority, it grew to symbolise Southern resistance to authority from without. As Pete Daniel writes, 'racing culture was characterized by disrespect for authority that had been the underpinning of bootleg culture and the worldview of the working class'.[68] Perhaps fans loved stock car racing because it was dangerous and violent in ways other sports were not, because, replete with racist imagery, it was dominated by white Southern talent.

Another, more historical, coincidence used by race event promoters helped popularise regional distinction among NASCAR fans. As NASCAR stock car racing began to consolidate in the South during the mid-1950s, a fresh wave of nostalgia celebrating the centennial of the Confederate States of America brought symbols and discussion of the Confederacy into the public sphere. Racetrack promoters brought this symbolism to NASCAR racing to sell tickets. Beginning in 1958, events began to carry names evoking the romanticism and racial legacy of the 'lost cause'. Thus events known as the 'Rebel 300', 'Dixie 400', 'Mason-Dixon 200', 'Volunteer 300' and 'Southeastern 250' came into being during the era of greatest racial tension across the south-east.[69] In keeping with this trend, during the late 1950s and early 1960, photographs of stock car races began to show more

Confederate battle flags flying among infield fans; victory lane ceremonies now sometimes featured 'Confederate honor guards' in grey uniforms sporting the confederate battle flag and race queens dressed as Southern Belles.[70] Though perhaps simply a nostalgic ploy staged by promoters to sell more tickets, the presence of these symbols in conjunction with political pressure from outside the region, and an increasingly regional schedule of events, helped cement the adoption of NASCAR stock car racing by Southern working-class fans.

With the withdrawal of overt factory support for racing teams after the AMA ban in 1957, NASCAR temporarily abandoned hopes for a national racing series with races throughout the nation. The Southern states, which offered little in the way of competing professional sports, or even amateur motor sport, were a logical place to regain momentum. Instead of building a championship with events in every state or even every region, a goal first defined at the formation of NASCAR, the National Stock Car Championship became a series contested mainly on Southern soil. Though stock car races were sanctioned in 17 non-Southern states during the first five years of NASCAR's existence, between 1955 and 1959 races were held in just nine states outside the South[71] (see Figure 2). During the next five-year period, from 1960 to 1964, cultivation of an eager fan base within the South continued, with a total of only 22 of 266 race events occurring outside the South. Concentrating NASCAR Grand National events in the South marked a logical return to a region with a tradition of support for production-based racing.

Review of the locations of races within the South suggests that the popularity of stock car racing below the Mason-Dixon Line had less to do with broadly accepted moonshine-and-magnolia mythology than with the high concentration of willing fans in particular locales. It seems that NASCAR depended on the expanding disposable income of the emerging working class, a working class rooted in Piedmont textile mills rather than the rural South as has been occasionally suggested.[72] During its first 30 years, NASCAR staged no races in Mississippi, and but one race in Louisiana, both agricultural states without significant concentrations of industry. Instead, the heaviest concentration of races occurred in the mill country of the Piedmont. Between 1955 and 1964, over one-third of all NASCAR Grand National racing events were staged in the mill towns of North Carolina.[73] More than half of all NASCAR Grand National races conducted during the first 30 years occurred in the four states of Virginia, North Carolina, South Carolina and Georgia.[74] Significantly, these same four states contained the highest concentrations of textile weaving and spinning mills in the nation.[75] These mills offered a concentration of potential fans that became the core fan base for NASCAR.

Arranged parallel to the Appalachian Mountains and diagonally across Virginia, North Carolina, western South Carolina and north Georgia into Alabama, the textile industry of the southern Piedmont created the largest, most established industrial working class in Dixie.[76] In 1950, Davison's Textile Blue Book listed 412 'cotton manufacturing' businesses in North Carolina.[77] In the same year, Massachusetts, the cradle of mechanised American textile production, had but 234 cotton mills.[78] By 1967, North Carolina had 994 textile mills of all types, while Massachusetts had only 381. Yet as textile manufacturing jobs moved south during the first half of the twentieth century, the diversions possible for the workers in the North did not move with them. Without competition from professional football, basketball or major league baseball, Southern labourers, some workers enjoying disposable income for the first time, found diversion at stock car races.[79]

Through the crucial years after NASCAR's initial foray into nationwide acceptance and before the onset of tobacco sponsorship in 1971, areas with the most cotton mills had the highest frequency of density of NASCAR stock car races. A map of 'Textile Mill Towns' from 1955 shows strong correlation between NASCAR event venues and the textile industry. Towns such as Rockingham, Martinsville, Charlotte, Darlington, Weaverville and Hillsboro, among others, all hosted multiple NASCAR events between 1955 and 1971, and all contained large textile mills. The distribution of races by county throughout Virginia, North Carolina, South Carolina, Georgia and Alabama suggests that the highest concentration of fans with an unlimited demand for stock car racing was the mill region of the southern Piedmont. Here, race promoters and NASCAR found a willing audience among working-class white men seeking entertainment, redemption of identity and escape.

Development of a strongly loyal fan base was essential for the long-term success of NASCAR. Patrons across the southern Piedmont, who financially sustained the sport after the loss of industry sponsorship in 1957, now claimed it as a regional development. Part of this association with the South, the violent action accepted as a part of the sport, remained a controversial yet fundamental attraction. When NASCAR again began cultivating a national audience during the 1970s, it would be as a sport cast as a regional phenomenon.

Notes

1. France and Britt, *The Racing Flag*, 16.
2. Eugene Jaderquist, 'NASCAR Primer', *Motor Trend*, May 1952, 19.
3. Sammy Packard interview, 'Speed and Spirit: NASCAR in America,' Smithsonian Transportation Collection, National Museum of American History (hereafter NMAH), Washington, DC.
4. 'AAA Contest Board Bulletin', 7 Jan. 1948, AAA Correspondence, Smithsonian Institution Transportation Collection, NMAH.
5. Ibid.
6. Russ Catlin, 'History of AAA Championship Racing', *Speed Age*, Dec. 1954, 40–1. It should be noted that these teams were supported by factories, but they seldom campaigned with equipment available to the general public. They were largely engineering and publicity exercises for the parent company.
7. Minutes of the First Meeting, International Speedway Corporation (ISC) Archives, Daytona Beach, Florida, 2.
8. Ibid., see also Humpy Wheeler interview, 'Speed and Spirit'.
9. Minutes of the First Meeting, ISC Archives, 2.
10. American Automobile Association Contest Board, *AAA Official Competition Rules*, 13.
11. *NASCAR Newsletter*, 12 Jan. 1957, 1: *NASCAR Newsletter*, 21 Dec. 1953, 1; John Painter, 'NASCAR Prexy Talks', *Speed Age*, Aug. 1954, 55; 'Summary of 1955 activity', AAA Correspondence, Smithsonian Insitution Transportation Collection, NMAH.
12. NASCAR, *1948 Stock Car Racing Rule Book*, 2.
13. Ibid.
14. Though many accounts suggest that Bill France planned from the beginning to develop a strictly stock racing series, there is no evidence of such prescience in the minutes from the meeting to form NASCAR. See, Minutes of First Meeting, ISC archives; 'NASCAR News Bulletin – The Story of NASCAR 1948–1970', ISC archives; Fielden, *Forty Years of Stock Car Racing*, vol. 1, 6.
15. Minutes of First Meeting, 12.
16. American Automobile Association Contest Board, *AAA Official Competition Rules 1947*; NASCAR, *1948 Rule Book*, 9.
17. Roger Huntington, 'How Did it Get this Way?', *Speed Age*, June 1952, 37–8.

18. United States Auto Club, *Official Competition Rules, 1958*, 13.
19. NASCAR, *1948 Stock Car Competition Rule Book*, 4.
20. Yunick, *Best Damn Garage in Town*, 106.
21. Ibid., 257.
22. *American Automobile Association, AAA Official Competition Rules1947.*
23. American Automobile Association Contest Board Official Bulletin, 9 March 1950, AAA Correspondence, Smithsonian Transportation Collection, NMAH.
24. Roger Huntington, 'The Truth About Stock Car Records', *Speed Age*, Feb. 1950, 18.
25. Don O'Reilly, 'NASCAR's History', *Stock Car Racing*, Oct. 1973, 78.
26. *American Automobile Association Contest Board Official Bulletin*, 30 Jan. 1951, AAA Correspondence, Smithsonian Transportation Collection, NMAH.
27. Eugene Jaderquist, 'NASCAR Primer', *Motor Trend*, May 1952, 18–19; 'Association Regulations', *Speed Age*, Feb. 1952, 60; 'News and Forecast', *Speed Age*, April 1951, 47.
28. 'AAA Late Model Stock Car Circuit', *Speed Age*, Aug. 1952, 25.
29. As listed in the 1950 rule book, rules for the 1949 strictly stock racing season were not available when the 1949 rule book was printed.
30. Weak systems – racing hubs as made by Holman Moody; innovations – fuel injection and supercharging.
31. 'Sanctioning Body of America's Most Important Stock Car Races', *Speed Age*, Feb. 1951, 51.
32. Eugene Jaderquist, 'NASCAR Primer', *Motor Trend*, May 1952, 46.
33. Ibid, 18.
34. Fielden, *Forty Years of Stock Car Racing*, vol. 1, 40, 207.
35. American Automobile Association Contest Board, '1955 Summary of Activity', AAA Correspondence, Smithsonian Institution Transportation Collection, NMAH.
36. Ibid.
37. NASCAR did not use the 'purse per mile' measure that the AAA did, but according to the data for the 1955 season (Fielden, *Forty Years of Stock Car Racing*, vol. 1, 208), the NASCAR number of dollars paid out for each racing mile in NASCAR was $39.12
38. 'NASCAR', *Speed Age*, April 1952, 74.
39. Barclay Inglis, 'The Facts about the LeMans Incident', *Speed Age*, Nov. 1955, 74–6.
40. Senator Richard Neuberger, speech on the Senate floor, 12 July 1955, reprinted in Russ Catlin, 'How To Save Racing In America', *Speed Age*, Nov. 1955, 13.
41. Fielden, *Forty Years of Stock Car Racing*, vol. 1, 173; *American Automobile Association Contest Board Official Bulletin*, 4 Aug. 1955, AAA Correspondence, Smithsonian Institution Transportation Collection, NMAH.
42. NASCAR even sanctioned 'modified' races in Hawaii, NACAR Newsletter, 1 Nov. 1953, 3.
43. Yunick, *Best Damn Garage in Town*, 27, 37, 57, 143. In 1951, 1952 and 1953 Hudson sponsored NASCAR teams and by 1955 Ford and Chevrolet were developing teams of their own.
44. Though NASCAR completed fewer races overall (modified, sportsman and Grand National) in 1956, it awarded $1,626,993.54 – an increase of $331,000 over 1955: *NASCAR Newsletter* 7, no 1 (12 Jan. 1957), 1.
45. Senator Richard Neuberger, speech on the Senate floor, 12 July 1955.
46. 'Detroit Censors Speed', *Speed Age*, Oct. 1957, 15.
47. AAA Contest Board, '1955 Summary of Activities', AAA Correspondence, Smithsonian Transportation Collection, NMAH.
48. In this instance, the Sports Car Club of America (SCCA) and road racing events it sanctioned were unaffected while the AAA contest board was quickly reorganised as USAC and continued with business as usual.
49. Howell, *From Moonshine to Madison Avenue*, 11–12.
50. Data from, Fielden, *Forty Years of Stock Car Racing*, vol. 1.
51. NASCAR, *1950 Stock Car Competition Rule Book*, 3.
52. 'Dimitry's Extinct Sports Leagues', http://www.geocities.com/Coloseum/Arean/6825/
53. Staff Report, 'Farewell to Midgets', *Speed Age*, Feb. 1951, 28

54. Cobb, *Industrialization and Southern Society*, 79.
55. US Department of Transportation, *Highway Statistics Summary to 1975*, 44, Dimmick, 'Traffic Trends on Rural Roads', 225.
56. US Department of Transportation, *Highway Statistics Summary to 1975*, 68.
57. Ibid.
58. During the ten-year span from 1955 to 1964, NASCAR staged 515 Grand National races, of which 179 or 34.84% were staged in North Carolina. Data from Fielden, *Forty Years of Stock Car Racing*, vols 1–2.
59. Data from Fielden, *Forty Years of Stock Car Racing*, vols 1–4.
60. Grantham, *The South in Modern America*, 233.
61. Ibid., 238.
62. Simon, *A Fabric of Defeat*, 219.
63. 'Exploratory Research on Motivations and Characteristics of Stock Car Racing Fans', 65/F-32-S, Ford Motor Company Archives, Motorsports Collection, Dearborn, MI.
64. Grantham, *The South in Modern America*, 321.
65. Reed, *The Enduring South*, 46.
66. In this survey Reed shows that 69% of Southern, urban, uneducated skilled labour favoured corporal punishment in schools whereas 37% of non-South urban, uneducated skilled labour favoured corporal punishment. While there is some difference between wrecking an automobile while racing and spanking a child, the important similarity is an underlying acceptance of violent methods to achieve a desired end. See Reed, *The Enduring South*, 54.
67. Grantham, *he South in Modern America*, 240.
68. Daniel, *Lost Revolutions*, 117.
69. Fielden, *Forty Years of Stock Car Racing*, vol. 2, 3.
70. Ibid.; *NASCAR News* 1958–1970, *passim*; ISC photograph collection.
71. Fielden, *Forty Years of Stock Car Racing*, vol. 2, 3.
72. Johnson, *Encyclopedia of Southern Culture*, 1241. Like some other historians, Johnson suggests that 'Throughout its history, stock car racing has been identified with rural white southern males'.
73. Fielden, *Forty Years of Stock Car Racing*, vols 1–3.
74. Ibid.
75. *Davison's Textile Blue Book* (1950), 302–35.
76. Cobb, *Industrialization and Southern Society*, 83–4.
77. *Davison's Textile Blue Book*, 302–35.
78. Ibid., 272–84.
79. The scale of stock car racing, and the strong attachment to the Piedmont fan base, suggests that it offered strong competition to minor league baseball, a very popular diversion throughout North Carolina.

References

American Automobile Association Contest Board. *AAA Official Competition Rules 1947*. Washington, DC: American Automobile Association, 1947.

American Automobile Association Contest Board. *AAA Official Competition Rules*. Washington, DC: American Automobile Association, 1953.

Cobb, James. *Industrialization and Southern Society*. Lexington, KY: University of Kentucky Press, 1984.

Daniel, Pete. *Lost Revolutions: The South in the 1950s*. Chapel Hill, NC: University of North Carolina Press, 2000.

Davison's Textile Blue Book. Ridgewood, NJ: Davison's Publishing, 1950.

Dimmick, Thomas. 'Traffic Trends on Rural Roads'. *Public Roads: A Journal of Highway Research* (US Department of Commerce, Washington, DC), Dec. 1951.

Fielden, Greg. *Forty Years of Stock Car Racing*, 4 vols. Surfside, SC: Galfield Press, 1992.

France, Bill, and Britt Bloys. *The Racing Flag: NASCAR – The Story of Grand National Racing*. New York: Pocket Books, 1965.

Grantham, Dewey. *The South in Modern America: A Region at Odds*. New York: Harper Collins, 1994.

Howell, Mark D. *From Moonshine to Madison Avenue: A Cultural History of the Winston Cup Series*. Bowling Green, OH: Bowling Green State University Popular Press, 1997.

Montgomery, Michael and Ellen Johnson, eds. 'The Encyclopedia of Southern Culture, volume 5: language', in *The Encyclopedia of Southern Culture*, eds. Charles Reagan Wilson and William Ferris. Chapel Hill, NC: University of North Carolina Press, 1989.

NASCAR, *Stock Car Racing Rule Book*, 1948. ISC Archives, Daytona Beach, FL, 1948–1979.

NASCAR. *1950 Stock Car Competition Rule Book*. Daytona Beach, FL: NASCAR, 1950.

Reed, John Shelton. *The Enduring South: Subcultural Persistence in Mass Society*. Chapel Hill, NC: University of North Carolina Press, 1974.

Simon, Bryant. *A Fabric of Defeat: The Politics of South Carolina Mill Hands, 1910–1948*. Chapel Hill, NC: University of North Carolina Press, 1998.

United States Auto Club (USAC). *Official Competition Rules, 1958*, ISC Archives, Daytona Beach, FL, 1958.

US Department of Transportation. *Highway Statistics Summary to 1975*. Washington, DC: US Department of Transportation, 1976.

Yunick, Smokey. *Best Damn Garage in Town: The World According to Smokey*. Daytona Beach, FL: Carbon Press, 2001.

Epilogue: The Evolution of Motor Sport Research

David Hassan

University of Ulster at Jordanstown, UK

The careful reader of this collection will have observed the evolution of motor sport history outwards, from its original codification in France, through its further development in the Benelux countries and beyond to the rest of Europe. Whilst developments were certainly unfolding in other parts of the world in the latter part of the nineteenth century it is to this continent that scholars of motor sport will turn to uncover the early years of what presently is one of the most pervasive sporting disciplines in the world. It is also interesting to note the manner in which auto racing, in particular, redefined itself depending upon the national context in which it emerged. The latter essays in this collection have begun to unpack the rich and complex history of motor racing in the America's and there is unquestionably more valuable work to undertake in this field regarding the social and cultural influence that certain motor sport disciplines, specifically NASCAR, have waged upon the southern states of the USA and elsewhere on that continent.

Ó Cofaigh's powerful opening essay highlights the decisive role played by the French aristocracy in locating this nation in the vanguard of motor sport development, despite the engines used to power these vehicles having been designed and built in neighbouring Germany. What is interesting in this case is that despite the original impetus emerging from the bourgeoisie, very quickly the history and development of motor racing became democratised and indeed promoted by the turn of the twentieth century by the ever stronger influence of the popular press in France and throughout Europe. What is equally significant at this time, and is a point highlighted in Aja's later work on motor sport in Spain addressing the same period, is the growing popularity of city-to-city races and again this serves as a platform for the promotion of the sport and indeed engenders a sense of national pride amongst its patrons.

Existing alongside the formative years of the famed Tour de France were comparable automobile races linking some of Europe's leading cities whilst the early popularity of auto races between Paris and Madrid, for example, easily eclipsed their cycling equivalents. It highlights an interesting issue worthy of further research which is the influence original city-to-city races of the form detailed here played in the social, cultural and political developments of each and asks the reader to consider what precisely were the consequences of these in terms of industrial development, trade links and national enhancement. It is in the early part of the twentieth century, as Ó Cofaigh correctly observes, that certain key developments in the promotion of motor racing unfolded and which together serve to assure France of its preeminent role in the history of the discipline. One is the personal influence of Gordon Bennett and his pioneering advancement of European, albeit primarily French, city-to-city racing and thereafter, secondly, is the iconography associated with the famed Le Mans circuit, which played host to the first ever Grand Prix in 1906. More than a century later the track still holds a central place in the minds of motor sport enthusiasts the world over. In 2007 more than 250,000 spectators attended the Le Mans 24 hour race, reflecting the enduring popularity of the event but also galvanising a crucial link between the past and the present. More pertinent perhaps is the importance of the concept of authenticity in the minds of motor sport followers in that Le Mans remains one of the few tracks that still utilises public roads and in so doing appears to constitute an important factor in the popular psyche of its supporters.

The early history of motor sport in central Europe is a theme further developed by Ameye, Gils and Delheye who use the period universally referred to as the Belle Époque as the conceptual backdrop to the emergence of motor sport, in a variety of forms, throughout Belgium. In profiling the personal histories of key figures, notably Pierre De Caters, Ameye et al. confirm the France/Belgium axis as being fundamental to our appreciation of the early emergence of motorized sporting forms. These detailed and insightful biographies highlight a very appropriate mechanism to illustrate the full extent of the interrelationship of various sporting codes – in this case cycling, motor sport and the aviation industries – and again constitute an opportunity for the further development of this approach in uncovering the nuances and interlinked nature of motor sport's remarkable history in a variety of settings.

This piece also underlines the gentrification of early motor sport – a theme previously unpacked in Ó Cofaigh's opening contribution where the importance of resources, principally finance, meant that only relatively wealthy individuals could afford to become involved in the sport during these formative years. As many of these same individuals were also motivated by a spirit of adventure and a commercial imperative it ultimately meant that a history of early motor sport in central and northern Europe was also a portrayal of the considerable influence of certain key figures, a relationship ideally captured by Ameye et al in this groundbreaking piece. Again it is clear that similar stories remain as yet untold in other countries and where this collection has sought to make an initial attempt at illuminating the key birthplaces for the development of motorized sport – primarily automobile racing – it is equally clear that much more research is yet to be undertaken to complete what is a hugely complex picture.

Amid the growing popularity of motor sport throughout Europe it was perhaps not surprising that in certain countries political figures would seek to align themselves with heroic individuals engaged in sport, not least those who appeared to personify many of the characteristics such leaders wished to be promote themselves. Hence for many such reasons the work of Aja, in capturing the influence of Angel Nieto, is worthy of close scrutiny by those wishing to build upon the iconography of key sportsmen and women and how their experiences were seen as embodying much greater meaning for a nation and its people. Here the focus is on motorcycling and it is apparent that this sport, in contrast to auto racing, experienced much greater difficulty in becoming initially established throughout Europe. Indeed it is well into

133

the twentieth century, 1923 to be precise, before the sport was organised on a national scale in Spain. Very quickly though the sport became more prominent and shortly thereafter Franco's victory in the Spanish Civil War ensured that Spain entered a period of considerable upheaval. Needing to align the regime to expressions of Spanish popularity Nieto, like many other athletes at this time, became an unwitting adjunct to a wide political movement. Yet Aja makes clear that Nieto was a man capable of forging his own path and remarks how the Spaniard was much more than a political actor, displaying instead considerable personal qualities that have resonance for the watching public.

In the sport of auto mobile racing, particularly Formula 1 (F1), it is arguable that few nations have exercised more of a profound influence than Brazil. Indeed it is reasonable to assert that its profile is disproportionate to the economic standing of the country – certainly historically – and the early part of de Melo's analysis of the considerable history of the sport in Brazil touches briefly on this phenomenon. Understandably he forgoes an in-depth discussion of this fascinating concept in favour of a considered portrayal of the early history of motor sport in the country. Yet he also opens the way for future research into the exact reasons why Brazil has succeeded in producing so many outstanding drivers. Of course this is likely to bring any such enquiry back to the genesis of the sport, which is located amid the country's largest cities, specifically Sao Paulo, during the first decade of the twentieth century.

Interestingly de Melo argues it was again the strong influence of European modernity, especially in France, that inspired within the Brazilian population 'a desire to be modern'. Indeed de Melo highlights a further issue worthy of further investigation, which is the way that the automobile industry – pointing to the influence of the American car manufacturers Ford and General Motors (GM) to illustrate his point – can exercise considerable influence at a political and cultural level within a given nation. He suggests that at the time Ford and GM – the latter in the personal guise of Albert Sloan – was establishing their manufacturing base in Brazil that this coincided with an era of increased importance of the USA within Latin America, albeit he makes clear that this was by no means a uni-directional process and in fact Brazil and other South American countries were adept at negotiating the full extent of the former's presence to ensure their economic and cultural well being. Yet again there are further opportunities here to undertake a more detailed enquiry into the way in which auto sport facilitated a wider social and cultural shift in the outlook adopted by sections of the Brazilian population notwithstanding the manner in which the indigenous culture remained capable of resisting and negotiating this process for their own ends.

In highlighting the historical latitude of motor sport development in South America and indeed the extraneous influences that flow from this, it is perhaps pertinent to consider the full extent of the responsibilities held by the motor sport industry towards the environments in which it operates. This debate is profiled in the piece by Hassan and O'Kane who as part of a more focussed examination of the famed Paris to Dakar rally highlight the considerable responsibilities held by the event's organisers, as well as its participants, concerning the setting in which the event takes place. The ever growing importance of corporate social responsibility has become more pertinent in recent times on account of the omnipresent debate around the environmental impact, often of delicate eco-systems, that emerge as a result of staging major sporting events. In the case of the Paris-Dakar rally however such considerations extend to include the protection of the environs through which the event passes as well as the safe guarding of its competitors following an increased terrorist threat that has emerged over the last decade. Again opportunities exist for those engaged in examining the social and cultural significance of motor sport to consider the full extent of its influence, across a range of domains, including the sustainability of major events traditionally held in certain ecologically delicate settings.

O'Kane takes the opportunity, in a single authored piece, to provide a considered analysis of three events that combined form the so-called 'Triple Crown of Motor Racing' which extends upon the earlier commentary by Ó Cofaigh around the Le Mans 24 hour race as well as casting an appropriate light upon the famed Indianapolis 500 race and the Monaco Grand Prix. O'Kane's detailed portrayal of the cultural significance of the 'Indy' 500 is particularly arresting, helping the reader to fully absorb the importance of the event nationally, locally and even at the level of the nuclear family, providing as it does an annual focal point for motor sport followers. Here again there are indications of a wider social role for motor sport in America – a point highlighted by Shackleford in the ensuring article – that perhaps is absent in other settings. Whilst having moved away from its exclusively gentrified image of the early part of the twentieth century motor sport in Europe – primarily it should be said F1 racing – remains the preserve of an upwardly mobile section of the population. In North America, with both Indy Car racing and NASCAR, the situation is evidently quite different and with this distinction comes opportunities for researchers to examine the exact nature of such fault lines and the implications for the study of issues around race, ethnicity and gender in the context of motor sport.

Thus having highlighted the telling contribution of America to the history of global motor sport its perhaps appropriate that the collection should conclude with a piece by Shackleford who, in his examination of NASCAR, does initiate a process of unpacking the particular forces at work in the southern states of the USA, which suggest this region may provide a rich resource for others keen to explore the full impact of this organisation. Indeed, as alluded to already, it appears appropriate that this collection should end with a piece on North America as it is little coincidence that this country is one of the few developed nations in the world that as yet has failed to embrace the 'jewel' in the motor sport crown – F1. Instead the indigenous codes continue to hold sway and thus the future will be marked by an ongoing battle between the forces behind the commercial and financial imperatives of F1 and the protectionist approach and apparent ambivalence of the world's largest democracy. For students of sport, not least those engaged in the study of motor sport, this struggle should make for a fascinating future.

Index

Page numbers in **Bold** represent figures.